D0707005

Some Measure of Justice

ALSO BY MICHAEL R. MARRUS

The Politics of Assimilation:
The French Jewish Community at the Time of the Dreyfus Affair

Vichy France and the Jews
(with Robert O. Paxton)

The Unwanted:
European Refugees in the Twentieth Century

The Holocaust in History

Mr. Sam:
The Life and Times of Samuel Bronfman

The Nuremberg War Crimes Tribunal, 1945–46:
A Documentary History

Some Measure of Justice

The Holocaust Era
Restitution Campaign of the 1990s

MICHAEL R. MARRUS

THE UNIVERSITY OF WISCONSIN PRESS

Publication of this volume has been made possible, in part, through support from the George L. Mosse Program at the University of Wisconsin–Madison.

The University of Wisconsin Press
1930 Monroe Street, 3rd Floor
Madison, Wisconsin 53711-2059

www.wisc.edu/wisconsinpress/
3 Henrietta Street
London WCE 8LU, England

Copyright © 2009 by Michael R. Marrus
All rights reserved. No part of this publication may be reproduced, stored in a retrieval system, or transmitted, in any format or by any means, digital, electronic, mechanical, photocopying, recording, or otherwise, or conveyed via the Internet or a Web site without written permission of the University of Wisconsin Press, except in the case of brief quotations embedded in critical articles and reviews.

1   3   5   4   2

Printed in the United States of America

Library of Congress Cataloging-in-Publication Data
Marrus, Michael Robert.
Some measure of justice : the Holocaust era restitution campaign
of the 1990s / Michael R. Marrus.
p.   cm. — (George L. Mosse series in modern European cultural and
intellectual history)
Includes bibliographical references and index.
ISBN 978-0-299-23404-1 (pbk.: alk. paper)
ISBN 978-0-299-23403-4 (e-book)
1. Holocaust, Jewish (1939–1945)—Reparations.
2. Restitution—History.
3. Reparations for historical injustices—History.
I. Title.   II. Series: George L. Mosse series
in modern European cultural and intellectual history.
D818.M37   2009
940.53´18144—dc22
2009010256

For

CAROL RANDI MARRUS

CONCORDIA UNIVERSITY LIBRARY
PORTLAND, OR 97211

Contents

Foreword

History and law are a tangled web. Michael Marrus, who is a professional historian with legal training, deconstructs the relationship between the two disciplines in the context of the Holocaust restitution phenomenon of the past decade and a half. Lawyers tend to prefer simplistic solutions, because they argue for one side or the other and expect the judge or jury to provide them with a black or white answer, a *veredictum,* which means "to say the truth." Once an issue has been decided by a court it is *res judicata,* and without new and undiscovered evidence the "truth" cannot be revisited. Sometimes the law gets the history right, or almost right, as it did at Nuremberg. But as Professor Marrus points out, it is also a rather blunt instrument that sometimes gets the history wrong.

Historians prefer more nuance, disputing simplistic attempts to describe complex realities. In principle, they remain open to reconsidering past assessments, conscious that historical narratives themselves tend to change over time, a result of some strange synergy between the past and the present. This fascinating study reveals Michael Marrus to be a bit of both, lawyer and historian. On one hand, he is profoundly frustrated by the framework of the legal regime which sometimes seems to create almost as much injustice as it eliminates, yet with the subtlety of the historian he is also respectful of law's potential to offer *some* measure of justice.

"It's not about the money." This phrase and variations on it figure repeatedly in the Holocaust restitution litigation. Michael Marrus is sceptical. Of course, civil claims for damages are inherently "about the money." They attract, as this volume convincingly demonstrates, those who are driven by financial reward and its ugly half-brother, avarice. This may take the form of dubious or fraudulent plaintiffs, high-end shysters who thrive on lucrative class action lawsuits, and immoral corporate executives indifferent to the past wrongs and modern-day consequences of the organisations they direct and control. Money is certainly significant for the survivors. Its importance, for often the payouts are quite modest, may be on the more symbolic end of the spectrum. Yet many are concerned that attempts to monetize atrocities ultimately trivialize the horror of the crimes and risk cheapening or demeaning the victims.

Finally, when the focus is on the Holocaust as thefticide, whereby prosperous Jews lost their artworks and antiquities, their large homes and their Swiss bank accounts, we lose sight of the fact that most Jewish victims of the Nazis were indigent. These "Jews without money" made up the majority of the six million, and they and their heirs and successors are marginal players at best in the campaigns to recover valuable assets or provide compensation for their loss.

Professor Marrus questions whether the fascinating phenomenon of the Holocaust restitution litigation is unique or whether its understanding can contribute to broader insights. Here too, the answer is probably a bit of both. Debate continues about whether the Holocaust itself is a distinct crime or rather part of a broader category, to which international law has given the name "genocide." The 1948 Convention for the Prevention and Punishment of the Crime of Genocide recognizes "that at all periods of history genocide has inflicted great losses on humanity."

Many of the insights and observations in this book are of more universal interest. They go well beyond the limited issue of Holocaust claims, bearing on broader themes of our time relating to accountability for international crimes, compensation to victims of atrocity, and the right to truth and justice. In this respect, I am reminded of the Truth and Reconciliation Commission of Sierra Leone, of which I was a member. We heard much testimony and considered other evidence of the outrages committed during that country's decade-long civil war, in the 1990s. When we asked victims about their own suffering, there was an almost endless list of brutality, rapes, gratuitous murders, and the hallmark of the conflict, random "amputation" of the limbs of innocent civilians. Not quite the Holocaust, perhaps, but certainly a species of the same genus. After the victims had recounted the crimes that had been perpetrated, we asked what they now expected from the process of peace, reconciliation, and justice. The answers were quite stunning, I felt. Instead of answering with the mantra of compensation for loss, which derives from fundamental concepts of European legal traditions, we were told: "I want education for my children. We require adequate housing. I need medical care for my family."

Sierra Leone is one of the poorest countries in the world, and victims of its civil war lost little in the way of rare canvasses by Klimt or Picasso. Compensation for loss, in the sense of provable claims in a civil court, was a meaningless notion. What they required was a vindication of their fundamental rights, to health, to housing, and to education. Similar issues arose in South Africa, where that country's Truth and Reconciliation Commission ordered commercial corporations to fund what were quite modest payments to individual victims. Few were satisfied with the process, although arguably it too delivered *some* measure of justice.

This is not to say that peculiar circumstances do not at least partially explain why Holocaust restitution became so important in the 1990s. For example, a rather rarified judicial atmosphere had been created in the United States that lent itself to high stakes class action lawsuits. There were talented and entrepreneurial lawyers to take the cases, in exchange for handsome percentages of the takings. The post–Cold War political climate was also propitious. The fall of the Berlin Wall had the consequence of opening up huge new archival sources, providing much new information and insight into the Nazi crimes. And there were enormous amounts of money and other valuable assets at stake. So perhaps this was the proverbial "perfect storm," whose repetition was at best unpredictable and whose lessons are of doubtful relevance elsewhere.

But that would be to overlook another more general process that was at work in international law and politics. This is variously described as the movement for accountability and to combat impunity. It began to surface within international human rights institutions in the 1980s. Victims are entitled to truth, to justice, to memory, and to restitution, it was contended. Previously, the human rights movement had been almost preoccupied with the rights of defendants before the courts and their treatment as prisoners upon conviction. The focus began to shift, and the justice system was held out not only as a source of human rights violations but also as a remedy for them.

With the momentum of the accountability movement, interest began to grow in criminal justice as a mechanism to address atrocities. In 1989 the United Nations General Assembly reactivated a project to draft the statute of an international criminal court. This process had lain dormant more or less since Nuremberg. Although it moved ahead quite quickly, impatience led to the establishment of temporary or ad hoc tribunals to deal with the war in the former Yugoslavia and the Rwandan genocide. In 1998 the Rome Statute of the International Criminal Court was adopted. This permanent institution provides not only for punishment of the offender but also reparation for victims. It even sets up a Trust Fund for Victims, which is intended to provide, in real time rather than sixty years after the fact, financial and other forms of compensation. The Trust Fund for Victims began its work a few years ago and has already made modest awards in the Democratic Republic of the Congo, even though no defendants have yet been convicted. Somewhat in parallel to criminal prosecution are the truth and reconciliation commissions, discussed above. They are a cognate to criminal prosecution, often resorted to when full-blown trials are impossible as a practical matter or legally blocked by amnesty or the death of the perpetrators.

It is surely more than a coincidence that the Holocaust restitution movement is contemporaneous with the revival of processes for international justice and accountability. As Professor Marrus explains, "Holocaust restitution carried with it a distinct flavor of human rights." Like the more general human rights campaigns, the litigation took place surrounded by other elements, making it difficult to determine whether courtroom victories were attributable to skilled advocacy and good facts or simply foregone conclusions resulting from overwhelming political factors. As a general rule, the cases were settled out of court. Thus, the Holocaust claims can be understood as part of a much greater phenomenon, involving truth commissions, international criminal trials, and claims to justice for historic wrongs.

The natural process of human aging means that there are fewer and fewer Holocaust survivors able to make claims and to participate in judicial settlements. This parallels another related development: Nazi war crimes trials are also drawing to an end, as few suspects remain alive. In contrast with many atrocities to which recent generations were subject, it cannot be said that justice was never delivered to the Nazis. At the criminal trial level, the International Military Tribunal provided a judgment of great historical and judicial significance in 1946, barely eighteen months after the first concentration camps were liberated by the advancing Allied armies. Justice was swift and effective, although it did not address restitution or individual claimants at all. Victims were hardly present in the Nuremberg courtroom, and only a few of them testified. Shortly afterward, Germany agreed to provide extensive compensation both to Israel and to individual survivors, as this book explains. In other words, there was already *some* measure of justice long before the restitution dimension arose in the 1990s.

The same observation cannot be made about many other victims of atrocities over recent decades. Not only do they remain without monetary compensation but their tormentors have gone unpunished and, in some cases, retained their power and prestige. A tribunal dealing with Khmer Rouge atrocities in Cambodia is only now underway, hastening to finish before all of the potential defendants die out. Bangladesh proposes to prosecute crimes committed in the civil war that resulted in its separation from Pakistan in 1971. Victims of horrendous massacres in Indonesia in 1965 seem to be entirely forgotten. In none of these is there any issue of restitution. As in Sierra Leone, talk of recovering lost assets seems even beyond the irrelevant in the context of poor, developing countries.

While criminal prosecution basically comes to an end when the suspects and the witnesses die, restitution claims and other forms of civil litigation can linger long into the future. Much of the Holocaust litigation has been the work of plaintiffs who often (but not always) had legitimate family ties to those who perished in the camps and could claim to be legal heirs. Beyond that their claim to victimhood was more remote, based on the chance of genealogy rather than any genuine persecution. It makes an interesting parallel with the defendants in the litigation, as Professor Marrus so ably points out, who were also much removed from the perpetrators. The connection between the Nazi plunderers and modern-day managers, directors, and shareholders in Swiss banks and German manufacturing companies is often quite remote. Like so much litigation, the debates are not about principle but rather the quirks of anachronistic legal documents and laws, norms on statutory limitation, and other technical matters. To return to the question Michael Marrus asks, it sometimes seems to be "all about the money."

Leaving the battle for remembrance of past atrocities in the hands of legal heirs, as the Holocaust litigation tends to do, has both appealing and unpleasant features. Descendants of victims of atrocities, even those without any legal entitlements, have an entirely legitimate connection to the victimization of their ancestors. To this day, young Armenians campaign for recognition of the suffering of their antecedents under the Ottoman Empire in 1915. In Ireland there is still a great collective attachment to the memory of the terrible famine of the 1840s and the belief that it bore some connection to the fact the country was not yet independent. The Irish no longer associate their current difficulties with the oppression of the past, unlike Blacks in the United States. African

Americans point to the Middle Passage, by which their forefathers and foremothers were brutally transported from one continent to another, and to centuries of enslavement and subsequent discrimination. Similar remarks apply to aboriginal peoples in Canada, and elsewhere, in that contemporary oppression seems to bear an obvious relationship with historic persecution.

How long can, and should, such claims go on? Perhaps the answer can be found in the interface between history and law. There is a point when law recedes deeply into the background, when we assess the wrongs of the past without much reference to legal entitlements. For example, there is no credible claim from the descendants of those who were made slaves under the Roman Empire to compensation from today's Italian government. Why is this an absurd suggestion, whereas we still entertain the logic of some form of financial recognition for the exploitation of slaves in the American south until their formal emancipation in 1863, or the unequal treaties between Europeans and Indians some one or two centuries ago?

The Genocide Convention, to which reference has already been made, says that the crime of genocide has been committed "at all periods of history." But we do not seriously quarrel about whether the Athenians perpetrated genocide in 416 BCE when they exterminated the people of Melos (nor do their heirs and descendants pursue civil claims), as Thucydides describes. Or whether the 1948 definition of genocide fits the pogrom of Saint-Barthélemy in France in 1572. Yet the debate rages about how to characterize the 1915 genocide of the Armenians. There is surely a point when such controversies end, or become insignificant, but it is hard to know when that point is reached. Perhaps the lessons of Holocaust restitution can generate some insights here.

At the purely technical level, law contributes some mechanisms or norms in this respect. Civil claims, and often criminal prosecutions, are time-barred or prescribed after a certain period of time. Law acknowledges that with the passage of time, the issues grow cold, or perhaps we simply need to move on. The reasoning makes great sense with respect to a loan of money to an old friend that was never repaid or the theft of a lawnmower that had been carelessly left outside. However, we largely reject the idea when atrocities are concerned. International treaties declare that there can be no statutory limitation upon prosecution for war crimes and crimes against humanity. Nazis continue to be apprehended and judged, although very few are even healthy enough to make the journey overseas, let alone withstand the rigors of a prolonged trial. Even Chile's erstwhile dictator, Augusto Pinochet, managed to escape judicial accountability in Spain because medical experts said he was no longer *compos mentis*. Where money and property, rather than a living defendant, are at stake, the claims seem to have a longer shelf life. Maybe this is not a bad thing, and merely a feature that helps provide an explanation.

From all of this it is difficult to distil the kind of rules and principles that lawyers are comfortable with. My reading of this book by Michael Marrus leaves me much enlightened, and his stimulating questions generate more doubts than simple answers, which is as it should be. The idea that justice is measured is a valuable one, as is the point that victims may not get the full measure they deserve. The title is, I think, an allusion to Shakespeare's play *Measure for Measure,* in which Vincentio, the Duke of Vienna, demonstrates the need to balance law with related concepts like fairness, equity, justice, and truth. The idea is of course rather more ancient, and Shakespeare probably got it from the Book of Matthew. Michael Marrus ends the book by reprising his title, but I will end with his final line in chapter 4: "Meanwhile, the effort to understand the Holocaust in all its complexity continues."

WILLIAM SCHABAS, OC MRIA

Oughterard, Ireland
April 11, 2009

Preface

This book originated in a gracious invitation, extended to me by my
friend Steven Aschheim of the Hebrew University of Jerusalem, to deliver the George L. Mosse Lectures at the Van Leer Institute in Jerusalem in November 2008. I was extraordinarily honored by him and his
committee and am very grateful as well for the opportunity to present
this work in the series of books based on these lectures inaugurated by
my distinguished colleague Christopher Browning, whose *Collected Memories: Holocaust History and Postwar Testimony* appeared under this imprint
in 2003. Most important, I am deeply touched and honored that the
lectures and this book are associated with the name of the late George
Mosse—friend, mentor, colleague, and professional exemplar to several
generations of historians around the world. To those of us who were
lucky enough to have crossed paths with George, to have spent time
with him, to have been taught by him, or simply to have enjoyed his
company, he is a continuing presence and guide to the practice of the
historian's craft. Often, as I wrote these pages, I found myself wonder-
ing, "Whatever would George think?" Like so many, I was lucky enough
to have discussed historical matters with him, and to have engaged with
his good-humored but razor-sharp critical disposition. I will never know
the answer to my question, but just posing it was, I believe, an encouragement to me to make this as good a work as I can manage.

I have benefited greatly from many who have helped me contend
with a subject that arouses strong feelings and about which there is little
consensus. All the more do I appreciate that those from whom I received assistance did not always agree with me at the time, and in some
cases still do not. Yet, while taking full and sole responsibility for what is
here, I know that they saved me from mistakes, omissions, and infelic-
ities. My thanks in particular go to Claire Andrieu, Yehuda Bauer, Michael Bazyler, Doris Bergen, Lawrence Douglas, Roger Errera, Antoine

Garapon, Judah Gribetz, Peter Hayes, Marilyn Henry, Nick Humez, Miriam Kagan, Mayo Moran, Mark Osiel, Jonathan Petropoulos, Anna Porter, Seymour Reich, John Roth, Anthony Sebok, Virginia Solomon, John Torpey, Lorie Waisberg, Ernest Weinrib, Richard Weisberg, and Katrina Wyman. My Canadian compatriot, William Schabas of the National University of Ireland, Galway, has honored me greatly with a foreword to this volume; having so much appreciated his sure hand on other subjects, often far afield from my own work, I am particularly delighted to find myself in his company on a topic close to home. I want to add to this list Master John Fraser and the Fellows of Massey College in the University of Toronto for having provided an extraordinarily congenial environment in which to work. I am also grateful to the Ford Foundation and to the Faculty of Arts and Science at the University of Toronto, which provided welcome financial support. Thanks, too, to my wonderful literary agent, Beverley Slopen, and the very helpful editorial staff at the University of Wisconsin Press, especially copyeditor Mary Magray and managing editor Adam Mehring. And finally, one more time, with all my heart, I gratefully acknowledge the support and encouragement of my wife, Carol Randi Marrus, to whom this book is dedicated.

Massey College
Toronto, March 2009

Some Measure of Justice

Introduction

S pit at it," wrote Leon Wieseltier, a sophisticated Jewish writer not known for extreme views, advising his mother, a Holocaust survivor, about how to respond to a query about possible restitution payments for wartime wrongs committed against Jews. Apparently, Wieseltier's mother needed no persuasion. At issue, as is clear from his November 1999 article on the subject in *The New Republic,* was not so much the alleged insufficiency of the proposed payment from the "Swiss Fund for Needy Victims of the Holocaust/Shoa," but also, as often in the sometimes heated discourse on this subject, the *principle* of the matter.[1]

"I am sick of hearing about the fate of gold," Wieseltier complained. He was also sick of hearing about the Jewish claims for restitution of paintings by the Austrian Expressionist artist Egon Schiele, at the time a major preoccupation of the New York art world. And similarly about the claims for stolen insurance payments and demands of German corporations for payment for wartime slave labor. "In the discussion of the Holocaust now, the authority of the philosophers and the historians is being usurped by the authority of the lawyers and the museum directors; and the subject, more and more, is money," Wieseltier protested. "I agree that there will be no justice in letting the 'neutrals' and the opportunists and the collaborators get away with it; but there will be no justice also in not letting them get away with it. Whatever happens, in the matter of what transpired in Europe between 1933 and 1945 there will be no justice."

3

Wieseltier's problem, he stressed, was not so much with the justice of the claims. Rather, it was that money was displacing more appropriate reactions to the Jewish catastrophe. "The emergence of the new reparations industry represents the strange and sapping illusion that certain elements of Jewish destiny in the blood-field of Europe may be reversed. I understand that the money that is the object of all this litigation is 'our' money, but what has litigation to do with sorrow? I really cannot bring myself to care about where the Monets of the martyrs will hang. I would rather grieve than sue. It seems more lucid." He had no more to say than that. It all came down to money because "money is swamping everything now. . . . We are fat and we are acting fat." There was nothing really to be done, although, as his article finished, "a little nausea would go a long way."[2]

What Wieseltier was reacting to is the subject of this book. My focus is a wave of Holocaust-era restitution, triggered by legal and then political action in the United States. Beginning in 1996 Jewish plaintiffs launched a series of claims in American courts against Swiss banks, focusing first on dormant accounts from the Holocaust era and then extending to other wrongs against the victims of Nazi persecution, including slave and forced labor and insurance claims. And shortly after, as a leading student of this process notes, "the floodgates of litigation have opened."[3] These have included actions against the banks of other European countries and against German and other corporations as well as demands for the return of works of art stolen from Jews during the Nazi era.

Remarkably, the actions begun in American courts were crowned with success. The Swiss settled in August 1998 for $1.25 billion, which at the time, it was noted, was "the largest settlement of a human rights claim in U.S. history."[4] Other banks settled similarly, as did corporations for their use of slave and forced labor and, to a much lesser extent, the insurance companies for their failure to honor obligations to clients who were victims of the Nazis. In all, the total awarded to Holocaust survivors and other persecutees amounted to some $8 billion paid or promised to survivors, a particularly impressive level of reparation in a relatively short period of time.[5] Proceedings to return stolen works of art have proceeded more unevenly, although I think most specialists would agree that, no matter what the results in specific cases, the general environment has improved significantly over the past decade for claimants seeking to gain possession of their own or their family's stolen treasures.

At issue here is not just the resolution of lawsuits—resulting in the $8 billion or so—but rather, to use a phrase frequently heard when settlements were finally achieved, the realization of "some measure of justice for the Holocaust." But in what way *were* such settlements "justice for the Holocaust"? That is what I want to discuss. About ten years ago I wrote about the latter subject, attempting to survey Holocaust-related trials since the end of the Second World War. My conclusion, in the mid-1990s when I first turned to this matter, was that the law's involvement with the Holocaust—I focused on criminal prosecutions—was essentially finished.[6] The courts had largely run out of perpetrators to try. The major directors of the massacre of European Jewry had passed from the scene. Some criminals were at large, to be sure, but the few that remained were aging, lower-level killers, about whom there was sometimes insufficient evidence for full-blown prosecutions and against whom legal proceedings were generally unsatisfactory encounters with the larger history and significance of the Holocaust itself.

But how wrong I was! For just as I was completing my consideration of this topic, masses of litigants and their lawyers were opening up a major new front in the United States—claims for restitution that had seldom been broached in the courts of any country, yielding results with a global impact scarcely even contemplated in the half century or so that had elapsed since the collapse of the Third Reich. To consider these I have taken up my previous subject once again. This time, to be sure, my focus is not criminal proceedings but, rather, civil actions and their accompanying resolution in the United States. And this time I am reluctant to declare that this will be the final concerted effort to come to terms with the Holocaust through legal processes. There are indications, especially with regard to looted art and Jewish communal property in Eastern Europe, that such efforts will continue, and not just through legal channels in the United States.

Throughout, I will refer to "restitution," not because the term is a precise terminological fit with what is usually at issue but because it is very widely used and because it is probably better suited than any other to refer to the broad spectrum of issues at stake. The more familiar "reparations" usually signifies a wider spectrum of remedies in international law. In its discussion of this subject, the United Nations International Law Commission's "Responsibility of States for Internationally Wrongful Acts" identified three kinds of reparation—restitution, compensation, and satisfaction.[7] In common parlance, "reparation" usually signifies an effort, arguably impossible for the Holocaust, to "repair" wrongs that were done, while "compensation," at least in the UN definition, suggests a similarly inappropriate effort "to cover any financially assessable damage." "Satisfaction" refers to apologies and other acknowledgments of wrongdoing. While "restitution," in the UN's definition, entails an impossible undertaking "to re-establish the situation which existed before the wrongful act was committed," in practice it may signify a more modest goal than "reparation," something closer to "recompense"—a term that has no legal currency at all but was admirably used by the American diplomat Sumner Wells in reference to the Jewish people in 1945.[8] "Restitution," in addition to its generally accepted reference to the restoration to a previous condition (*restitutio in integrum*), can also mean "the act of making good . . . for any loss or injury"—begging the question, to be sure, of what "making good" actually entails.[9] The latter, indeed, is the subject of this book.

Settling for second best in terminology should be a sign that with Holocaust restitution we are entering relatively uncharted and hence hazardous legal and historical waters. This is, indeed, one of the findings of my inquiry. I want to stress, at the outset, the wide range of legitimate views on this subject, extending far beyond questions of terminology. Reflecting on his several years of constructive involvement, the Clinton administration's point man on this subject, Stuart Eizenstat, observes that the entire subject of the Holocaust "is politically radioactive."[10] That is why, several years into this process, there were views on all sides of the question—many of them held by survivors who differed strenuously among themselves.

Leon Wieseltier was certainly not alone. From across the Jewish spectrum there were strong opponents of the entire process. Abraham Foxman, national director of the Anti-Defamation League, spoke as a Holocaust survivor to denounce "a new 'industry' . . . spearheaded by lawyers and institutions, in an effort to get what they call 'justice' for Holocaust victims."[11] In Jerusalem, Efraim Zuroff, director of the Israeli office of the Simon Wiesenthal Center that emphasized the hunt for Nazi war criminals, argued that restitution diminished the message Jews should relay about the Holocaust: "We've been telling the world for the last fifty years that the Holocaust is important. Is this why we're doing it? So that in the end we'll get paid back? Or is it because the Holocaust is a watershed in the annals of human history, and that everything has to be done to see that it doesn't happen again—I'm talking about the genocide aspect, not the grand larceny aspect."[12] In Paris, the Jewish author and human rights activist Marek Halter said much the same thing, decrying the suggestion that Jews were killed for any other reason but that they were Jews. "Enough of bargaining about their money," he told the readers of *Le Monde*.[13]

"My family belonged to the middle class but we did not have a bank account in Austria, let alone in Switzerland," grumbled Raul Hilberg, dean of Holocaust historians.[14] On the right, Charles Krauthammer described how "what began as an attempt to locate actual confiscated Swiss bank accounts of individual Holocaust victims has turned into a treasure hunt for hungry tort lawyers and major Jewish organizations."[15] Similarly, Christopher Hitchens sneered about "Holocaust profiteers."[16] According to Israel Gutman, Israel's most senior and respected Holocaust historian, the restitution campaign "was a big mistake. At most, an effort should have been made to see if compensation could have been secured through quiet discussions. It shouldn't have been made into a dramatic public struggle, as if it was the ultimate redress for the Holocaust."[17] In a lengthy article in *Commentary*, its senior editor, Gabriel Schoenfeld, described Holocaust reparations as "a growing scandal."[18] The entire exercise was wrongheaded, he suggested. Despite some good intentions, the campaign had gone off the rails in a misguided effort to extract "every last ounce of justice," with unseemly political tactics, questionable legal claims, and reckless disregard for historical truth. And on the far left, in an egregious and dogmatic rant against the entire process, which attributed much of the blame to political mobilization for Israel, maverick political scientist Norman Finkelstein lambasted "the Holocaust industry," a campaign "to extort money from Europe in the name of 'needy holocaust victims' [that] has shrunk the moral stature of their suffering to that of a Monte Carlo casino."[19]

Defenders of restitution responded vigorously. "If these injuries occurred," asked Eizenstat pointedly, "why should their victims not have the same right to sue for justice as victims of other and lesser catastrophes?"[20] To fail to pursue these claims, according to Michael Bazyler, "would be [to] let off the hook . . . some of the world's wealthiest concerns" and to permit them "to keep their ill-gotten gains."[21] Going further, Bazyler claimed that the Holocaust restitution cases could "serve as a template for a new era of relief to victims of war crimes and crimes against humanity—but this time without the fifty-year wait for justice." Similarly, Canadian political leader and human rights scholar Michael

Ignatieff, aware of the dilemma, came down on the side of restitution: "Financial restitution runs up against the idea that honor and dignity are beyond price and that once they are taken away, they cannot be restored by mere money. But if such things have no price, it is hard to undo the harm done when they are lost. The perpetrators can always say they are sorry, but that is too easy. They must be made to pay. So money becomes the sorry center of the whole restitution business."[22] Burt Neuborne, a distinguished legal academic and one of the lead attorneys in the Swiss banks and German corporations litigation, reminded critics that Jews received less than a quarter of the payment from the German settlement, with the rest going to non-Jewish victims of industrial forced labor.[23] Neuborne referred to the "vast profits" earned during the Holocaust and to similar wrongdoing by the Swiss banks. He also offered a strong defense of the theory behind the plaintiffs' case and a stout defense of the lawyers involved. "Lawyers worked extremely hard for years to develop novel legal theories and to uncover the facts sixty years after the events. Despite their enormous effort, more than half the lawyers in the Swiss bank cases have waived all fees." Similarly, in the settlement with German corporations, "the attorney's fees in the more than fifty cases will total 1 to 1.25 percent of the settlement figure. That is, I believe, the lowest fee structure in history for comparable levels of success."

Alongside these polemics and in part flowing from their Holocaust-related themes has come a torrent of analysis of human rights, historical memory, memory politics, apologies, and the reparation of historic wrongs.[24] Increasingly, these writings draw new attention to the victims of great persecutions and crimes against humanity, and how we contend with their grievances after the events themselves. "Restitution is in the air," writes one observer.[25] This suggests that we are likely to be dealing with a phenomenon that extends beyond the Holocaust in both its origins and its wider implications. To me it suggests as well that, with recent efforts at Holocaust-era restitution, we are in a domain that supersedes the demands for legal certainty and definitive answers that are integral to the legal process.

In the chapters that follow I will try to make sense of the most recent wave of justice seeking for the Holocaust: what it has been, why it has emerged when it did, how it fits with earlier reparation to the Jewish people, its implications for the historical representation of the Holocaust, and, finally, what its implications are in the wider project of justice seeking in our time. Up to this point, as the notes to this book will show, writing on this subject has mainly come from participants, lawyers, philosophers and social scientists specializing in restitution, and journalists. Most of these writings appeared when the campaign was under way, or just at the point of resolution. Now that the dust has settled somewhat, it may be possible to look at things with a bit more perspective—including historical perspective. I take up the issue as a historian first and foremost, but as a historian preoccupied with claims of historical justice that set this campaign in motion and with the larger questions of what happens to historical understanding and historical interpretation when they enter the legal arena.

1

Restitution in the 1990s

The restitution agreements discussed in this book may be likened to the "laws" in the famous quip attributed to Otto von Bismarck, the nineteenth-century Iron Chancellor of Imperial Germany: "Laws are like sausages," Bismarck is supposed to have said, "it is best not to see them in the making." The "laws," in this case, were outcomes of startling revelations, charges and countercharges, politics, campaigning, public and private threats, and litigation, followed by many months of arduous negotiations—in one important instance through the courts, in another with contending parties brought together by governments, and in still another with private industrial and organizational representatives working together. Different somewhat from other instances, restitution of works of art, which will be considered in the next chapter, could involve variations on all these pathways to resolution, and at least as much acrimony and notoriety, even if fought on a smaller scale. In every case, these settlements purported to achieve "some measure of justice" for survivors of the Holocaust or, in some cases, their heirs. To this day there remain disagreements over the extent that they managed to do so and about the processes by which these settlements were reached. By no means is everyone happy with what was achieved. But there *were* settlements, and I think there is a consensus, even among the defendants, that *something* positive was achieved. Instrumental in reaching this result were concepts and procedures of American civil law, often articulated in the idiom of human rights. This chapter examines the pathways to resolution and gives some sense of why, to many at least, and notwithstanding

10

the high moral purpose, these were unmistakably sausagelike, unap-
pealing at close scrutiny.

Swiss and Other Banks

The engine of the American restitution campaign, which drove the
issue forward from the mid-1990s, was the affair of the Swiss banks, the
global controversy begun in 1996 when the leadership of the World Jewish Congress decided to contest the issue of dormant accounts, originally held by Jews who became Holocaust victims, on which there had
never been proper postwar reporting or appropriate restitution.[1] To be
sure, this was not the first time the Swiss banking community heard accusations about Holocaust-era accounts. Nor was this the first time that
plaintiffs had sought to use civil courts in the United States to seek justice for the Holocaust. But the matter had remained largely invisible,
beneath the radar of international publicity and public controversy.
American courts had been unreceptive. Their reasoning was that without legislative direction it was not their business to reach back over several decades to right wrongs committed in faraway countries in circumstances that were on a scale and complexity ill suited to the application
of tort law.[2] It should be added that the Swiss were scarcely responsive
through this same period. It was only in the mid-1990s that this question emerged, full-blown, in the glare of American political, legal, and
social contention. Within a short time, as one analyst puts it, the Swiss
banks issue "came to symbolize how justice was denied to Holocaust
survivors."[3]

   Early revelations came in the spring of 1995 from Israeli historian
and journalist Itamar Levin, deputy editor of an Israeli business newspaper, *Globes*, and a student of Holocaust history. Levin disrupted the
phlegmatic world of Swiss inquiries into long-standing accusations of
mishandling Jewish accounts with a series of articles on how the banks
had mistreated heirs of deceased Holocaust victims and had wrongfully
retained heirless accounts.[4] His reports documented obstacles set by the
bankers in the way of accessing Holocaust-era accounts, most notori-
ously the cynical requirement of death certificates for account holders
who had been murdered in Auschwitz, Treblinka, Majdanek, and other
camps. And the amounts were potentially huge: from nearly 300 million
Swiss francs said to have been owed in 1946, Levin calculated, on the

basis of interest and changes in currency values, a total of 6.4 *billion* Swiss francs.[5] The international press carried the story first in 1995: London's *Jewish Chronicle* relayed the charges and noteworthy articles appeared in U.S. publications, including the *Wall Street Journal* and the *New York Times.*[6] *Newsweek* and *Time* gave prominent place to the issue two years later. The latter introduced its cover story on the issue with an image of emaciated survivors with a foreground of gold bars in the shape of a swastika. According to *Time,* while the "proximate cause" of the crusade against the Swiss bankers was money, "the soul-searing intent of the men and women who set the hunt in motion was to peel back the veil time had cast over the evils of Nazism and expose the truth."[7] Israeli leaders, including the prime minister at the time, Yitzhak Rabin, seized upon the matter, as did the flamboyant and energetic Rabbi Israel Singer, deputy to Seagram liquor magnate Edgar Bronfman at the head of the World Jewish Congress.[8] Within a short time, restitution became a global issue. "In the course of 1995–7," writes one participant, "Western media was flooded with information on stolen Jewish property which had not been returned. The phenomenon itself was amazing: material on confiscation of property, bank deposits and gold transactions, which would usually be suitable for historical journals, found its way onto the front pages of national newspapers, capturing international media interest with extraordinary intensity. It was as if the facts had been revealed for the first time, and material which in the past had been the basis of Hollywood action movies, suddenly appeared to be historic reality."[9]

Within little over a year of Levin's report, lawyers filed three class action lawsuits in a federal court in Brooklyn against the three major Swiss banks—Credit Suisse, the Union Bank of Switzerland (UBS), and the Swiss Bank Corporation—claiming tens of millions of dollars in damages and restitution and involving more than two dozen different law firms. A battle that would last for many months, which would extend to wartime forced and slave labor as well as insurance, which would reach into several countries and many different areas of wrongdoing during the Holocaust, and which was backed by some two million claimants around the world, had effectively begun.[10]

To the Swiss, these lawsuits did not come completely out of the blue. As historian Regula Ludi has shown, the Swiss had their own reasons, in the mid-1990s, to rethink the patriotic memories of the wartime period, with their celebrations of Swiss armed neutrality, heroic resistance to

Nazism, and principled services to humanitarianism.[11] Such views were in some quarters seen as outdated, out of keeping with more recent concerns for minorities and global preoccupations with human rights. While still widely held, traditional Swiss patriotic views were also contentious by this time. Other, more critical perspectives existed, and they could not help but spill over onto matters related to the Holocaust. There was even some rethinking in high places. In 1995, even before the Swiss banking scandal broke, Swiss Confederation president Kaspar Villiger apologized to the country's Jewish community for its treatment of Jewish refugees during the war and its refusal to accept more into the country.[12]

Historical interpretations were not permitted to evolve at a leisurely pace, however—assuming that is what they would have done. Rather, the Swiss were abruptly called to account in the contestations of high-stakes American litigation. To the lawyers for the plaintiffs, seeking what they understood as belated justice for the Holocaust meant fitting an unfathomable historic catastrophe more than half a century old into menacing legal threats and fierce accusations. And so rather than following a meandering path of historical revision, the Swiss enlisted historical interpretation, just as did their opponents, in a great class action struggle that unfolded in the United States.

Pressure mounted as attention focused on the litigation and the related issue of unreturned gold looted from the central banks of Nazi-conquered European countries, including gold that had been taken from the Jews. Among the latter was even gold that had been pried loose from the teeth of the murdered Jews in the death camps and that had disappeared into the Swiss bank vaults. Early on, Singer and Bronfman recruited the New York Republican firebrand Senator Alfonse D'Amato, chairman of the Senate Banking Committee. An enthusiastic champion of his Jewish constituents, D'Amato was running for reelection and resourcefully seized upon the issue. Amid charges that the banks held many hundreds of millions of dollars in Holocaust accounts, D'Amato's banking committee began to hold hearings on the matter.[13] Researchers from his office went to work—not infrequently going over ground that had been covered by academic researchers years before but that was little known to the wider public. "Toward the end of 1996," writes Isabel Vincent, D'Amato's investigators were feeding sensational stories "to an eager international press corps on an almost daily basis."[14] Later, when the campaign against the Swiss banks had intensified, he publicly urged banking authorities to block a proposed merger of two of the banks involved in the litigation, the Swiss Bank Corporation and the Union Bank of Switzerland, "pending the outcome of a thorough investigation [into] . . . the disposition of assets of Holocaust victims and their heirs, and their record of collaboration with the Nazis."[15] At a Democratic fund-raising luncheon at his apartment in April 1996, Bronfman, a major supporter of the administration, buttonholed Hillary Rodham Clinton and gained an appointment with President Clinton the next day. The Clintons were both, thereafter, onboard.[16]

Carried along by the momentum of litigation, increasing political support, and growing antipathy toward the Swiss, popular appreciations of the scale of the wrongdoing magnified significantly. Representatives of forty-one nations met at the London Gold Conference in December 1997 to discuss outstanding wartime issues, putting even more pressure on the Swiss. The more critics heard about the Swiss story, the more outraged they became. "This is the greatest robbery in the history of mankind," announced Elan Steinberg, one of Bronfman's deputies at the World Jewish Congress.[17] Steinberg, the aggressive champion of the campaign on a day-to-day basis, became a force to be reckoned with. "We know that a lot of people don't agree with our tactics," he told one interviewer, "but so what? It's not our responsibility to be nice to the Swiss and get them off the hook. We represent the Jewish people, and we are trying to achieve truth and justice for those who have been victimized for more than fifty years."[18]

As the campaign intensified, accusations broadened from the restitution of dormant accounts to include a wide range of wrongs against victims of the Holocaust. As law professor Michael Bazyler notes, "because the Swiss banks were accused in these lawsuits not only of wrongfully keeping . . . deposited funds but also of earning money by trading with the Nazis in goods made by slave labor and in possessions looted from the victims (including gold), the beneficiaries of the Swiss banks had to include victims of these Nazi policies as well."[19] Assembling a formidable case, the plaintiffs presented claims to the court that were enough to make any Swiss banker blanch: "breach of contract, breach of fiduciary duty, conversion, conspiracy, unjust enrichment, conspiracy to violate international law, complicity in violations of international law, negligence and violations of Swiss Federal Banking Law and the Swiss Code of Obligations." These involved not only demands for restitution and compensation but also damages under the Alien Tort Claims Act of

1789, according to which aliens could sue in American courts for a tort committed in violation of the "law of nations." Put simply, the plaintiffs sought to use American courts to seek compensation for Holocaust-era violations of human rights.[20] Reinforcing their claim, Israel Singer increased the pressure. During the autumn of 1997 there was talk of a boycott, regulatory pressure from New York City officials, and calls to block the proposed merger between the Swiss Bank Corporation and the Union Bank of Switzerland. Secretary of State Madeleine Albright added her voice, urging that the Swiss parliament follow the example of the United States in discovering "the truth about the Holocaust and events related to it." And Congress, too, sprang into action. From mid-1996 to 2001 the Senate and House of Representatives held some fourteen separate hearings on Holocaust-related restitution matters.[21]

Sensing early in the day that they had a major public relations disaster on their hands, the Swiss responded with three initiatives. First, an agreement between the Swiss Bankers Association and the major Jewish organizations established an international committee of experts, headed by Paul Volcker, the former head of the United States Reserve Bank, with a twofold mandate: "(a) to identify accounts in Swiss banks of victims of Nazi persecution that have lain dormant since World War II or have otherwise not been made available to those victims or their heirs; and (b) to assess the treatment of the accounts of the victims of Nazi persecution by the Swiss banks." The Volcker Committee's audit, it was later acknowledged by an American court, was "likely the most extensive audit in history, employing five of the largest accounting firms in the world at a cost of hundreds of millions of dollars to the defendants."[22] Second, as a gesture of goodwill while the dispute was being resolved, the Swiss government established a $200 million humanitarian fund (later raised to $400 million) for needy Holocaust survivors, administered by Swiss and Jewish authorities. And third, the Swiss parliament established a blue-ribbon international investigative commission, headed by a respected historian from Zurich, Jean-François Bergier, to examine Switzerland's role during the Second World War. The commission enjoyed a broad mandate and exceptionally good working conditions. And its report, ultimately released in final form in March 2002, proved devastating to the Swiss banks' case.[23]

Long before that happened, in the familiar scenario with lawsuits of this scale, the parties eventually found their way to negotiation and settlement, assisted and pushed and prodded by Judge Edward R. Korman,

Chief Judge of the United States District Court in Brooklyn, before whom the various lawsuits had been consolidated in March 1997, and assisted at critical junctures by Stuart Eizenstat, the delegate of the Clinton administration who was to play a vital role in subsequent restitution negotiations. An experienced civil servant who had served as American ambassador to the European Union, Eizenstat came to the issue from service as a special envoy of the American government on property recovery issues in Central and Eastern Europe in the mid-1990s. Later, he prepared two stinging reports on wartime collaboration with the Nazis: the first on looted Nazi gold deposited in Swiss banks and retained thereafter, including that which had belonged to murdered Jews, and the second on neutral governments' wartime involvement with the Nazis operating through Swiss channels.

The Swiss banks situation was complicated by, among other things, deep divisions among the plaintiffs' attorneys about how to proceed with the case. Some of the latter opted for a wider set of claims against the Swiss, including their involvement in slave labor, their assisting the Germans in looting Jews' assets, and their restrictive refugee policies. Others focused more narrowly for the restitution of bank accounts.[24] Following the Swiss banks affair, and with the blessing of the American government, Eizenstat helped bring the contending parties together on related restitution issues concerning other banks, German industry, insurance, and art—urging accommodation, identifying common ground, and shaping an outcome acceptable to the interests of the United States.

Eizenstat struggled to circumvent litigation and challenged the lawyers constantly—sometimes in extreme frustration. "Lawyers are lawyers the world over," he complained in his memoir on the restitution campaign. While full of sympathy for the plaintiffs' cause, he saw his role as promoting compromise among the contending parties and bringing as much calm as he could to the roiling legal waters.[25] For a time, in the summer of 1998, the talks broke down and at that point Judge Korman had a decisive impact. Many felt, however, that Eizenstat's involvement was essential for settlement. The *New York Times* even published an editorial praising his efforts, referring to him as "a long-serving American Government official who has brought a rare degree of energy and attention to these difficult matters."[26]

Judge Korman, before whom the Swiss banks parties came as litigants, used the authority of his office and the courts to clarify legal issues and to postpone ruling on some procedural matters, thereby pressuring the parties to settle and in the end to hammer out an agreement—which in this case he was responsible for administering. In Eizenstat's view, "it took Korman and the threat of sanctions to get the banks over the top."[27] Committed to righting the record of the history of the affair, Korman was a distinguished jurist who was appointed under President Ronald Reagan and who had worked with and respected Burt Neuborne, a New York University law professor and one of the lead counsel for the plaintiffs. Neuborne, in turn, thought Korman's handling of the negotiations "masterful" and, like many others on the plaintiffs' side, believed that he was the indispensable impresario of the final settlement. Critical of the Volcker Committee for what he felt was too indulgent a view of the Swiss banks, Korman preferred what he felt was the harsher judgment of the Bergier Commission. He was, therefore, not a disengaged arbiter, but he was widely believed to be fair.

Following a colorfully recounted dinner with the lawyers of both sides in August 1998, hosted by Korman at the famous Gage & Tollner steak house in Brooklyn near his courthouse, the judge brought the two sides to what eventually became a Settlement Agreement.[28] "The judge basically told us—and he was only half joking—that no one would leave the room until there was a deal," recalled one participant.[29] And so there was, ensuring that the matter would not come to trial, following the pattern of virtually all class action lawsuits.[30] The Swiss banks (Credit Suisse and the Union Bank of Switzerland) agreed to establish a Settlement Fund of $1.25 billion for the compensation and relief of several categories of plaintiffs. As agreed to in a distribution plan under the auspices of a Special Master of the court, Judah Gribetz, five categories of claims were identified: a Deposited Assets Class to which the bulk of the money would go, made up of those with unresolved Swiss bank accounts; a Slave Labor Class I, made up of those forced to work for German companies whose profits were sheltered in Switzerland; a Slave Labor Class II, made up of those forced to work for Swiss-controlled companies in Germany; a Refugee Class, made up of those who had been mistreated as refugees by Switzerland; and a Looted Assets Class, made up of those whose property was looted by the Nazis and disposed of by Swiss institutions.[31] The plaintiffs agreed to dismiss all their claims, and Eizenstat found a way to reassure the Swiss through an "all Switzerland" release that precluded subsequent litigation.

To the initiated, what was remarkable about the settlement was that the substance of the wrongdoing was never definitively resolved in court.

To be sure, Judge Korman was hardly silent on matters of substance. Evenhanded before the settlement was reached in August 1998, he took public exception, several years later, to what he believed was a continuing whitewashing of Swiss wrongdoing during and after the war. Korman continued to spar with the Swiss over the implementation of the settlement, vigorously challenging the bankers on their interpretation of the historical record.[32] However, the judge's decisions on procedural issues were no substitute for a final resolution in court. "Except for the Volcker audits, conducted independently from the lawsuits," writes Eizenstat, "the evidentiary essence of the legal process that could have lent legitimacy to the massive settlement was utterly lacking. Not one shred of traditional legal discovery was made. Instead, external pressures and the intervention of the U.S. government compensated for the serious flaws in the legal cases."[33]

To the lawyers and much of the public, however, the settlement was momentous: not only because of its considerable magnitude—$1.25 billion—but also because of the pathway that it opened for other lawsuits then being contemplated or even under way. "By settling the litigation, UBS and Credit Suisse had set a precedent for the rest of Europe's corporate establishment," write John Authers and Richard Wolffe. "They had also provided the perfect tactical template for the Jewish advocates. The deadly matrix of strategies used against the Swiss—lawsuits backed by high-pitched public relations, governmental pressure, and threats of sanctions—could be used again and again."[34]

Many of the lawyers involved with the Swiss banks went to the courts in the late 1990s with subsequently filed lawsuits against German, Austrian, French, Belgian, and even British and American banks. Their claims had to do with so-called "Aryanized accounts"—deposited money and valuables that had been confiscated by the banks, acting under Nazi directives or general policy, together with other acts of alleged complicity with the wartime persecution and attendant profiteering at the Jews' expense. Sometimes the banks involved were the direct successors of wartime banking houses. But sometimes, too, the relationship was cloudy. Institutions such as the German Deutsche Bank or the Austrian Creditanstalt were familiar to all students of banking history in Germany and Austria, for example, and their complicity with Nazi persecution fit people's general understanding. But this was hardly the case with the American Wells Fargo & Company. A claim against the latter appeared when Wells Fargo acquired a Belgian bank in 1996 and balked at paying obligations under a settlement reached with some twenty-two different banks in Belgium.[35] Other cases, against Barclay's Bank, Chase Manhattan, and J.P. Morgan, arose because of the activity of their Paris branches during the wartime occupation of France.

Associated with almost all these claims were not only the wartime robberies but also their cover-up—hiding or destroying evidence both in the postwar period and subsequently, as highlighted in one egregious case in January 1997 when a Swiss security guard and subsequent whistleblower, Christoph Meili, caught a Zurich branch of the Union Bank of Switzerland red-handed, in the dead of night, shredding some relevant wartime documents.[36] As we shall see, these charges led to some painful encounters, both in Congress and the court of public opinion. The Swiss banks affair involved some of the most flagrant instances of what Judge Korman later found to be "decades of improper behavior"—hiding the existence of bank accounts of Holocaust survivors, stonewalling on claims, destroying records, and deceiving external agencies seeking to discover the truth.[37] The case of the French banks was also important because of the symbolic significance of bringing the proud French bankers and the French government to account before American courts, legislators, and the wider American society, and also because of the legal precedents deployed when a federal judge allowed the case to go forward. As with the Swiss banks, eventually these lawsuits were settled, mostly in early 2001, at the end of the Clinton administration and through the Herculean efforts of Stuart Eizenstat.[38]

Slave and Forced Labor

Throughout the 1990s, the largest Nazi-era claims by far were those filed against German corporations on behalf of Jewish and non-Jewish wartime survivors who had been dragooned into wartime labor for private corporations in the Third Reich. As historians have come to appreciate, the employment, often under duress and in terrible conditions, of as many as twelve million Europeans was one of the fundamental policies of the Third Reich and an essential requirement of its war making and imperial strategy during the Second World War.[39] "Employment of foreign forced laborers was not only limited to large-scale enterprises," according to the leading German authority, Ulrich Herbert. "It was applied throughout the whole economy; from the small farm and locksmith's shop with just six workers, to the national railway system, the local authority districts, the big armament companies and also many private households."[40] In all, the Nazi regime employed foreign workers in virtually every walk of life, from farms to churches to heavy industry and concentration camps. In the late summer of 1944 these numbered close to eight million and represented one-quarter of the workers in the entire German economy. This was, it has been noted, "the largest use of foreign forced labor since the end of slavery in the nineteenth century."[41] In the case of Jews, the term "slavery" is to some degree a misnomer, as their veteran advocate Benjamin B. Ferencz pointed out years ago: Jews were regularly employed simply as another means of mass murder; they were supposed to be worked to death, with the products of their labor squeezed out of the victims as a by-product of the murderous process.[42] As to the many hundreds of thousands of surviving workers, most had never received any reparation whatsoever.[43]

Beginning in March 1998 with a spectacular lawsuit against the American automotive giant Ford and its German subsidiary, lawyers went to courts in five different states, from New York to California, to win compensation and damages for the use of their clients' wartime labor.[44] The defendants included familiar pillars of German industry— Siemens, Daimler Benz, Volkswagen, Degussa, Hugo Boss, Bayer, Hoechst, and so on. The claims were astronomic, amounting to some $37 billion at the beginning of the process.[45] Significantly, 80 percent of the claimants represented in the various classes were non-Jews, coming from the various East European nationalities that had never been compensated by their home governments for their wartime labor and suffering at the hands of the Germans. For a time the defendant companies, including some prominent American firms such as Ford, sued because of their relationship with their wartime German branches, put up a stout defense, mainly arguing, along with procedural challenges, that the claims should have been made against the German government, representing the regime that had been responsible for the persecution of Jews and other peoples of Europe. In the months that followed there were legal ups and downs, political pressures, and political intervention on both sides of the Atlantic—from Bill Clinton in the United States and the German chancellor Gerhard Schröder, whose Social Democrats had favored restitution in the federal election and triumphed over the more recalcitrant Helmut Kohl's conservative Christian Democrats in October 1998. Unlike the case with the Swiss banks in which governments maintained an arm's length, Washington and Berlin urgently pressed for a resolution and involved themselves in the process, which soon extended to other governments as well—those of Eastern Europe as well as Israel, representing their citizen-claimants.

Negotiations began in early 1999 and, in addition to the litigants and victims' groups, involved no fewer than eight sovereign governments—those of Germany, the United States, Israel, the Czech Republic, Poland, Russia, Belarus, and Ukraine. After close to a year of arduous deliberations, the logic of settlement prevailed. The agreement reached with German industry at the end of 1999, amounting to DM 10 billion or about $5.2 billion in all, made an important distinction between two classes of plaintiff: a smaller class, the slave laborers, mainly Jews who had toiled in concentration camps and who were intended to be worked to death, and the much larger class of forced laborers, mostly Slavic people who had worked elsewhere for the German war machine under a variety of conditions, ranging from the most cruel to the relatively favorable. The former, said to number some 240,000, received a token payment of $7,800 per worker, and the latter, of whom there were about 1.2 million still alive, $2,600 each. The settlement was wide-ranging, extending also to some life insurance obligations as well as claims of some business owners who had not previously been compensated for wartime robberies. A German Foundation Fund, referred to as "Remembrance, Responsibility and Future," was to take charge of the process of compensation at the German end and was to conduct educational and commemorative programs about the Nazi persecution. Remarkably, the lawyers, the victims' groups, the Anglo-American lead negotiators (Eizenstat for the United States and Count Otto Lambsdorff for Germany), and the diplomatic representatives all managed to agree. To the industrialists, in addition to winning back a measure of goodwill in the United States, the prize was "legal peace"—the dismissal of the existing lawsuits and the promised intervention of the American government to prevent such cases from going forward in the future. This last, although not easy given American constitutional restraints, was eventually achieved.[46] To the victims, the result was a no doubt symbolic, but nevertheless tangible, recognition of their sufferings that was long overdue.[47] And from the German government, in line with a series of important declarations that extended back to those of Konrad Adenauer, there was an apology by German President Johannes Rau before an assembly of survivors: "I pay tribute to all those who were subjected to slave and forced labor under German rule and, in the name of the German people, beg forgiveness. We will not forget their suffering."[48]

Insurance

Claims against European insurance companies, amounting originally to billions of dollars, proved to be more complicated, more contentious, and more difficult to resolve than the slave and forced labor cases, possibly because, at least when viewed in general terms, the wrongdoing was less clear cut and more difficult to measure than the confiscation of bank accounts or the human rights violations of German industry. Prior to the Holocaust, Jews may have owned as much as $2.5 billion in insurance policies, used at the time as a convenient vehicle for savings and investment.[49] This money was placed in literally dozens of companies headquartered in several European countries. These included the Allianz AG, headquartered in Munich and the second-largest insurance company in the world, and the giant, Italian-based Assicurazioni Generali S.p.A., known as Generali, founded by Jewish merchants in Trieste in the nineteenth century and headed, until recently, by a survivor of Auschwitz.[50] But there were also smaller concerns, the names of which were usually unknown to the more than ninety thousand claimants who eventually sought compensation for Holocaust-era losses.[51]

First filed in the spring of 1997 and eventually consolidated in New York before Judge Michael Mukasey (later U.S. Attorney General under President George W. Bush), the class action suits against the insurers alleged that the companies had colluded with the Nazis to confiscate the policies of Jews and facilitate their persecution and that they had covered up their wrongdoing after the war and blocked appropriate restitution through legalistic, bureaucratic, and other subterfuges. The insurers offered several responses. Many claimed that they had no choice but to operate under Nazi directives and that they had often done their best to preserve the interests of their clients. As to prewar accounts for which they claimed to lack evidence or responsibility, they usually explained this by their wartime and postwar situation: some claimed that their records had been destroyed during the war; some companies had merged with others; some had been nationalized by the Soviet-dominated countries of Eastern Europe; and some insisted that claims had been resolved in earlier agreements between Germany and global reparations agreements of earlier times. Some of the original insurers, it was noted, had simply gone out of business. The companies did, however, acknowledge that they had no alternative but to address outstanding claims.[52]

For a time it looked like the insurance companies were on the same road to settlement as the Swiss banks. Pressure came from state regulators and on occasion legislators, highly susceptible to opinion on the state level where the industry was regulated. On the companies' side, insurance associations tried to make their members' case. In August 1998, six major European insurers reached agreement with U.S. insurance regulators, the Claims Conference, the World Jewish Restitution Organization, and the Israelis to constitute the International Commission on Holocaust-Era Insurance Claims (ICHEIC, pronounced "eye-check") to facilitate the resolution of claims.[53] It appointed as its chairman Lawrence Eagleburger, a veteran State Department official, diplomat, and experienced negotiator who had been Secretary of State under George H. W. Bush. Pointedly, ICHEIC left the lawyers outside this process—a decision that appealed to the insurers and the Jewish organizations and that was supported by Eizenstat but was later blamed for the delays and for a resolution not satisfactory to many claimants.[54] In a radical departure from the path taken with the banks and German corporations, ICHEIC agreed to work by consensus, to the extent possible. Discussion proceeded slowly, however, and the two sides skirmished. Several states, notably California, passed laws to require the insurers to disclose information about unpaid Holocaust accounts. The companies sought to have those laws invalidated. In its *Garamendi* decision, in 2003, the U.S. Supreme Court did so, finding California's statute in conflict with the right of the federal government to conduct foreign policy.[55]

ICHEIC began to implement its claims process for policies of Nazi persecutees in February 2000, promising to do justice to account holders without cost to the claimants and agreeing to use relaxed standards of proof for policyholders in well-defined cases. Notably, the process was to be inclusive not only of policies issued by the participating companies but also of *all* prewar and wartime insurance, including nonparticipating companies and companies no longer in existence—a breathtaking commitment by present-day insurers. Determining valid recipients was not easy. ICHEIC published the names of some 500,000 potential policyholders; 90,000 applied before a deadline of March 2004. Both the process of identifying possible claimants and assessing claims drew criticism.

Critics also blamed ICHEIC for its allegedly expensive overhead, its lack of transparency, its occasionally stringent rulings, and its unwillingness to publish more complete prewar and wartime lists of policyholders. Most of all, critics complained that the process was moving at a snail's pace.[56] At one point, Eagleburger stormed out of a meeting with representatives of the European companies and resigned from his chairmanship of ICHEIC, charging that the commission was making insufficient progress on the seventy-nine thousand claims it had received to that point. Returning to his post the next day, he continued to struggle with the insurers. In 2001, after two years of battering from both sides, Eagleburger expressed his frustration to a largely Jewish audience: "I have negotiated at one point or another in my life with the North Vietnamese, with the Soviet Union; you name it, I've met with them. I don't think I've found any of them more difficult or more frustrating than have been the companies."[57] For their part, the companies defended the confidentiality and professionalism of their policies, although they insisted on operating from a head office in London, outside the reach of U.S. regulatory authority and litigation subpoena power.

Rejecting the "rough justice" approach of the German corporations on slave and forced labor, ICHEIC sought a much more precise determination about what was owed. As Eagleburger explained in ICHEIC's final report, "there was no instruction manual" for spreading the word, in many languages, to people around the world, and for identifying valid policyholders among tens of thousands of claimants. Adjudicators "were constantly juggling the need for speedy resolution (particularly given the advanced age of the survivors) with the importance, intricacies, and need for fairness and justice of the issues being discussed." But as he freely admitted, the commission "sacrificed time efficiencies for process effectiveness."[58] Clearly, not everyone was satisfied with the balance struck.

But in the end there *was* restitution, through a process that was unprecedented. In their final accounting, ICHEIC announced awards on insurance policies to more than forty-eight thousand survivors of the Holocaust and their heirs around the world, amounting to over $306 million. Elaborating, ICHEIC noted that among those who received payments totaling nearly $100 million were eight thousand claimants who had not been able to name a specific insurance company; in addition, the commission designated $30 million for East European claimants for cases in which "policies had been written by companies that had been nationalized or liquidated after the war and for which no present day successor could be identified." Thirty-one thousand persons also received "humanitarian awards" totaling $31 million, in cases "that contained a high level of anecdotal information regarding insurance but could not be matched against any company records." And finally, ICHEIC contributed $169 million to various humanitarian programs for Holocaust survivors, supporting welfare, health services, and other social programs.[59] Roman Kent, a member of ICHEIC and chairman of the American Gathering of Holocaust Survivors, presented both the positive and the negative. "Survivors had waited too long for insurance companies to address the theft of thousands of policies," he said, in a less than enthusiastic commentary. Still, he added, "the ICHEIC process has, at last, provided some small acknowledgement of this theft and restored what is possible for those survivors and their family members who are still alive."[60]

An American Campaign

The story that I have told to this point cannot be properly understood without reference to a critical element of its context—the overheated atmosphere of American high-stakes, class action litigation. Extensively questioned and even detested by some in the United States, mass litigation of this sort, in which lawsuits are brought on behalf of a large group of plaintiffs, was alien, though not unfamiliar, to most of the seasoned business leaders in these contests and deeply unappreciated by European academic and practicing jurists.[61] Put simply, to many Europeans the practice of U.S. civil litigation was "justice run amuck."[62] Begun with consumer-related litigation and reaching spectacular heights with settlements for injuries caused by tobacco, asbestos, and pollution, this kind of lawsuit has extended widely into other fields, stimulated by the ingenuity, resolve, and combativeness of plaintiffs' counsel. For an introductory guide to this culture I can do no better than to refer to a set of guidelines crafted for a professional journal by one of the most energetic of these legal gladiators, Morris A. Ratner, a very bright young San Francisco lawyer who represented plaintiffs in the Swiss banks and German corporations cases and who worked closely with the veteran Michael Hausfeld, a widely respected lead attorney in the Swiss banks and German corporations cases.[63]

As Ratner freely admits, central to this high-powered system is the arrangement of contingency fees, by which lawyers are paid only when there is a favorable outcome and through an agreed percentage of the settlement that must be approved by the court. Structured in this way, contingency fees mean that attorneys' already robust competitive urges are fueled by economic necessity—and in some cases, it must be said, by the attraction of huge earnings in the event of gigantic settlements. "Lawyers pursuing human rights or individual class action cases on a contingency basis cannot afford to select the wrong cases, or to posture those cases in an unfavorable manner," Ratner candidly indicates.[64] Put more bluntly, aggression is practically built into the system. Up against defendants with generally deep pockets, and sometimes expending millions of dollars both to wage these legal battles and comply with the ground rules for them, plaintiffs' lawyers can often not afford to lose— or to soften the arguments made on behalf of their clients. At the same time, plaintiffs' counsel, often portrayed as pit bulls in the fight, can see themselves as underdogs. "Wielding greater resources," Ratner observes, defendants "are usually capable of purchasing big-firm legal representation, accompanied by the large volume of offensive legal work often intended to delay proceedings, bury plaintiffs' counsel in paper, and scare over-burdened courts into dismissing or limiting victims' claims."

"The case law is riddled with the legal equivalent of train wrecks, where victims' claims have been dismissed on numerous grounds," Ratner notes. "Conversely, there is also a danger in victims' advocates' being too timid, and failing to creatively use the judicial system to obtain justice, even in tough cases." Need one add, selecting defendants does not derive from a careful weighing of historical responsibility. Facing countless legal hurdles, the lawyers must identify defendants over whom the courts will accept jurisdiction and who will ultimately make the investment of legal talent, time, and money worthwhile. "For example," notes Ratner, "in the Nazi-era slave labor litigation, plaintiffs sued only a fraction of the German companies that were involved in the use of slave labor during the Holocaust; plaintiffs sued those companies that they believed had sufficient contact with the United States to justify an exercise of personal jurisdiction by the court over those defendants."[65]

After describing the formidable legal challenges, Ratner goes on to outline the importance of "government contacts and support" in the resolution of these battles. Cooperation with government enabled the plaintiffs to apply "the maximum pressure," notably in the Swiss banks case by Senator Alfonse D'Amato. "Victims' advocates' relationships with the United States State Department, banking committees in New York, insurance commissioners and other public figures also played prominently in the dynamics that ultimately prompted the settlement of the Nazi-era litigation," he noted.[66] Similarly, "media coverage" was a crucial part of the overall strategy "to complement the political activities and grass roots activism." Lawyers had to be prudent, however, and Ratner recommends against showboating: "counsel should be wary of becoming the target of media attention which risks the inevitable anti-lawyer, anti-legal fees type of coverage that plagued the Holocaust cases."[67]

The operatic contest suggested in Ratner's advice to his colleagues was in fact staged during the Holocaust-era litigation, negotiation, and settlement in the late 1990s. From the Olympian heights of the German philosophical tradition, Hannah Arendt once noted the inadequacy of "juristic concepts" to deal with matters such as genocide and the Holocaust.[68] For participants in the struggles against the Swiss and other banks and corporations, however, the restitution campaign of the 1990s had precious little to do with "juristic concepts." Elan Steinberg of the World Jewish Congress put it brutally. "Why did it work?" he asked. "Because we beat their brains out. It's like Pharaoh. This is punishment."[69] Robert A. Swift, a litigator who acted for the plaintiffs in the Swiss banks case and in later suits suggested more elegantly that the outcome "may owe more to political, diplomatic and media pressure than to the likelihood of a court verdict"—although he insisted that nothing could have happened without "credible, triable and quantifiable claims" being presented.[70] Burt Neuborne, recently referred to as "one of the nation's leading public interest lawyers," allowed that "the litigation was as much about politics as it was about law." Indeed, it was "an untidy mixture of law, politics and raw emotion."[71] Whatever their emphasis, both plaintiffs and defendants would have agreed: it was impossible to ignore the public pressure, the bluster, and the various kinds of collective mobilization utilized to promote final agreement.

How people reacted to this depended in part on their views of lawyers and the American practice of tort law, not to mention the substantive issues of restitution for the Holocaust. In my view, we should at least accept that there were reasonable grounds to feel uncomfortable about the process. Occasionally, when negotiations became especially heated, the word "blackmail" passed the lips of defendants or their representatives. Although such charges are hardly unusual in litigation, this prompted furious objections and insinuations of corporate greed and wrongdoing. What I think one should keep in mind about this part of the restitution campaign is that it was part and parcel of a legal culture that is widely contested, that has both strong defenders and critics, and that marks a particular moment in the American legal tradition.[72]

During the campaign itself, it is important to note, not all the proponents of restitution felt comfortable with the aggressive posture of the litigators. Stuart Eizenstat, who had a ringside seat in the battles of the lawyers, saw the lawsuits as the perhaps unavoidable catalysts for the real process—negotiation among representative groups, facilitated also by diplomatic engagement. "The lawsuits were simply a vehicle for a titanic political struggle, which was messy, sometimes unseemly, and constantly frustrating," was his summation. The lawyers could be outrageous; he decried "their often infantile, ego-driven maneuvers, quarrels, and manipulations, peppered with accusatory words like 'scandalous, double-crossed, poisonous, evil,' and worse"—although he conceded that without them there would have been no settlements.[73] The litigators "hijacked the Swiss bank dispute"; they were "a witches brew of egos and mutual jealousies, greatly complicating my responsibility to keep the Swiss affair from careening out of diplomatic control and . . . impeding my ability to develop a coherent bargaining unit with which the Swiss could deal."[74] His preference for resolving the disputes, and his own personal expertise, was diplomacy—the value of which was, in his estimation, one of the major lessons of the entire Holocaust restitution movement.[75]

The public posture of the plaintiffs' lawyers was of course part of the negotiating process. Referred to by one journalist as "the attack dog of the class action world," Michael Hausfeld, of Cohen, Milstein, Hausfeld and Toll, was known as the "most feared lawyer in Washington, D.C.," according to an article posted on the firm's own Web site; the celebrated Melvyn Weiss, referred to by *Forbes* as "Mr. Class Action," framed a newspaper article in his office referring to himself as the "Crocodile Lawyer."[76] Paul Volcker, whose pivotal investigation set the framework for the Swiss banks settlement, "despised the class-action lawyers" according to Eizenstat, "seeing them as greedy egomaniacs more interested in burnishing their shingles than serving their long-suffering clients."[77] At the World Jewish Congress, Singer and Steinberg harbored deep suspicions about the lawyers, in one view disliking them for stealing the Jewish organization's show.[78] Seeking mediation, Eizenstat "felt like the manager of an insane asylum; if the inmates had not actually taken it over, they certainly had been let out of their rooms."[79] The most outrageous personality, according to almost everyone, was an energetic personal injury specialist named Edward Fagan who emerged as the advocate for tens of thousands of survivors and other claimants and whose signature strategy was a media appearance alongside Holocaust victims, together with demonstrations, prayer vigils, and a disruptive, attention-grabbing unwillingness to defer to his more experienced colleagues.[80]

As the contests widened, aggression was not limited to the fight between the two sides. By the time the Swiss banks affair moved close to a settlement, according to one well-informed observer, "not only were the two sides not talking to each other—neither were some of the plaintiffs' lawyers."[81] Prior to the final discussions, the claimants' attorneys fought furiously with one another to sign up the most clients and to gain the upper hand in strategy. By the autumn of 1998 these battles were reaching a boiling point. The *New York Times* headlined one story "Jewish Groups Fight for Spoils of Swiss Case." As the report described, "competing lawyers from the United States barnstormed across Europe soliciting clients, publicly castigating each other and privately maneuvering to oust their adversaries."[82] Two main factions emerged, one headed by Michael Hausfeld and Melvyn Weiss, two lions of the class action world, and the other by Edward Fagan, a loose cannon whose stylistic vulgarity went hand in hand with his inexperience in this scale of class action litigation. "The two teams were spending their time denigrating each other, their ability, parentage, ethnic heritage, you name it," according to Burt Neuborne. European Jewish leaders were often aghast as the class action lawyers came to town: not only were these quarrelsome outsiders signing up local claimants, they claimed to speak for masses of survivors, confronting local and national institutions. Antisemitism, some said, would be the inevitable result.[83]

Congressional hearings were an occasion for politicians to enter the fray. Survivors of the Holocaust made emotional appeals. Meetings of banking and insurance regulators offered platforms for new interventions. Along with the politicians, public officials joined their accusations. New players appeared: Alan Hevesi, the chief financial officer of New York City emerged as an important force, orchestrating regulatory challenges to the Swiss banks. In California, flanked by the state's governor Gray Davis, the state's insurance commissioner Chuck Quackenbush, a prominent Republican, took on the insurance companies: "We come to send a message," he told them. "You can pay now or we guarantee you will pay more later."[84] Campaigns against the banks, corporations, and insurance companies involved petitions, full-page advertisements in newspapers, and threats of punishing sanctions. Pension fund managers threatened the Swiss with a boycott on the scale of the divestment campaign against the apartheid regime in South Africa.[85] Insults were common. According to Eizenstat, the worst came with negotiations over money: These were "like a boxing match, with many rounds but few rules, certainly not those of the Marquis of Queensberry. There were rabbit punches, low blows, and verbal insults on all sides. It took us months to move from the opening round to the final round about money, and each negotiating session featured the pounding of heavyweight prizefighters."[86]

Reactions

To the litigators who argued on behalf of the plaintiffs and to those who favored Holocaust restitution, the settlements were a triumph of American jurisprudence and a fitting conclusion of a historic campaign. At a moment of satisfaction in Berlin in July 2000, celebrating the culmination of negotiations with the German government and corporations, Stuart Eizenstat was exceptionally generous to the representatives of the Holocaust survivors, particularly given what we have already seen of his harsh views on the matter: "It was American lawyers, through the lawsuits they brought in U.S. courts, who placed the long-forgotten wrongs by German companies during the Nazi era on the international agenda. It was their research and their work which highlighted these old injustices and forced us to confront them. Without question, we would not be here without them." And he added with regard to their remuneration—the object of no little contention: "The legal fees they will receive are far less than would normally be received for such a large settlement and represent only about one percent of the total [settlement]. This is eminently reasonable given their contribution."[87] Judge Korman's similarly generous assessment of American counsel, particularly the more junior among them, prompted a historical reflection when he chastised senior Swiss judges for being insufficiently generous to survivor claimants: "It's because of young Americans that every mess in Europe was cleaned up in this century," he lectured his Swiss counterparts.[88]

"The real hero of this story is the American justice system," wrote Michael Bazyler. "The unique features of the American system of justice are precisely those factors that made the United States the *only* forum in the world where Holocaust claims could be heard today."[89] Melvyn Weiss, later to fall afoul of the justice system himself as we shall see, also believed that the outcome was a tribute to American law. "The litigation against Swiss banks, German industry, and others reinforces my strong belief in the precious role of the American legal system as a significant cornerstone of modern society," he wrote. The settlements demonstrated "the vital role of America's legal system in protecting and, indeed, safeguarding human rights and the rule of law." He even added a warning to those who wanted to trim the sails of litigators like himself: "Any attempt to constrict access to the American court system, or otherwise limit the efficacy of the class action device should be resisted as an attack on a cornerstone of American greatness."[90] American greatness was similarly on the mind of Burt Neuborne as he contemplated the link between the outcome of the Holocaust-era litigation and "the astonishing success of our economic and political models":

> Measured by prosperity, freedom, innovation, tolerance and the simultaneous achievement of social mobility and political stability, the American experiment is a remarkable success. It is so successful that no major economic player on the world stage can hope to succeed without participating vigorously in our market and reaping the benefit of our economic prosperity. But that market, and the resulting prosperity, did not spring up by accident. Our success flows from a social and political commitment to fairness and the values of decency that find their expression in the American respect for the rule of law—a virtually unique legal system that provides a genuinely level playing field for a poor Holocaust survivor seeking to confront a corporate giant. In short, I believe that we are prosperous in large part because we have enjoyed—and dispensed—the blessings of "Equal Justice under Law" and have built a legal system that provides the weak with a fair chance of victory, at least sometimes.

To be sure, Neuborne conceded, it would have been better to have litigated these cases in Europe, where the crimes occurred. However, "the

legal systems of Switzerland and Germany are so stacked in favor of defendants and so hostile to the claims set forth in the Holocaust cases that
it would have been suicidal to litigate in those forums." Those countries
simply lacked the legal machinery by which to resolve such claims. In
both Germany and Switzerland, "class actions are perceived as a symp-
tom of American madness. The mindset of the judiciary is timid and
rigidly locked into the status quo. In short, the European courtroom is
not currently a level playing field; it is a fortress for the powerful. Until
European justice evolves into a level playing field, lawyers have no choice
but to resort to an American courtroom as the only game in town."[91]

In the debate on the role of the United States in the resolution of
these disputes, no one denies the special receptivity of American courts
and the American public environment for Holocaust-related claims.
However, both American critics and many Europeans have challenged
the moral and legal claims that I have noted here. In fairness, it should
be stressed that such criticisms make sense when applied to class actions
in general, rather than to anything particular to the Holocaust-related
suits. Europeans often see the United States as a "litigation-driven society," of which multiparty lawsuits are a primary expression. "A prevailing view amongst European experts," according to one analyst, "is that
the U.S. style class action can simply be used to leverage large sums of
money from a corporation to claimant attorneys through contingency
fees 'earned' in return for settling a large number of claims sometimes
of speculative value."[92] Particularly irksome in the view of these commentators is that none of the Holocaust restitution contests have ultimately been resolved on the merits of the case. In the end, the defendants simply calculated that it was cheaper to settle than to continue.
Owen Pell, a counsel for the defendants, noted that his clients simply
had drawn the obvious conclusion: "Companies have learned you don't
judge a lawsuit by its merits. . . . You judge it by the potential public relations damage."[93] To critics, this result is "one of the last steps along
this path toward the lawsuit as a business deal."[94]

Companies and their lawyers, one should add, were not only dis-
comfited by the mobilization outside the courts; they were not too
happy with what happened inside them as well. It is not hard to see,
just beneath the surface, the unease of those who come from the civil
law jurisdictions when plunged into the heated arena of adversarial
justice. On occasion, lawyers for the plaintiffs ventured forth with
barely a legal leg to stand on: in some cases this was fully in keeping

with an Anglo-American "tradition of tort suits that go against the current of law and that welcome 'justice as struggle'"; but for the Europeans, as University of Pittsburgh legal academic Vivian Curran notes, "courts which hear tort actions are neither the best equipped nor the best accepted for adjudicating issues of public and historical importance."[95] As well, the Europeans could be extremely uneasy with American lawyers pressing for "rough justice"—broad agreement on liability, without laboring over individual cases. In the Swiss and French banks case, for example, the bankers' instincts were to resolve each and every claim, however long it took, to as precise a degree as possible. The Americans preferred a negotiated settlement resolved around the bargaining table. "It didn't sound like justice," was the reaction of a member of the French delegation upon hearing the American plan.[96] "The class action suit is unknown here in Germany," reported historian Gerald Feldman as he tried to understand the reactions of the Allianz, the insurance company that engaged him to assist their case, "and the adversarial system employed in American civil law makes it possible for lawyers to make broad charges, insinuate all kinds of misbehavior, and present very shallow and even implausible arguments. Their purpose is [to] open up every conceivable area to discovery and force the opponent to disgorge information that will improve the plaintiff's case."[97] And behind that, the major goal was, as always, to settle, and to do so on the best possible terms for the claimants.

The problem here, from the perspective of those unaccustomed to or uncomfortable with resolution through the rough-and-tumble of the American system, is that such outcomes arguably undermine the rule of law. In the words of Samuel Baumgartner, an academic with both Swiss and American legal experience, the result is "a litigation system in which power (including judicial power), money (who has it and who does not), and tactics seem to be more important in the outcome of litigation than a finding of who is right and who is wrong."[98] What for Bazyler, Neuborne, Weiss, and others is the admirable reach of the American courts in calling others to account as well as a leveling of the judicial playing field is for many Europeans an unwarranted mobilization of political and economic power, the imposition of a *lex americana* or an exercise of judicial imperialism.[99] Defendants and their publics resent American sponsorship of a "courthouse for the world," practicing what has been termed "the blackmail of oppressive aggregation."[100] "Imagine how we would feel," asks Joseph G. Finnerty, a lawyer for the defendants in a class action suit, "if courts in another part of the world decided they had jurisdiction over alleged actions by America, in America, against other Americans. We would be affronted, and rightly so."[101]

Finally, in response to American claims about bringing the Europeans to a reluctant acknowledgment of their wartime pasts, critics have pointed to the allegedly lackluster results of the United States' own efforts to organize restitution for its own shortcomings during the Holocaust—not to mention other cases of extreme violence in the American past. "Having held other countries up to the harsh light of history," observes Stuart Eizenstat, "we have a special responsibility to hold ourselves to the highest standard."[102] But this has not always been realized. Notably, a proposal to establish a fund for needy Holocaust survivors to be supported by American corporations that had been sued or threatened with litigation failed to attract support or indeed any private donors.[103] Also, the Presidential Advisory Commission on Holocaust Assets (PCHA), the Clinton administration effort to assess United States dealings in Holocaust-era assets, ended in what was widely seen as disappointment. Between 1998 and 2001 a panel of experts chaired by Edgar Bronfman labored away to produce a report that, in the views of many at least, failed to get to the bottom of American responsibilities and to promote American-sponsored restitution.[104] In Bazyler's judgment, PCHA's "track record has been poor."[105] According to an account in the *New York Times*, "objections to the panel's work were so strong that some staff members said they contemplated writing a minority report." "We didn't do as good a job as we could have," Bronfman admitted, referring particularly to American involvement in looted art. Lack of time, too narrow a mandate, and insufficient documentary evidence were cited as reasons for the failure to meet expectations. According to Gerald Feldman, the commission "had some good scholarship but didn't do anything with it."[106]

Rosner v. United States was a high-profile lawsuit over alleged American wrongdoing concerning property stolen from Holocaust victims.[107] At issue was the famous Hungarian Gold Train, a Hungarian fascist transport of Jewish valuables seized before Hungarian Jewish deportations and allegedly pocketed by some American soldiers at the end of the war.[108] Finally settled in September 2005, the issue of the Gold Train, which had been the object of investigations by PCHA, much publicity, and a book by the Israeli historian Ronald Zweig, was finally put to rest with a settlement mediated by the Justice Department. After protracted negotiations the Americans agreed to the payment of some $4.5 million a year for five years to some sixty thousand needy Hungarian Holocaust survivors around the world—and this without admitting the theft or even that any law had been broken. Had the United States set an example to others for the resolution of such disputes? Some thought not.[109] Attempting to penetrate the fog of rhetoric associated with the Gold Train—the vastly inflated mythology of "Jewish gold," claiming billions of dollars worth of disappeared assets, the hyperbolic accusations of theft and greed, and the dark allegations of reparations withheld—Zweig struggled admirably to bring the affair down to earth. A Hollywood film appeared on the Gold Train not long after the war. In Zweig's view, "When the story of the Hungarian Gold Train resurfaced in the 1990s it was strongly influenced by these images of drama and excitement skillfully created on film. In the popular reconstruction of the past, Hollywood is more important than history."[110] So thought some about the class action lawsuits.

2

Art, Law, and History

Introducing a 1995 symposium at Bard College called "The Spoils of War," Dr. Jeanette Greenfield, a lawyer specializing in the ownership of cultural property, put the question of Second World War plunder of artworks and postwar restitution into historical perspective. The heart of the matter was not in the taking: "The act of plundering in time of war is ancient, timeless, and pandemic," she reminded her listeners.[1] "In the past, objects were taken on any pretext—'indemnity, ransom, punitive expedition, sacred and religious crusade.' Monstrous greed and barbarism were common denominators." It was partly the scale of the Nazi seizures that was unprecedented, amounting it is said to over $20 billion in today's values. And so, as well, was "its ruthlessness, its planning, and even its recording."[2] According to Lynn Nicholas, an American writer, the Nazis' plunder of European cultural artifacts led to "the greatest displacement of works of art in history"—as many artworks carried away as by the rampaging armies of both the Thirty Years War and the Napoleonic Wars combined, in the words of another investigator, Hector Feliciano.[3] In the name of the higher civilization they believed they represented, the Nazi occupiers had trashed, officially seized, or simply helped themselves to what they wanted across the entire continent. Historian Jonathan Petropoulos has calculated that the Germans carted off more than six hundred thousand pieces of art ("paintings, sculpture, *objets d'art*, tapestries, but excluding furniture, books, stamps, or coins"), possibly as much as one-fifth of the European art of the day, from museums, galleries, dealers, and private individuals.[4]

At the center of the European art market, one-third of the privately held works in France disappeared. To carry out this transfer in France, the German occupation employed a staff of sixty, who classified, photographed, stored, and transported the loot. And it was not just the scale of the looting that was so important. As Feliciano emphasizes, the losses involved "symbols of the soul and breath of a country." In France as elsewhere, "the Nazis stole much more than mere assets. These wily and tenacious confiscators were also stealing the soul, meaning, and cultural standards of these collectors."[5]

But apart from the scale and significance, what was also new about this colossal wartime thievery, Greenfield has suggested, was how countries reacted. She detects a striking movement away from an acceptance of this time-honored practice of spoliation as part of the natural order of things. Through shifts of opinion and through international agreements such as The Hague Convention of 1907, "the idea has emerged that cultural property is a matter of international concern, part of the 'heritage of mankind.' This concern has centered on looting from and destruction of archeological sites, cultural heritage, the illicit traffic of art in the international market, and the return of cultural property."[6] In January 1943, the Allies arrayed against Hitler issued a historic commitment "to do their utmost to defeat the methods of dispossession" of the Axis powers, serving notice that they could "declare invalid any transfers of, or dealings with, property, rights and interests of any description whatsoever" in occupied territories.[7] Particularly as it has developed in the wake of the Second World War, this new conviction about the importance of cultural property and the corresponding determination to reverse the tide of spoliation derives partly from rejections of colonialism and calls for the rectification of the imperial past of the Western countries. Less and less, since the end of that conflict, are the spoils of imperialism regarded as an unquestioned entitlement of Western societies. As Elazar Barkan has noted, cultural property "is now recognized as being bound up with national, ethnic, and individual identity, and disputes over its ownership, in turn, shape those identities."[8] Stolen art, therefore, had to be restored to its original owners.

Attitudes such as these, together with outrage at the Nazis' treatment of subject peoples, intensified in wartime and shaped official views and practices of postwar restitution. In April 1945, in preparation for postwar arrangements, General Dwight D. Eisenhower received a directive on the military rule of Germany to impound "works of art or cultural material of value or importance" for eventual repatriation and restitution.[9] Thanks to the commitment of governments and individuals, restitution was considerable following the end of hostilities. Despite immense practical difficulties, lack of cooperation among the Allies, and occasionally outright theft, much was returned. Petropoulos estimates that between 1945 and 1950 the Americans and the British restituted 2.5 million cultural objects, including 468,000 paintings, drawings, and sculptures. The Soviets returned over 1.5 million, and the Germans claimed to have given back over a million. However, tens of thousands of works were never recovered, including incalculable numbers that the Soviets carried away with no intention of restitution, considering this booty as compensation for the vast hoards that the Germans had taken away and/or destroyed.[10]

To be sure, the Allied military command did not return works to individual claimants. The Allies, usually in fairly short order, handed back to the governments of the countries of origin those works that could be identified as having been taken from their territories. Thereafter things did not always work out well. Some of the works were thereupon restituted to the individuals or families from whom they had been taken, but sometimes they were not, either because neither owners nor heirs could be found or the owners could not properly be identified, or else because original ownership could not be established to the satisfaction of local authorities. Perhaps most important, much that was lost was not returned because original owners, and often their heirs as well, had disappeared in the Nazi Holocaust—or the few who had survived were scattered, demoralized, and too busy reconstituting their lives to hunt for what had been taken away. Staggering numbers of works deemed to be "heirless" were auctioned off, sometimes for the benefit of Jewish survivors, but sometimes not.[11] Some individuals, it needs to be said, did search for their lost property from the very first opportunity. Original owners, or in some cases their survivors, scoured the works transferred to various countries when this was possible, or searched private and public collections where many works had ended up. Sometimes they were successful, but often they were not. Some efforts to recover lost works proved to be particularly difficult because the artwork, possibly acquired by new owners in good faith, was difficult to trace and was passed from hand to hand, making identification even more difficult. In addition, many who wanted to search simply lacked the means to do so. As a result, many who sought lost art simply gave up.

Sometimes, too, greed intervened along the way, and those responsible for restitution had other ideas about the final disposition of what had been taken. State institutions, auction houses, and private collectors, it must be said, often failed to prioritize restitution and declined to cooperate with efforts to find works that had been lost. Speaking of Austria, but the observation may be applied to Germany as well, historian Oliver Rathkolb identified "a strange mixture of ignorance and stubbornness to admit the Nazi policies and brutal Austrian collaboration on all levels" as affecting postwar restitution.[12] Original claims were therefore sometimes forgotten, in some cases intentionally so.

Changes in the 1990s

In the view of Gideon Taylor, the executive vice president of the Claims Conference, "the issue of restitution of art and looted cultural property has lagged behind that in other areas."[13] The reasons for this are various: "the ease with which art can be moved across international borders, the lack of public records documenting original ownership, the difficulty of tracing art transactions over the years, and the absence of a central authority to arbitrate claims for artwork." To this he could add the traditional secretiveness of the art market, with many transactions undocumented and conducted out of the public eye, and the sometimes low priority of art restitution in the grand scheme of things. Still, there have been some important successes. As with Swiss banks, insurance, and slave labor, the latter part of the 1990s witnessed a surge of litigation in American courts to achieve the restitution that had stalled in previous decades. The 1990s, notes one observer, "saw an exponential growth in the number and political sensitivities of claims by original owners of stolen art against good-faith purchasers of that art. These cases have challenged jurists, impacted international relations, created public relations nightmares for museums, and have generally shaken the art world."[14]

Although each of the cases for art restitution is distinct, based on a unique set of circumstances, the overall movement for the return of Jewish cultural property lost during the course of the Nazi era no doubt reflects a deeper understanding of the significance of the persecution and murder of European Jews that has emerged in the years since the war. In this perspective, the particular zeal with which the Nazis sought to strip Jews of their artwork is increasingly seen as deriving from the same impulse as the Holocaust itself; it was part of "a systematic plan to rob [the Jews] of their lives, their culture, and their identity."[15] Similarly making this case, the cultural critic Eric Gibson contends: "The Nazis weren't simply out to enrich themselves. Their looting was part of the Final Solution. They wanted to eradicate a race by extinguishing its culture as well as its people. This gives these works of art a unique resonance, the more so since some of them were used as barter for safe passage out of Germany or Austria for family members. The objects are symbols of a terrible crime; recovering them is an equally symbolic form of justice."[16] There is therefore a particular moral imperative, concludes one analyst, to restore to its rightful owners artwork stolen as an integral part of genocide conducted against the Jews. "All of the participants in this story, from individuals to institutions, should be willing to make efforts to make a terrible and continuing wrong a right."[17]

Notwithstanding links with justice seeking examined so far, Holocaust-era art restitution raises particular problems having to do with the complex circumstances of most disputes. As veterans of this process know well, each case requires careful and sometimes prolonged investigation. "People with claims want you to dive right in, but we have to make sure we know enough before we dive in," observed Ronald Lauder, chairman of the World Jewish Congress's Commission for Art Recovery in 1998 and a long-time collector himself when he made this observation. A multibillionaire cosmetics heir, philanthropist, and former U.S. ambassador to Austria who succeeded Edgar Bronfman as chairman of the World Jewish Congress in 2007, Lauder appreciated how art restitution involved sometimes exquisite legal refinement and entailed uncertain resolution—both of which fit uneasily with the history of the Holocaust.[18]

To much of the public, the issues were still understood as confrontations of original owners and Nazi or pro-Nazi confiscators; more often than not, however, the disputes were better characterized by shades of gray, with each side having a strong case and with the evidence being thin and difficult to assemble. "It's a Solomonic situation. You have one piece of property and two innocent parties. You have a situation where the law has to pick which one gets it," commented attorney Randol Schoenberg, whose victory in a case involving a famous painting by the Austrian painter Gustav Klimt was a major success for claimants.[19] Often, the contests were between "two relative innocents," says one analyst, their arguments forming a "chaotic palette" in which good faith, greed, generosity, determination, the public interest, just restitution, tactical ingenuity, strategic vision and compromise were often to be found all together in various combinations.[20] Often, too, as one journalist observed, "the families involved don't always know the truth. To avoid discussing painful experiences, Holocaust survivors often mixed lore with reality. Family branches were sometimes separated, leaving one side in the dark about the other's activities. Many works have changed hands many times."[21]

Far from the questions of Nazi goals and the extraordinary experience of Jews in the art world of the early and mid-twentieth century, litigation over art restitution took disputants into complicated issues of property law, statutes of limitation, jurisdiction, and civil procedure. Frequently disputed, for example, were the circumstances of the original owner's sale, or forced sale of art, often in the years immediately after the Nazis took power in Germany. Were such transfers of ownership made under duress? If so, then the sales could be seen as invalid and the works deemed to be stolen. Or were works sold by choice, either because of financial reverses or part of the collectors' ongoing sales and purchases of paintings?[22] To some degree this was often the case. But how should one measure or define "duress" in the Nazi era? And what if the motives were mixed? Should one simply assert that antisemitic pressure always governed sales of Jewish art? Other questions: What about instances in which there were multiple paintings bearing the same title and therefore no way of conclusively establishing whether a contested work was stolen or legitimately sold?[23] Should restitution litigation take place in Europe or in America? Or should it be in, say, Illinois or New York? Or should it be in New York applying Illinois law? These choices involved far more than convenience, for quite often critical determinations about when the statute of limitations on claims began to accrue turned on the question of which state law was applicable. According to one rule, the statute of limitations did not begin to run until the location and identity of the possessor were discovered; according to another, this did not apply until the original owner demanded its return and the possessor refused.[24] Most often, given the expense and trouble involved in litigation, the parties decide to settle their disputes. Often, this leaves the "principle of the matter" or the "history" essentially unresolved. To adapt anthropologist Clifford Geertz's observation on law, not only do such settlements not get at the whole story, that is, the story and significance of the what happened to the work itself, they are not even *related* to the whole story![25]

Culturally significant as the disputed art of Jewish collectors may have been, it was often extraordinarily high priced as well. In most cases, of course, art lost during the Holocaust was not particularly costly, was irrevocably lost, and those who believed they had claims either never tried to recover their property or tired of seeking what had been stolen or destroyed. But at least part of the drama of art restitution derives from that small set of cases of extraordinary and subsequently deemed extremely valuable stolen works collected in the 1920s and 1930s by a relatively small but significant number of astute Jewish collectors in the major cities of Europe. In some outstanding cases these collectors assembled spectacular collections of Modernist works that have come to be recognized as masterpieces of Western art. Works such as these were sometimes purchased for practically nothing in the prewar or postwar period and are now among the most expensive pieces in the world.

During the 1990s a very small number of original owners or descendants or distant descendants of owners sought to recover works that were worth millions or tens of millions of dollars in a billion-dollar global art market—"second in scale and profitability," it has been said, "only to the trafficking in illegal drugs."[26] These included scions of great and wealthy collectors and dealers such as the Parisians Alphonse Kann and Paul Rosenberg, the Mendelssohn-Bartholdys of Berlin, the Viennese Ferdinand and Adele Bloch-Bauer, and others. Operating in sometimes overheated markets where all sorts of predators lurked, seeking to capitalize on the trading of extraordinarily valuable works of sometimes dubious provenance, where secrecy was often the rule and intrigue commonplace, litigants tried, and continue to try, to find their way, with the courts offering at least the possibility of secure title and fabulous treasure.

Unsurprisingly, critics suspect that battles over art were motivated exclusively by money. As is widely appreciated, just a hint of contestation over the ownership of a painting could call public attention to the work and possibly drive up its value. The notoriety of a Nazi provenance—or even just a rumor of a shady past—might similarly increase the value of the painting. Alternatively, such claims could render a work impossible to sell.[27] Hardened veterans of the art market looked cynically on some claims and regularly suspected the worst. In a recent case, Judge Jed

Rakoff of the federal district court of Manhattan dismissed an appeal to bar Christie's in New York from auctioning a Picasso painting claimed by a great-nephew of the original owner, the banker Paul Mendelssohn-Bartholdy who died in 1935. "I know that no one in the art world is just interested in money or in buying and selling paintings for profit," observed the judge tartly. "They're guided by their belief in truth and beauty. But nevertheless, one might suspect that this is just a fight about money." The painting, Picasso's *Absinthe Drinker*, was said to be worth between $40 million and $50 million.[28]

Ownership disputes in the 1990s involved various scenarios. Michelle Turner outlines four of these: first, looted art in a state-owned museum or public institution; second, looted art in the possession of a thief or a descendant of a thief; third, looted art in the possession of someone who knew, or ought to have known, about its questionable provenance; and fourth, looted art in the possession of what is known in the trade as a "good faith purchaser" or "innocent buyer."[29] During the 1990s and subsequently, claimants most commonly faced counterclaims, either that the works in question were legitimately acquired during the 1930s and were not sold under the duress of persecution or forced emigration, or that the claimants themselves were not the legitimate heirs of those who were the original owners of the work and who often perished during the Holocaust, or that the claimants failed in some manner or other to conform to the procedural requirements of restitution.

As with other restitution campaigns, claimants turned hopefully to American courts. "If you want to sue, you sue in this country," says Willi Korte, an independent Washington-based expert in stolen art who specializes in restitution.[30] Along with the factors that we have already examined that made these courts receptive to these litigants were several peculiar to the field of art. Notably, American law embraces the principle that a thief cannot pass along title, and therefore even good-faith purchasers cannot normally acquire ownership of works taken from the Jews by the Nazis. As Michael Bazyler observes, by comparison with the United States, "continental Europe is much more protective of the innocent buyer and adheres to the legal rule that a good-faith purchaser may acquire a legitimate title to stolen goods."[31] Also, because of more expansive rules regarding the time period for the bringing of claims, American courts often agree to hear cases when European courts do not.[32] In addition, many galleries or museums against which claims have been filed have proven more amenable to settlement than their

European counterparts, because the latter were usually state institutions, enjoying not only government resources but also the support of the broader public for whom public institutions were considered to be custodians of the national patrimony.

To be sure, there were limits to even American courts' flexibility and effectiveness in deciding very difficult matters of ownership. In 2004, representing the Association of Holocaust Victims for Restitution of Artworks and Masterpieces (AHVRAM), the flamboyant and obstreperous attorney Edward Fagan threatened to bring class action suits against the German government and Sotheby's in New York over their failures in art restitution—a maneuver doomed not only to failure but also to the derision of much of the legal profession that followed these matters and took an intense dislike to Fagan's showman tactics.[33] Unlike the Swiss banks and other cases that I have noted to this point, the various steps along the road to Holocaust-era art restitution for the most part involved individuals or small groups of family members making claims against defendants who were far indeed from the perpetrators of the Holocaust.[34]

Generally, the outcome of claims for the recovery of Holocaust-related art stolen during the war has not favored the plaintiffs suing in American courts.[35] State laws governing the recovery process differ considerably, and the litigation is expensive, difficult, and time consuming. Moreover, leaving statutes of limitation aside, the courts have difficulty with evidentiary issues after the passage of so much time. Lynn Nicholas admits that, "realistically, some fifty years after the fact, some thought should be given the present holder of the work, who may not have anything to do with the original confiscator or receiver of stolen goods. By now, proving absolutely that something was or was not a good faith acquisition is extremely difficult."[36] In one famous case in 1999, the Seattle Art Museum spontaneously decided to return a Matisse painting to the heirs of a French family from whom it was stolen in 1941.[37] But such cases are rare. Recently, several American museums have taken the initiative, appealing to the courts preemptively to establish their rightful ownership of works that are in dispute.[38] Finally, as veteran observers have noted, this litigation is also intensely emotional. As Gilbert Edelson, director for the Art Dealers Association of America once noted, "I know of no lawsuit which engenders more passion, this side of the bedroom, than an action involving a work of art, especially one involving possession of the work."[39] In the end, there is the "principle of the matter."

Too often battles for Holocaust art restitution do not produce outcomes that elucidate history or contribute decisively to justice over the Holocaust. This is particularly so when the parties agree to "settle," for any number of reasons not necessarily having to do with the merits of the case.[40] Put differently, efforts to return Holocaust victims' art to their proper owners may be sorted out in legal terms, but often leave the larger historical and moral questions unaddressed. Here are three examples, illustrating major themes.

American Litigation over Holocaust Art: Three Examples

In the first case of 1990s Holocaust art restitution to be settled in the United States, one that highlights an important and recurring theme of Holocaust-era litigation, claimants and defendants reached agreement in August 1998 in a dispute over the ownership of a delicately rendered landscape of 1890—pastel over monotype on textured paper by the famed French Impressionist painter Edgar Degas and known as *Landscape with Smokestacks*.[41] Purchased for $850,000 in 1987 by a Chicago pharmaceutical magnate, conservative philanthropist, and collector, Daniel C. Searle, a member of the Board of Trustees of the Art Institute of Chicago, the work was sought by Lili Gutmann and Simon and Nick Goodman of Southern California, the daughter and grandsons, respectively, of Friedrich Gutmann, the grandson of the founder of the Dresdner Bank whose family had converted to Christianity, and his wife Louise von Landau, daughter of a famous Jewish banking family. After the First World War Friedrich and Louise settled in Amsterdam, where Friedrich carried on his banking business. In 1939, fearful for the future and with his banking business having failed, the Gutmanns sent several paintings from their distinguished collection, including the Degas monotype, to Paris, allegedly for safekeeping. During the war the Germans captured and eventually murdered the Gutmanns—first Friedrich in Theresienstadt and then Louise in Auschwitz.[42]

Thanks to the persistence of their descendants, the Gutmanns' terrible ordeal with Nazism came to exemplify a family's quest for art lost in the Holocaust. The CBS television program *60 Minutes* carried the story of *Landscape with Smokestacks* and presented the case for the Goodman family as a relatively simple case for restitution. In this view, the painting was stolen by the Nazis in Paris between 1940 and 1942. As the litigation proceeded, however, the story of *Landscape with Smokestacks* became increasingly murky. Searle's lawyers, led by a distinguished senior attorney, Howard J. Trienens, presented evidence to suggest that Friedrich Gutmann may have dispatched the Degas to Paris not for safekeeping but, rather, to be sold, probably because of business reverses. Further, it was not clear that the Germans' Einsatzstab Reichsleiter Rosenberg had actually stolen the painting at all. It is quite possible that the monotype was overlooked when the Germans took what they wanted and was then sold at Gutmann's direction. New issues also arose that were crucial for the litigation: there was the question of whether the case should be heard in New York or Chicago (very important because different state laws applied, particularly with regard to statutes of limitation); there was Searle's genuine effort to obtain guarantees about the work's provenance before he purchased it; and further testifying to Searle's good faith was the extensive public exposure of the work before it came into his hands.[43] As the case neared trial in February 1998, the fight over the monotype gave every indication of becoming a cause célèbre, the outcome of which was difficult to predict. Newspaper reports repeated the contentions of the claimants. *60 Minutes* aired their account of the dispute, followed by a documentary on U.S. public television. The Goodmans published advertisements in the Jewish *Forward,* seeking financial support to carry on the fight. For the defendant, as so often in these cases, the public exposure was increasingly intolerable.

In the end, after three years of costly litigation, the suit was settled— as most civil suits are. Quite possibly what precipitated this resolution is that the Gutmann heirs simply ran out of money to pursue the case. In what the *New York Times* referred to as a "split the baby" solution, the litigants agreed to share ownership of the painting. Searle donated his half interest to the Art Institute of Chicago, and the Institute bought the Goodmans' half. Thereafter in the possession of the Art Institute, the Degas monotype would be exhibited accompanied by a notice that it was a "purchase from the collection of Friedrich and Louise Gutmann and a gift of Daniel C. Searle."[44]

According to one estimate, the claimants and the defendant together spent about $1 million in the litigation—for a work purchased by Searle for $850,000.[45] Oft-quoted about this complicated case is an observation attributed to the counsel for the Goodmans, Thomas Kline, as advice to prospective litigants: "If the art is worth less than $3 million, give up." Trienens contests this recommendation, noting that the case of the Degas monotype was particularly time consuming, complicated, and difficult, but the general point almost certainly stands, that litigation of this sort is extremely expensive and should not be undertaken lightly.[46] Nor is it clear how to evaluate a "settlement" in this and so many other cases, given the very high costs of going to trial and the adverse publicity likely to be incurred in doing so to one or the other of the parties, irrespective of the trial results—or for that matter those of appeals. Most interesting, so far as the substance of the issue in this case, is the ambiguity of the evidence, the fact that what seemed to be might not have been, and more particularly that we will probably never know precisely what transpired with respect to the Gutmanns' *Landscape with Smokestack* during the Second World War.

Historically, and as a morality tale, the litigation over *Landscape with Smokestacks* failed to clarify anything except the disposition of the painting. As in so many such cases, much turned on the circumstances in which the painting was lost—a crucial issue, which it turned out was very difficult to establish. Was *Landscape with Smokestacks* sent to Paris to be sold? Was it sold, and sold legitimately? Was it stolen? Was the settlement an example of "Holocaust justice"? On all these essentials, uncertainty persists. That is why the last line of Howard Trienen's book on this subject is: "Draw your own conclusion."[47]

—————

Different kinds of questions, at least as perplexing, arise in what is probably the most important of the Holocaust-related art restitution matters ever to come before the courts—the case of the Austrian Expressionist Egon Schiele's paintings loaned by the government-associated Leopold Foundation in Austria to New York's Museum of Modern Art (MoMA) for a special exhibition in 1997. Part of a stunning collection built by a former ophthalmologist, Rudolf Leopold, an octogenarian art lover who has been collecting since the 1950s, the works in question are housed in the Leopold Museum, which opened in 2001 and is one of the prized cultural centers of modern-day Vienna. For the organizers at MoMA the nightmare descended in the last days of the exhibition, when the heirs of two Holocaust victims demanded two of the paintings, *Dead City III* and *Portrait of Wally*, which they claimed had belonged, respectively, to Fritz Grünbaum, a famous Jewish cabaret entertainer murdered in Dachau in 1941, and Lea Bondi, a Viennese gallery owner who escaped to London in 1938. At issue with these paintings were the claims of the families of the original owners that the paintings did not rightfully belong to the Leopold Foundation and should not be returned to Austria with the rest of the exhibition but should be held in New York pending a final resolution of their ownership. With respect to *Wally*, a haunting portrait of Schiele's young mistress Wally Neuzil, there was a complicated and serious allegation that the painting had been mistakenly dispatched to the Austrian authorities by the American military after the war, instead of being treated as having come from the Bondi gallery and subject to restitution. As a result of ramifications from this mistake, Lea Bondi had been unsuccessful in recovering the painting, despite considerable efforts before her death in 1969.

Fully aware of the serious ramifications of acceding to this request, MoMA director Glenn Lowry rejected it, insisting that he had a contractual obligation to return the borrowed works to the Leopold Foundation in Austria. Two days after the exhibition closed, Manhattan district attorney Robert Morgenthau blocked the return of the paintings, now alleged to be stolen property. Red flags flew everywhere. MoMA contested the grounds for the district attorney's seizure, which is prohibited in civil disputes. Morgenthau insisted that he was able to do so because this was a criminal, not a civil matter. On appeal, the district attorney won. But then MoMA, joined by other museums, including the Jewish Museum in New York, fearing the chilling effect of seizure on their capacity to borrow art from abroad, appealed to the New York Court of Appeals, which overturned the seizure. Thereupon, the New York state legislature passed a special law permitting the seizure after all. The federal government also brought its own suit, alleging that *Wally* had been illegally imported into the United States in the first place.[48] After more legal maneuvering, *Dead City* was finally released for return to Vienna, but *Wally* remains in the custody of the U.S. Customs Service to this day, involved in prolonged and expensive litigation between the private litigants and awaiting a much-delayed decision in a forfeiture proceeding brought by the U.S. government in the Federal District Court of Manhattan. The impact of this imbroglio on the art and the museum world has been extraordinary, and no one seems happy with things being in limbo. "If there were habeas corpus for paintings, 'Portrait of Wally' would have been released by now," recently grumbled one respected art news blogger.[49]

As time has passed, the arguments over *Wally* have piled up on both sides. MoMA and the museum community remain deeply aggrieved at the idea that the return of a painting on loan to an American museum could be blocked and the painting spirited away. "It is always difficult to persuade individuals and institutions to lend art, and this is just another factor that will discourage them," declared the counsel for MoMA.[50] Detailed arguments have been made regarding the status of the painting and whether it should indeed be considered "stolen" property, so that its future could be determined by United States courts. The Austrian government and the Leopold Foundation want the painting returned and have always believed that Austrian law should apply with respect to ownership. Members of the Leopold camp insisted on their good faith as purchasers: "We bought 'Dead City' and 'Wally' from good people, and we could not know that they were stolen by the Nazis," Mrs. Leopold told the *New York Times* in 1998, and in any event the painting ceased to be stolen property after it was recovered by American forces.[51] And the Leopold Museum reminds their opponents of the "total and unbroken silence" of the Bondis about their claim between the mid-1950s, when the latter allegedly decided to drop their effort, and 1997, when they took it up again. On the other side, the Bondi heirs' claim for *Wally* persists. They maintain that the Austrians knew about the mix-up after the war but did nothing about it, and that Leopold ignored obligations to the family to recover the painting in order to get it for himself. In support of that position lawyers for the United States now claim that Rudolf Leopold knew he had shaky title to the work and that he spurned repeated appeals from Bondi asserting her claim.[52]

Stepping back from this exceedingly complicated affair, the seizure of *Wally* put museums on notice that restitution could mean serious trouble for them, however responsive they were to legitimate claims. Here is Glenn Lowry in February 1998, for example, fresh from having received the claims from family members, testifying before the New York House Banking and Financial Services Committee in what turned out to be a vain effort to win their sympathy for the gallery whose paintings had been seized: MoMA "does not and will not knowingly exhibit stolen works of art." Together with other museums, Lowry insisted that MoMA adhered to strict guidelines in provenance research. But this research could be complicated, and making determinations was not always easy. And then, among other grounds for resistance, was the allegedly weak standing of the claimants:

Although we had assumed from the start the good faith of the people claiming the pictures, it now appears likely that neither family had a bona fide claim. In the case of one of these two claims, the painting was claimed by a former reporter for *The New York Times*. As it turned out, her claim was based upon her being the widow of a son of the pre-war owner's cousin, who in turn was not an heir to the painting.

The other claim is even more convoluted. The man who asserted his family's rights in the painting wrote to us about his vivid recollections of seeing the picture in his aunt's house in Vienna before the war. But, according to the pre-war owner's grandson, the claimant never saw the painting, never set foot in the house in Vienna, and is not, as a matter of fact, an heir—a fact the claimant recently conceded in a British newspaper interview. Despite all this, the U.S. Justice Department has commenced a forfeiture proceeding to reclaim this alleged heir's painting, making it almost impossible to engage in the kind of meticulous and dispassionate research required to ascertain the exact history of this painting immediately before and after the Second World War, and who today is the rightful owner.

I mention this example not to discuss the merits of the claim, or to delve into deeply sensitive moral and legal questions of who may rightly assert claims and when they should do so, but to demonstrate that the process of determining what, if any, art in American museum collections was looted by the Nazis and never returned to the proper owner, and then trying to determine who the proper owner might be, is an extremely complex undertaking, and is made even more so when the works in question are loans to, rather than objects owned by, the relevant institution.[53]

One can almost feel the exasperation.

————

A third example, at the very top of the art restitution ladder both in terms of the value of the paintings and the importance of the legal determinations made in the case, was the successful struggle of a determined Los Angeles woman, Maria Altmann, to obtain restitution of five family paintings by the Austrian Symbolist artist Gustav Klimt, valued at tens of millions of dollars, from the Austrian National Gallery, known as the Belvedere Gallery in Vienna.[54] The story of the Klimt paintings, and especially the portrait of Maria Altmann's aunt, a famous and beautiful Viennese hostess and Social Democrat named Adele Bloch-Bauer, exemplifies the complexities to which Lowry referred. Painted by Klimt in 1907 and known as *Adele Bloch-Bauer I* or the *Goldene Adele,* the portrait was of Adele, the wife of the wealthy Czech-Jewish sugar industrialist Ferdinand Bloch-Bauer, who allegedly became the mistress of the artist after the work was completed. The painting is a dazzling, shimmering, gold-flecked masterpiece—"the ideal emblem of opulence," as one observer put it—eventually purchased in 2006 by Ronald Lauder for the Neue Gallerie in New York for $135 million, said at the time to be the highest price ever paid for a work of art.[55]

When Adele Bloch-Bauer died suddenly of meningitis in 1925, aged forty-three, she willed her property to her husband, asking that he, in turn, bequeath five Klimt paintings, including the famous portrait of herself, to the Austrian National Gallery upon his death. Ferdinand fled Vienna after the *Anschluss* of 1938, when the Germans marched into Austria and Austrians welcomed the absorption of the country into the Reich. He found his way to Czechoslovakia, then France, and eventually settled in Switzerland in 1939. In danger not only because of his Jewish background but as an opponent of the new regime, Ferdinand left behind his famous art collection, which was then subjected to Aryanization. Representatives of Viennese museums and top Nazi officials showed up at the Bloch-Bauer Palais on the Elisabethstrasse and made their selections. Other works were sold, and some ended up both in Hitler's personal collection and his proposed Führermuseum in Linz.[56] When Ferdinand died in Zurich in 1945, alone and crushed by his wartime experiences as a refugee, his will did not carry out his wife's wishes of twenty years before. Instead, and in rejection of the country that he felt had so badly mistreated his family, he left all his possessions to three of the five children of his older brother Gustav, a lawyer and noted cellist who, as it happens, had married Adele's older sister.[57] The youngest of Gustav's children, Ferdinand's niece Maria, born in 1916, was also a refugee from Nazism and had settled in Los Angeles. For years, while the portrait of their aunt hung in the Austrian Belvedere Gallery as a prized Viennese icon, Maria and her brothers sought to reconstitute Ferdinand's art collection, and in particular battled the Austrians to obtain the spectacular portrait of Adele Bloch-Bauer.

Stung by the seizure of the Schiele paintings by Robert Morgenthau in 1998, the Austrians began to conduct serious investigations of the provenance of disputed works in their national galleries and museums. Far from exonerating the National Gallery and other institutions, these inquiries raised serious and public questions about Austrian policies and the provenance of various disputed works. Critical for Maria Altmann's case, the investigative journalist Hubertus Czernin showed that the Austrian Gallery had obtained the Klimt paintings through some shady wartime transactions with a Nazi property custodian, Dr. Erich Führer. The Austrians seem also to have forced the family to relinquish some of their claims in order to permit the export of other works of lesser value and importance.[58] Using this information, Altmann began legal proceedings in Vienna to recover several Klimt paintings, acting through her Los Angeles attorney, Randol Schoenberg, a family friend and grandson of the Austrian Jewish composer Arnold Schoenberg. Then, frustrated by procedural difficulties, not to mention the obdurate response from the Austrian authorities for whom these paintings were considered national treasures, Altmann and Schoenberg turned to the federal court in Los Angeles.

Surprisingly for those who followed such matters, Altmann won the first round of this contest, when a judge disallowed the defense of sovereign immunity—saying in effect that the Austrians could not have the case thrown out because of legal protections afforded to sovereign states. The court agreed with Altmann that it would be unjust to force her to sue in Austria because of the unreasonably high procedural hurdles for the plaintiffs in that country.[59] Eventually the vital question of whether Mrs. Altmann was entitled to sue Austria in the United States was argued before the United States Supreme Court. In June 2004, in a landmark ruling, the Court declared that she could, and that the Foreign Sovereign Immunities Act of 1976, which allows suits against foreign nations in cases involving "rights to property taken in violation of international law," could be applied to actions that took place before its enactment.[60] So long as foreign agencies conducted business in the United States they could therefore be sued in U.S. courts. With the way now open to further American litigation, the parties agreed to submit the dispute to an Austrian arbitration panel, and after careful consideration the three arbitrators unanimously awarded the paintings to the then ninety-year-old Maria Altmann.[61]

In this case, there is no doubt that the seizure of the Schiele paintings in New York had a dramatic and salutary effect on the process of Austrian art restitution, nudging the managers of a difficult, uncooperative restitution regime very gradually, and not without difficulty, into a new deal in art restitution. However, the Austrian rules of the game remained highly impractical for claimants such as Maria Altmann, involving astronomic filing fees, for example, calculated as a percentage of the value of the works being sought.[62] Randol Schoenberg, reflecting on his arbitration award—which was unanimous, as he told an audience at the Neue Galerie in New York—had some thoughtful observations about the manner in which this outcome was achieved. "In Austria, very much like here, people latch onto a winner. As soon as we won, of course, everyone had been on our side from the beginning. . . . In terms of public opinion, I heard that people were generally supportive. We had resolved this in an Austrian way, through arbitration. I think that helped considerably for the people of Austria. If we had a U.S. judgment saying these paintings have to come back, there would always have been a question about those crazy Americans trying to stick it to us. They don't understand us, and they don't understand our language and our documents and things. But to have three Austrians say that we were right, really had an impact. So public opinion afterward was very favorable."[63]

The outcome illustrates another theme that is part of the restitution process in the United States. Although it is exceptionally difficult, it can also be exceptionally remunerative. While undoubtedly owing much to the determination of Maria Altmann and her supporters, most particularly her lawyer Randol Schoenberg, one paradoxical reason the case moved forward was that the painting was so important to the defendants and its value was so great. Because this was the case, the claimants decided to invest heavily in the campaign to restore it to the family. Randol Schoenberg spent seven and a half years working on the case, and he must have often had doubts about the final outcome. "The blockbuster claims are going forward," says Thomas Kline, who has represented both sides in these disputes, "those based on the biggest prewar dealers, the biggest collectors, and claims against national collections." Claimants in lesser cases, it is widely felt, do not do so well.[64] In the end, the Klimt paintings sold for an enormous sum. Randol Schoenberg reportedly received 40 percent of the sale price, which means that he earned $54 million from the *Goldene Adele* alone.[65]

As to the substance of the dispute, it must be said, Maria Altmann's odyssey turned out to be a far less momentous Holocaust-related battle than might be suggested both by the value of the paintings and the dreadful context in which they were lost—not to mention the admirable fortitude and commitment with which she and her attorney pursued her cause. For once one left aside the questions of national immunity and Austria's punishing treatment of claimants, the core issues specifically in dispute in the quest for restitution were quite humdrum matters, although legally important, having to do with burden of proof, the interpretation of wills and contracts, definitions and documentation of ownership, laws governing allegedly stolen property, and mind-numbing questions of legal procedure. At bottom, these were the issues— although, to be sure, against a backdrop of expulsion, theft, mass murder, and cover-up. In the end, I think most people would agree, justice was served. As for the historical record, however, and as for justice for the Holocaust, the case of the Klimt paintings had much less weight and significance. The question of who would ultimately own the paintings turned upon significant questions of law, but these had much more to do with the interpretation of a will and with matters of jurisdiction than with broad principles of historical justice and restitution of property stolen by the Nazis.[66]

Some footnotes on the latter: Four of the five Klimt paintings restituted to Maria Altmann went to auction at Christie's in Manhattan on November 8, 2006. The reported price of the Klimts caused a sensation, amounting to a record $192 million. The purchasers were probably private collectors, and the four paintings have not been seen since they were sold.[67] The fabulous *Goldene Adele* was purchased earlier as we have seen by Ronald Lauder, reinforcing the suggestions of some that there were conflicts in his involvement in restitution matters. The problem was not only that Lauder declined to publish the ownership histories of his own, vast collection of German Expressionist and Viennese Secession paintings, works "whose provenance was at best ambiguous and at worst unknowable," according to the *New York Times*. The problem was also that, as a prominent, public champion of Maria Altmann's moral claim to the Klimts, he had a private interest in the matter—namely a long-standing desire to acquire the Adele Bloch-Bauer portrait for his Neue Gallerie in Manhattan.[68] As one commentator noted: "During the legal maneuvering, Ronald Lauder remained a staunch supporter of Mrs. Altmann, and his loyalty was richly rewarded in the privately arranged sale."[69] This is not the first time that questions have been raised about Lauder's strong advocacy of restitution and his activities as an avid collector, but this was undoubtedly the one that was most closely associated with a particular work—in this case, one of the most expensive paintings in the world.[70] Once the work was acquired, according to one source, attendance at the Lauder museum increased sixfold, to ten thousand visitors per week. "It was clearly a picture destined to be at the Neue Gallerie," said Glen Lowry of the MoMA.[71]

American Government Involvement

Not every effort to restitute art lost during the Holocaust involved litigation or even the threat of legal action. Some simply entailed breaking through decades of indifference or opposition to such claims and presenting a reasonable, well-documented case. The Claims Conference's Austrian affiliate (the Committee for Jewish Claims on Austria) raised the issue of Nazi-looted art with Austrian authorities in the mid-1980s, following a strongly accusatory report in the New York-based *ARTnews* magazine in 1984 entitled "A Legacy of Shame."[72] A few years later, the reunification of Germany and end of the Cold War prompted "the renewal of investigations all over Europe," according to Lynn Nicholas.[73] In a survey of his own work on Holocaust restitution, Stuart Eizenstat posited a "wall of silence" on the issue, referring to the lack of discussion of the question following the very substantial return of stolen art in the 1940s, silence that he says was broken by the publication, beginning in the mid-1990s, of books by Jonathan Petropoulos and Lynn Nicholas on the Nazis' plunder of art, Konstantine Akinsha on the Soviets', and Hector Feliciano on the French retention of many works.[74] At the end of 1997 Morgenthau's seizure of the two Schiele paintings and the beginning of a criminal investigation into paintings exhibited in an important New York gallery prompted international discussion of the issue.

The result was a major breakthrough. About this time New York State authorities expanded the mandate of an office of the New York State Banking Department, the Holocaust Claims Processing Office, originally set up to deal with Swiss bank issues, to include other assets, including lost art.[75] Similarly, Stuart Eizenstat gave the debate on stolen art additional momentum within the art community and the general public by linking art restitution to the highly publicized issues of Swiss banks and looted gold. He aired the issue at the London Conference on Nazi Gold in December 1997 and, most importantly, gave a major platform for the question at a conference on Nazi looted assets at the United States Holocaust Memorial Museum in Washington a year later in November 1998. These high-profile discussions put Holocaust-looted art into a far broader perspective than did litigation in American courts—broader, and also more nuanced. Eizenstat had some sympathy for museum directors who feared that a tide of aggressive private efforts to recover paintings might significantly reduce the prospects of international borrowing and lending of art and, in the highly secretive art market, might have driven some works even further underground than was already the case. For their part, museum authorities were particularly alert to the possibility of spurious claims and to the need for guidelines that would put all their institutions on the same footing. To that end, the Association of Art Museum Directors, prompted by the director of the Metropolitan Museum of Art in New York, Philippe de Montebello, began considering such policies in early 1998. Similarly, the American Association of Museums set to work on guidelines for provenance research, focusing on the Nazi era.

Most important, Eizenstat's efforts and those of the American government helped to lift the question of art restitution, gently, to international significance. The Washington Conference, assembling the representatives of forty-four countries at the Holocaust Museum, was a major landmark on the road to a new regime for Nazi-confiscated art.[76] At the meeting J. D. Bindenagel, a veteran State Department official assigned to work on this project, worked hard to protect national sensibilities. "The bottom line of our effort," he told the delegates, "is historical honesty, memory, and openness. We recognize that it is painful for any country to confront historical events that reopen old wounds or raise new questions that affect national identity or international reputation. We know, too, that the horrors of the Holocaust and the fate of its victims' assets inescapably touch on sensitive memories. We hope, as Under Secretary Eizenstat said last night, that we can join together in this noble cause."[77] Following intense behind-the-scenes discussions and very difficult negotiations at the conference itself, and with the path having been smoothed by Eizenstat's diplomatic efforts, European and American representatives agreed to what became known as the Washington Principles, drawing on the work of the Association of Art Museum Directors.[78] The upshot, as one State Department representative later put it, was "to provide guidelines that could be applied by all countries under their own national laws, procedures and practices."[79] Counting on moral authority rather than on any formal enforcement mechanism, the signatories agreed to cooperate in the tracing of looted art, publishing provenance research, resolving disputes, and reaching fair solutions when owners could not be found. The principles included nonbinding guidelines for the search and return of looted art. "The art world will never be the same," Eizenstat quotes Philippe de Montebello as having whispered to him at the meeting.[80] Time will tell, and it should be noted that not everyone was satisfied with the force of these principles or the degree to which they have been followed.[81] Still, it does seem to be the case that there is perceptible progress as compared with the period before the mid-1990s.

Since 1998, optimists can point to significant signs of national and international cooperation in the effort to recover art stolen by the Nazis. Hundreds of works have been returned from European and American museums. American lawyers, some of them pioneers in cultural property law, have been at the forefront of recovery lawsuits internationally— often having honed their skills with Holocaust-era restitution and having moved from there to other restitution work.[82] After the Washington meeting in 1998, a follow-up conference in the Lithuanian capital of Vilnius urged governments to pursue actively the restitution of Holocaust era cultural property.[83] And there were some signs that other institutions were following suit. "Major art dealers and auction houses report a complete overhaul of acquisition standards for European art during the wartime period, and no respectable American museum will even look at an art object for sale from Europe unless its ownership between 1933 and 1945 is documented beyond doubt," according to Stuart Eizenstat.[84]

Along with the cooperation among museums and respect for the Washington Principles, increased awareness of the issue of looted art through American initiatives has promoted the work of nongovernmental agencies committed to the provenance research and/or recovery of works stolen by the Nazis and sometimes other cases as well. Perhaps the most important of these is the Commission for Looted Art in Europe, a nonprofit agency established in 1999 by a documentary filmmaker, Anne Webber, which, as its Web site states, is an international, research, and recovery agency that has assisted in finding over three thousand looted Nazi artifacts since its inception. Founded in New York in 1997, the Commission for Art Recovery affiliated with the World Jewish Congress and the World Jewish Restitution Organization focuses on the lobbying of European governments to promote restitution. The Art Loss Register, a commercial agency based in London established in 1991, registers pieces of art and does investigative and recovery work, with clients ranging from auction houses, museums, galleries, and individuals. Other organizations, each with slightly different foci and terms of reference and some with only a nominal presence, include the International Foundation for Art Research the Holocaust Art Restitution Project, and the New York State Banking Department Holocaust Claims Processing Office.

"The whole meaning of provenance has changed," reports one New York gallery director. From having been a perfunctory listing of previous owners, sometimes with gaps overlooked, this history is now carefully researched by experts in the field. Provenance investigation has shown great potential as a genre of family and social history, contributing significantly to our knowledge of the Jewish world before the Second World War.[85] Databases about the history of ownership of works of art are increasingly important in the art world, and there is a growing recognition that, as Lynn Nicholas put it at the Washington Conference, "justice depends on information."[86] "Most major museums in the United States have posted on their websites the provenance of their holdings known to have changed hands in Europe between 1933 and 1945," reports a State Department official in 2007, and "a portal operated by the American Association of Museums links these websites, so that a potential claimant can check all participating museums for a particular work simply by entering the identification data on the portal website."[87] Major auction houses now have experts on provenance who check the background of artworks they sell. European institutions have made restitution in some notable cases, part of the new climate of receptivity to such claims.[88]

In March 2007, in one of the largest resolutions of claims based on such investigation, galleries in the Netherlands agreed to return 202 works of art to the heirs of the Amsterdam art dealer Jacques Goudstikker, whose paintings were taken by Hitler's lieutenant Hermann Göring and who died accidentally on a ship on the way to safety in 1942.[89] And a year later, France loaned more than fifty paintings to the Israel Museum for an exhibition entitled "Looking for Owners: Custody, Research and Restitution of Art Stolen in France during World War II," organized in cooperation with the Israelis. These pictures went on display together with a separate Israeli show, "Orphaned Art: Looted Art from the Holocaust in the Israel Museum," which provides an Israeli counterpart of unclaimed Holocaust-related art.

Notwithstanding these signs of progress, it is clear that not all art looted by the Nazis will be identified or returned to those who have made persuasive claims or who might do so if they could be made

aware of the whereabouts of their property. Worse, the pace of art restitution seems to be slackening. One-sixth of the artworks stolen by the
Nazis remained missing in 2006, according to a widely cited estimate —
amounting to an astonishing one hundred thousand pieces. Much of this
art was destroyed during the war, but much of it, too, has knowingly or
unknowingly passed into others' hands. According to the *New York Times*,
"experts have become increasingly pessimistic that much more of it will
ever be recovered and restored to its rightful owners."[90] Stuart Eizenstat
has been quoted recently as saying that, following a burst of restitution
after the Washington Conference, "the momentum we generated has
been lost."[91] In the United States, following the work of museums on
guidelines for tracking stolen art, there has been no push for Holocaust-
era art restitution outside the realm of individual litigation. In December 2000, the Presidential Advisory Commission on Holocaust Assets
issued its report, but apart from a discussion of the Hungarian Gold
Train it contributed little more to the movement itself than to survey,
briefly, the museums' commitment "to provide public access to information about Holocaust-era works in their collections." It did make a series
of recommendations about the identification, publication and research
on Holocaust-era assets, but these were never implemented.[92] European
institutions have not fully embraced the Washington Principles, either
because they have been unwilling to conform to those objectives or lack
the resources to do so. The Russians, although they made some conces-
sions in Washington in 1998, are probably in violation of international
law because of their retention of art taken as trophies at the end of the
war. Holocaust-related art in Russia remains uncatalogued, unposted
on the Internet, and has sometimes been seen on display in Moscow
and Saint Petersburg.[93] In Europe, in must be said, with a stronger
tradition of public institutions than in America, there was widespread
support after the war for the idea of entrusting national galleries with
Holocaust-related art for which there were no immediate claimants,
seen as a progressive, patriotic decision.[94] Some of these attitudes persist, and with them goes a strong resistance against the restitution of
works of art unless the claim is exceptionally compelling and the claimants appear as direct heirs of those who either perished in the Holocaust
or died before they were able to claim their former property.[95] And finally, art in private hands often remains untraceable until it enters the
marketplace. Meanwhile, the clock is ticking, and claimants become increasingly remote from those who lost their art during the Holocaust.

3

Restitution in
Historical Perspective

Why did it take fifty years? This is the question most frequently asked about the Holocaust-era restitution campaign of the 1990s. "Why this late concern for stolen money and wealth?" asks Elie Wiesel, in his preface to Stuart Eizenstat's book on Holocaust-era restitution.[1] Just putting such questions implies a grave accusation. Practically nothing was done, it is sometimes asserted: this was a grave injustice for which there must have been responsible parties. To be clear, the question rests on an assumption that for an entire generation statesmen and national leaders evaded redress of one of the greatest crimes in history, turning a deaf ear to reasonable appeals to restore what had been taken from the Jewish people. The usual explanations begin with an assessment of the shortcomings of the postwar victors over the defeated Axis powers, their widespread nonrecognition of the gravity of the Holocaust, their incomplete and unenergetic denazification, their preoccupation with the rise of the Cold War, and ultimately their lack of sympathy for the Jewish victims of wartime genocide. But did it really take fifty years to come to grips with the problems of restitution for the destruction of European Jewry? Is it true that "practically nothing was done"? Or that there was, as Stuart Eizenstat contends, "a fifty-year wait for justice"?[2] Or that Germany paid only "token reparations" to survivors after the war?[3] In what follows I take up some of these questions in an effort to put the restitution campaign of the 1990s into broader historical perspective.

Why now? is the complementary second question that is often put, and to complete my overview of historical perspective I shall examine it here. The question was publicly put in February 1998 by Rabbi Israel Singer, Secretary General of the World Jewish Congress, at a symposium dedicated to Holocaust restitution at Cardozo Law School in New York. To his audience of students, professors, and interested visitors, Singer explained the timing as a reaction to cumulative frustration and stonewalling. It was a case of not taking it anymore. It was time to push back. Abruptly, in his talk, Singer called attention to the presence in the audience of Daniel Jonah Goldhagen, whose celebrated and highly controversial book, *Hitler's Willing Executioners,* had been published a year before and who was still making waves for his militant insistence on German bloodlust during the Holocaust. "It takes a person like Professor Goldhagen to heighten the awareness of people throughout the world," Singer proclaimed to his audience. "He has done more to educate, to sensitize, to revolutionize, and to re-interest people in this world than any conference, government, or Jewish organization that I know. I am here to tell Professor Goldhagen that he is an institution, an academic institution that has changed Jewish history, and I congratulate him for it. It is an honor for me to know you."[4] If there was a unifying theme to Rabbi Singer's rambling remarks on "why now?" it was Jewish militancy, which would explain his spontaneous affinity for Goldhagen. "I believe that I have been appointed by my parents to make the lives of those who are here and still with us miserable, and I shall do that with every bit of strength that I have—both allies, neutrals, as well as those who are opponents, criminals, and varied villains," he went on. Singer's point was pushing people to do the right thing. "I learned from Lyndon Johnson," he added, "that there are two options: You either can be outside the tent or you can be inside the tent. You have a choice as to where you want to be. I found a third place, and that was outside, inside, as well as inside the tent, urinating on the President's shoe."[5]

The quality of these remarks aside, I think that Singer asked a good question. For the restitution campaign that was well under way in 1998 had not been predicted by those who had closely followed the broadening consciousness of the Holocaust in North American culture and had sought to understand and explain it. Restitution had no place in a collection on the history and memory of the Nazi era published in honor of Saul Friedlander in 1997.[6] The subject hardly appeared in Peter Novick's *Holocaust in American Life,* published in 1999.[7] It had little or no place in the burgeoning literature on the "memory" of the Holocaust until the Israeli historian Dan Diner began to bring some disparate themes together a few years later.[8] Restitution came to prominence as a matter of wide public preoccupation in North America rather suddenly. Why, then, the late 1990s? This is the issue I take up in the second part of this chapter.

Reparation for the Holocaust, 1940s to 1990s

While to Edgar Bronfman, president of the World Jewish Congress when it took on the hunt for Jewish assets in the mid-1990s, "nobody had looked at this question in 50 years," in fact efforts to secure restitution for Holocaust-era material wrongs had been under way since the end of the war itself—indeed had begun even before the defeat of the Third Reich and had continued practically uninterrupted to the 1990s.[9] The real issue was what had been demanded, the manner in which restitution had proceeded, and what had been accomplished. Certainly not everything had gone well. Sometimes this had been the result of a poor response from public authorities and sometimes claims had just not been pressed from the Jewish side. To understand this process, one needs to enter into the sometimes convoluted and historically shifting ground of restitution history, a subject that has itself been neglected and that I must survey briefly here.

While we contemplate restitution now as a core element of justice seeking, it is important to see how, immediately after the war, people were overwhelmed by the urgency of relief for the newly liberated—the emaciated, shattered survivors of camps and forests and hiding places and death marches, the displaced and broken remnants of European Jewry who remained in deep distress. Those who felt an obligation for the survivors thought first of relief, and only then, if at all, of the limited possibilities of restitution. "No recompense can be offered to the dead," wrote the veteran American diplomat Sumner Wells in May 1945. "The efforts today to right the wrongs which have been committed will be of all too little avail to the bereft, the orphans to the homeless, and to the wanderers on the face of the earth. But such measure of recompense as can be offered surely constitutes the moral obligation of the free people of the earth as soon as their victory is won."[10] When victory finally came, relief workers were swamped. Statesmen had never seen anything like it before. Preparations were thin, and relief institutions had to be hastily improvised. As to legal requirements, few had even given these much thought. As the Swiss historian Regula Ludi rightly notes, no one had any clear idea of what the rights of the victims were, and certainly the law did not provide a guide.[11] There was no clear pathway to redress. "International law was no more prepared for the dynamics of the present war than was the Maginot school of military strategy," wrote a senior Jewish expert on the subject, Jacob Robinson, in 1945.[12]

As so often happens when there is no obvious guide, people turned to the most immediate analogous past—the First World War. One of the great failures of the settlement of that conflict, the Allies believed, was the absence of criminal prosecutions. And so the Allies began trials—at the highest level before the International Military Tribunal at Nuremberg and, at the same time, others under the auspices of the various victorious powers. Meanwhile, there was little consideration of the victims or their rights. As in 1918, it was certainly accepted that civilians had a right to compensation for at least some of what they had lost and what they had suffered. But the means to achieve this, "reparations," were understood to be a matter of *interstate* negotiations and payments. Following the immediate provision of emergency aid, there would be agreements on reparation that would be written into peace treaties.[13] The defeated powers would pay reparations to the victorious states, who would in turn make payments to individuals. The keys to restitution were therefore in the hands of governments, not individual claimants. Moreover, Western perceptions of excessive political and economic impositions of the Versailles Treaty cast a long shadow over considerations of German reparations. A lasting peace and economic stability, it was believed, required moderate demands. That was why there were limits to reparation, which had to be prudently assessed. What mattered crucially was the capacity of the former enemy to pay. In the words of the legal scholar Rudolf Dolzer, "the parties acted on the belief that Germany's reparations would be calculated on the base of certain defined German assets, not on the basis of the full loss and injuries caused by the total war of Germany."[14]

With these basic constraints understood, reparations were therefore less a matter of justice to individuals than they were part of the restoration of global equilibrium, the construction of a new world order. As statesmen saw it, reparations depended upon internationally agreed obligations of the defeated aggressors and an appropriate allocation among the victors. There would be complicated negotiations, balancing the competing demands of the victorious powers and arranging global priorities. One particularly difficult issue, recognized from the start as problematic because it was unprecedented in scope, was the widespread victimization of many people, particularly Jews, who had been citizens of the defeated German state. This problem, like so many others, was consigned to the agenda of interstate negotiations. This was not a matter of shuffling off responsibilities to individual victims but was rather seen positively as subsuming these obligations under a wider framework of peacemaking after a terribly destructive war. American statesmen, who had the greatest influence on issues of global restitution, felt an awe-inspiring responsibility as they set about to deal with these issues at the highest international level. As Brian Urquhart comments about U.S. policymakers at the time, the latter was an idealistic and even visionary group of leaders, moved by universal challenges and inspired by a great vision. "They were pragmatic idealists more concerned about the future of humanity than being popular with one another or with the American electorate." Internationally minded, they put their hopes in international diplomacy, peacemaking, and collective security.[15] Restitution to individuals—understood to number in the millions and coming from every corner of Europe—was a question of relatively minor importance.

For further perspective, it makes sense to look at how Jewish observers considered restitution during the war and immediately after. Surveying this commentary one enters a world of only a handful of farsighted individuals, a tiny number who ventured beyond the catastrophic wartime slaughter to consider restitution for the Jews. One of the first to raise this issue was Shalom Adler-Rudel, a German Jewish refugee leader in London who in 1939 made the case for compensation to German Jews for the theft of their property before the outbreak of war. His first efforts, a call to collect information about demands for restitution, were poorly received.[16] A war had just begun, and statesmen had other things on their minds than the details of an eventual settlement. Later, as information about persecution and mass murder disseminated, some Jewish spokesmen insisted that Jews should be recognized for their victimization *as Jews*. In other words, there would have to be, as part of an eventual peace settlement, some recognition of the standing of a Jewish collectivity. As early as 1941, Nahum Goldmann, the urbane liberal internationalist and founder of the World Jewish Congress, made this case for reparations at the Pan-American conference of the Congress in Baltimore. "Who can doubt that we Jews have every right to international help for European Jewry after the war? If reparations are to be paid, we are the first who have a claim to them," he told the assembled representatives.[17] Thereafter, others took up the issue as oppression worsened. As one historian notes, the term *Wiedergutmachung*, referring to restitution, "began to appear in discussions and modest publications mostly by refugee Jews around 1943."[18] But those who commented on the matter during the war were literally scattered: Shalom Adler-Rudel wrote from London; Zvi Schreiber and Siegfried Moses published in Palestine; Louis C. Bial and Herbert Dorn in Havana; and Nehemiah Robinson and Hugo Marx in New York. According to a contemporary reviewer of some of their works in the *American Journal of International Law,* all of these were moved by the idea that "the torts and damages inflicted upon the Jews, first in Germany and then in Nazi-occupied countries, entitle them to reparations, for which the legal basis must be established."[19] Beyond that, however, there was very little agreement. And finally, their work seems to have had little or no impact on the few American officials who were concerned with postwar reparations during the war itself.

Sailing into uncharted legal waters, these commentators advanced tentative suggestions, aware that they had few precedents and perhaps even fewer supporters. The war was nearing an end, wrote Siegfried Moses in 1944. "However," he continued, "as soon as we make an attempt to picture restitution in any concrete fashion we find ourselves face to face with numerous misgivings and doubts. In fact, the problems appear so varied and complicated that we begin to ask ourselves whether the idea of restitution and reparation, striking and obvious though it may be, will not prove to be something beyond all realization."[20] Moses boldly made a case for restitution, as did all of our commentators. But they knew it would not be easy. Particularly toward the end of the war the overwhelming Jewish priority was the relief and settlement of the survivors. Planning and mobilization were for relief not compensation, for the immediate present and not the culmination of a lengthy, strenuous legal claim. And the Jews could count on very little if any support. Jewish restitution, Moses argued, depended almost entirely on the Jews' own lobbying campaign. "Those who will have to decide as to what ought to be the conditions of peace must be shown and made to realize what the provisions for restitution and reparation must be if the Jewish people and its members are to receive at least some degree of compensation for the damage inflicted upon them," he observed at the time.[21] Nehemiah Robinson, writing in 1944 for the newly established Institute of Jewish Affairs in New York and brother of its director Jacob Robinson, prepared a weighty study, *Indemnification and Reparations: Jewish Aspects,* in 1944. While detailed, Robinson's inquiry was cautious in its expectations. "No large scale transfers of money in favor of the Jews either from Germany or from any other country can be expected in the crucial period of reconstruction as long as no modification has occurred in the political trends in regard to Germany," he estimated. "Evidently, the Allies themselves have as yet no clear notion as to what they are going to do with Germany." Jewish policy on restitution, therefore, "had to be sufficiently elastic to adapt itself to changing circumstances." Much would depend on postwar social and economic conditions, he acknowledged, noting further that "the magnitude of dispossession may also greatly affect the possibility of restitution."[22]

"Property rights following this war will be far more shadowy and fluid than at the close of World War I," was a common alternative perspective — in this case articulated by a popular writer, Hiram Motherwell, a regular contributor to *Harper's* magazine. "Scores of millions of individuals will simply have to take their losses and start anew."[23] This was the estimation so stoutly opposed by the proponents of Jewish restitution, but it was not an unusual view, and Jewish proponents of restitution struggled hard to make the opposite case. Despite important differences in tactics and strategy, commentators eventually rallied around the controversial idea that, whatever their individual claims, the Jews should be thought of as a collectivity that had been grievously wronged. "The Jewish People, who were regarded and treated by Nazi Germany as its first foe, cannot be refused the right of being set on an equal footing in certain respects within the conditions of peace with the states and peoples who participated in the war," wrote Siegfried Moses, for example.[24] This was an obvious way to deal with the legal understanding of reparations as a matter for states to determine, with the added advantage for some of reinforcing Jewish nationalist claims that were being promoted on behalf of a Jewish state in Palestine.

Immediately after the war this argument on behalf of a Jewish collective claim was taken up by Nahum Goldmann and Dr. Chaim Weizmann, representing the World Jewish Congress and the Jewish Agency for Palestine, respectively. Writing to U.S. Secretary of State Dean

Acheson, Weizmann identified "a three-fold problem—of reparation, of rehabilitation, and of restitution." Making the case for the Jewish Agency, Weizmann demanded that it receive title to all heirless Jewish property, valued at around $8 billion. He also suggested "that a proper percentage of the reparations to be obtained from Germany should be allotted for the purpose of the resettlement in Palestine of Jewish victims of racial and religious persecution."[25] Goldmann did the same. Famously, he railed against the "frittering away" of German payments on "a winter coat here or a soup kitchen there," arguing that at least some of the money be used for the reconstruction of Jewish life.[26] His accent was on the future of a sorely wounded Jewish nation. "We demanded that Germany pay compensation wherever possible for any infringement of health, liberty or the opportunity to practice a profession suffered by individual victims of the Nazi regime, Jewish or gentile," he later wrote. While "unprecedented in scope," he noted, those demands were "more or less in line with contemporary ideas." But going further, as Goldmann did, demanding reparations to the Jewish *people*, was "as audacious as it was ethically justified."[27]

What Goldmann did *not* dwell upon for his readers, to be sure, were the bitter divisions among the Jews on this subject—on individual versus collective restitution, on the disposition of heirless and communal Jewish property, on the role of Jewish Palestine as a recipient of reparations, and on many other difficult questions for which there was no ready guide. From the ranks of the victims, there was relatively little pressure. "The survivors themselves were grateful to be among the living," wrote Benjamin Ferencz, a former war crimes investigator who took up the restitution campaign in the immediate postwar period. "Their main concern was to start a new life as quickly as possible in a land of freedom."[28] Some activists such as Ferencz who actively sought compensation for camp survivors, pressed for compensation. But others opposed any dealings with the Germans whatsoever. "In view of the situation among the Jews themselves, whose opinions in all these matters are strongly divided, there is no organization possible which can represent such a large section of the Jews of the world that such a tremendous power and wealth could be conferred upon it," noted one legal specialist at the time. Moreover, as the New York legal analyst Bruno Weil observed, the idea of a collective Jewish claim went against some basic economic assumptions. "In most capitalistically organized countries there would be a strong resentment against disposing of the assets of individuals, against existing international and domestic laws in favor of whatever collectivity could be created or exists," he wrote.[29] The way forward, clearly, would not be easy.

Allied decision making on reparations took as its point of departure a statement by some sixteen governments and the French National Committee in January 1943 declaring "their rights to declare invalid any transfers of, or dealings with, property, rights and interests of any description whatsoever" in territories occupied by Nazi Germany. For the Allies, the starting point was the "systematic spoliation of occupied or controlled territory [that] has followed immediately upon each fresh aggression"; there was no singling out of the Jews or their particular victimization.[30] And as the leading German authority on this subject, Constantin Goschler, notes, "a basic assumption prevailed that it would be impossible for the Germans to pay for every crime they had committed."[31] The challenge, for both the Allies and Jewish leaders, was to set priorities, notably who would be compensated and for what losses suffered.

In the immediate postwar period, there was only intermittent acknowledgment of a particular Jewish claim for restitution, or for that matter for any other kind of distinctive recognition of Jews. Within Germany itself, divided into four occupation zones, German state administrations set up by the occupying authorities, prodded by the Allies, moved unevenly and inconsistently to restore property taken by the Nazis, irrespective of its origins. Along with Jews, trade unions, churches, political parties, and charitable organizations all had claims. The Americans pressed hardest to address particular Jewish concerns, in the face of severe practical problems, disagreements among the Allies, and sometimes recalcitrance among the German authorities and the German population. With no overarching vision for Jewish restitution, there were intense debates among the occupying authorities over such matters as the disposition of heirless Jewish assets, the adjudication of conflicting claims and rights, and the transfer of assets abroad. Nevertheless, there was progress, led by the American military administration working through the various German state authorities, although more in property restitution than in compensation.[32] And although restitution was grudging and graceless in many instances, and certainly incomplete, it was also substantial. As we have seen, much of the stolen art was returned in the first four years after the war—although since so much was taken and the political and social climate so difficult, the priorities for art restitution often lagged behind other kinds of restitution. Goschler notes an estimate of DM 3.5 billion for identifiable assets restituted by the Federal Republic, including West Berlin, much of it involving Jews; additional restitution, for nonidentifiable Jewish property, was agreed upon in the mid-1950s, amounting to some DM 4 billion.[33]

Outside of Germany the Western Allies did acknowledge Jewish needs, but here, too, more in the form of relief than of restitution. At the Paris Reparations Conference in December 1945, following an agreement with the Soviets at Potsdam, the Western Allies took over German assets in neutral countries. From these, the Allies allocated the sum of $25 million to persecutees, generally referred to as the "non-repatriable victims of Nazism." At a later conference it was decided that 90 percent of this amount should be specifically allocated to Jewish rehabilitation and settlement. The governing principle was clearly one of social welfare rather than reparation, and the amount set aside for the Jews was considered at the time to be "pitifully small" by the American authorities, not to mention Jewish leaders.[34] The intention was clearly emergency relief and social welfare, not reparations, a view that remained in place for the next few years. Publishing in 1951, two sympathetic and experienced observers came to the conclusion that payments for the victims had to be wrapped up very soon, through global transfers rather than laboriously calculated amounts of what was owed to individuals. "The rectification of the evils of the Hitler regime is a fundamental Allied policy," they contended, "but it is a policy which is best implemented by being quickly implemented, and bulk sum settlements, gross though they may be, are the best instrument for the solution of the political problems which arise . . . out of the immediate and pressing needs of surviving persecutees."[35]

East and West failed to establish a common policy on Germany and on reparations in the first years after the war, with the result that two German states emerged in 1949 (the Federal Republic of Germany in the West and the German Democratic Republic, or DDR, in the East), each with its own approach to compensating the victims of Nazism. In the East, there was scarcely any recognition of a distinct obligation to Hitler's Jewish victims, and even after the establishment of the German Democratic Republic the very idea of restitution was considered a bourgeois holdover of capitalism, associated in any case with stereotypical Jewish associations with capitalism and private property rights. In the East, restitution and reparation meant German payments to the Soviets and to the Poles in compensation for the colossal damage that they had suffered at the hands of German fascism. Jews from abroad who inquired about restitution of German assets in the Soviet-dominated DDR did not even get a response.[36] In the West, restitution clearly took a second seat to the reparation demands of the Allies, but the return of Jewish property inside Germany, sometimes charting new legal ground, did make progress. An important step in this respect was the U.S. Military Law No. 59, in which the American authorities directed that heirless assets should be restituted to a successor organization, later designated as the Jewish Restitution Successor Organization, instead of accruing to the German state through a process of escheat.[37] In 1953, the federal government moved to harmonize the regulations and policies at work in the various states, or Länder, of West Germany, putting into law what would eventually, after various revisions, become the so-called "final compensation legislation," or *Schlussgesetz,* in 1965.

Seeking a respected place for Germany in the Western community, Konrad Adenauer, becoming the first chancellor of the Federal Republic in 1949, determined to address huge gaps that remained in the theory and practice of reparation for the Jews. Also in 1949, West German president Theodor Heuss helped prepare the way for the restitution to come. "We must not, we may not simply forget the things which people would like to forget because it is so unpleasant," he told a German audience. "We must not and may not forget the Nuremberg laws, the burning of the synagogues, the transport of the Jews abroad to misfortune and to death."[38] Beginning in April 1951, German and Israeli negotiators sounded each other out and quietly extended their contacts. In September, Adenauer made a historic speech to the German parliament acknowledging that "in the name of the German people . . . unspeakable crimes have been committed which require moral and material restitution [*Wiedergutmachung*]. These crimes concern damage to individuals as well as to Jewish property whose owners are no longer alive."[39] In December, believing that the way was now clear for more substantial discussions, Goldmann met with Adenauer to broach the issue of restitution to be paid to the Jewish state. "I told him that I knew I was asking something unusual, something that by conventional standards might be considered incorrect," Goldmann recalled telling the German leader. "But this is a unique case. . . . Until now, Chancellor, I did not know you, but in the twenty-five minutes I have been sitting here opposite you, you have impressed me as a man of such stature that I can expect you to override conventional regulations."[40]

A few months later, in the Dutch town of Wassenaar, German representatives began negotiations with the Israelis and with spokesmen for the Conference on Jewish Material Claims against Germany, a recently established Jewish umbrella body bringing together twenty-three mainstream diaspora organizations headquartered in New York.[41] After difficult discussions, and with the assistance of the Americans, who very much wanted the negotiations to succeed, the parties reached agreement in 1952, enshrined in the Luxembourg Agreement in September of that year between the Israelis and the Federal Republic. Together with changes made to it as years passed, this treaty and its protocols, referred to in Hebrew as *shilumim* (reparations), defined German compensation and restitution practice until the restitution efforts in the 1990s discussed in this volume.

Payments by Germany, it was stressed at the time, were for *material losses* and not compensation for moral wrongs suffered by the victims.[42] Indeed, so far as many Israelis were concerned, the very idea of payments to individuals was morally unacceptable; and from that perspective the main point was rather to compensate the Jewish state for costs of settling a half million Holocaust survivors. According to the Luxembourg settlement, the Germans agreed to pay some DM 3.45 billion ($820 million in the currency of the day) in goods and services to Israel. Of this amount, some DM 450 million ($107 million) was payable to the Claims Conference to be dispensed for the relief, rehabilitation, and settlement of Holocaust survivors outside Israel. The latter portion of the reparations payments would be turned over to the Israelis, partly in the form of goods and partly in both Israeli and foreign currencies, and the Israelis would then transfer this amount to the Jewish organizations, among whom were the Joint Distribution Committee and the Jewish Agency.[43] West Germany also promised to enact legislation to provide compensation and restitution to individual survivors of Nazi persecution—or at least those living in the Federal Republic or who had emigrated before an established deadline. These payments were to cover compensation for lost property, slave labor, wrongful confinement, damage to health, and many other personal injuries. Known as the *Bundesentschädigungsgesetz*, or BEG, the legally defined protocols for payments according to this law were progressively renegotiated, widened, and improved, resulting eventually in the payment of more than $70 billion, in all, by the early twenty-first century.[44]

Commentators at the time of the Luxembourg Agreement and subsequently have remarked upon its uniqueness. As a contemporary legal analyst noted, Luxembourg "is a treaty between two states which do not entertain diplomatic relations and do not even intend to establish such relations for the purpose of carrying out their mutual contractual undertakings. Furthermore, it is a treaty between states of which one was not in existence as a state and the other was not yet constituted in its present legal form when the events giving rise to the payment of reparations occurred."[45] At the time, reparations of this character were truly unprecedented, not only for their massive scale but also for their compensation for persecution and for their acknowledgment of the debt owed to the Jewish people.[46] Most Jewish contemporaries, therefore, considered the agreements with Germany to be a significant accomplishment. Writing to Nahum Goldmann about the treaty, Israeli Prime Minister David Ben-Gurion noted its historic character: "For the first time in the history of a people that has been persecuted, oppressed, plundered and despoiled for hundreds of years in the countries of Europe, a persecutor and a despoiler has been obliged to return parts of the spoils."[47] According to Goldmann, Ben-Gurion also confessed to him how unexpected was this prodigious achievement. "You and I have had the good fortune to see two miracles come to pass," the prime minister is supposed to have said, "the creation of the State of Israel and the signing of the agreement with Germany. I was responsible for the first, you for the second. The only difference is that I always had faith in the first miracle, but I didn't believe in the second until the very last minute."[48]

Even as they congratulated each other, neither Ben-Gurion nor Goldmann could have felt so well about a disturbing accompaniment to the negotiations and settlement with Germany, namely the uproarious, bitter, even violent controversy that erupted in the Jewish state, approaching the dimensions of civil war. "Rarely has an issue so divided the Jewish people, Goldmann later commented.[49] Political parties and factions opposing the very idea of talking to the Germans angrily denounced the very idea of the talks, let alone accepting payments from the perpetrators. Their claim, in a nutshell, was that German money would trivialize the Jews' loss, devalue the lives that had been eradicated. "The reparations money is dipped in Jewish blood," declared the Herut party, led by Menachem Begin.[50] He and his followers mobilized "to frustrate this horrible plot." Demonstrators besieged the Knesset and threatened to lynch the proponents of restitution. "May God help us all to prevent this Holocaust of our people, in the name of our future, in the name of our honor," Begin warned the Knesset in a terrible speech. Ben-Gurion, however, did not flinch. Violent demonstrators, who included both the right and the left, were "a wild mob," he told the nation in a radio broadcast, and the opposition leader, Begin, led a fascist-like effort by thugs and assassins to take over the country.[51] Moshe Sharett, Ben-Gurion's foreign minister and his faithful lieutenant both in the negotiations and the political storm that followed, "recognized the reparations' vital importance to a young state that was barely breathing," according to one recent evaluation.[52] In this view, Israel desperately needed the German funds, perhaps in order to survive. In the end the protesters failed, the deal was signed, and reparations flowed both to the survivors and also to the Israeli government that had absorbed a half million survivors at a precarious moment in the young state's existence.

Complementing the completion of the Luxembourg Agreement, and under pressure from Western countries, the German Federal Republic also negotiated treaties during the late 1950s to the mid-1960s providing payments to eleven former neutral or occupied states outside the Soviet bloc intended as restitution for their formerly persecuted citizens.[53] Notwithstanding the Americans' concerns lest West Germany be overburdened with financial obligations, these arrangements amounted to some $188 million in lump sum payments, a good portion of which went to Jews in those countries.[54] But beyond this there was no expansion of the overall conception of German restitution. With the London Debt Agreement of 1953, the Western Allies permitted Germany to defer additional payments, including reparations for crimes against civilians from East European countries or for slave and forced labor, until a future peace settlement.[55]

Three general themes put developments of the 1950s and 1960s in historical perspective. First, whatever the shortcomings of these agreements, and there were plenty, these were hardly seen at the time, and nor should they be seen now, as involving mere token payments, based on an evasion of responsibility. Rather, the sums involved were huge, unprecedented, based on innovative legal principles, and often considered by the Americans, who viewed the West Germans as their Cold War protégés, as pressing against the limits of what their new German ally would be able to pay.[56] "No similar case is recorded of the voluntary payment of indemnities by a state to its own subjects and to foreign subjects on account of crimes and outrages committed by a former government," observed the English Jewish barrister Norman Bentwich in 1965

looking over his broad perspective on Jewish refugee issues.[57] Speaking
of the restoration of his own family's stolen Jewish properties, the distinguished historian George L. Mosse commented in his memoirs on how
remarkable this was. "Such a restoration of the past seems miraculous,
a totally unforeseen irony of history. No other such restoration has taken
place in the last two centuries after any upheaval and revolution. The
Russians who fled from the Bolshevik Revolution, for example, were apt
to remain poor the rest of their lives, and this was also the case for those
who fled from fascist Europe. But our property was returned bit by bit,
not the moveable goods but the real estate which my Mosse grandfather
had accumulated."[58]

Second, and fully in keeping with the diplomatic and legal culture of
the day, German reparations were top-down negotiations, worked out at
the highest diplomatic and political levels, and notably for the Luxembourg Agreement, by two masters of statecraft, Konrad Adenauer and
Nahum Goldmann. The German public was largely disengaged and at
best lukewarm to the idea. "These were not talks between 'perpetrators'
and 'victims,'" according to the leading German authority on the matter, "but talks between political representatives of Germans and Jews
which were held in a cultured atmosphere and tried to revive an illusion
of German-Jewish prewar discourse."[59] This particular momentum to
restitution to the victims of Nazism may account for its ultimate patch-
work character: enormous sums have been paid, but the outcome is
oddly inconclusive. "Germany did not regard the compensation of Nazi
victims—Jewish as well as others—as a debt for which they should actively seek a solution. Instead they showed a strong tendency to wait for
claims first and then to try to beat down the price."[60]

Third, these restitution efforts, never understood as "complete" by
any of the parties, were seen as imperfect but reasonable global settlements at the time they were negotiated—one priority among many,
none of which could be fully or even adequately satisfied. As the agreement made clear in its opening section, the Federal Republic determined to make good the material damage "*within the limits of [its] capacity.*"[61] "The German Government and the German people realize that
there cannot be genuine and complete restitution, but only an effort to
reassert principles of justice," Bentwich observed.[62] "It was understood
that the standard for compensation would be imperfect," notes one
legal scholar, "for no amount of restitution could compensate the victims of Nazi tyranny for the egregious wrongs committed. German

internal legislation was built upon this premise."[63] But from this, Germans and Jews may well have drawn two different conclusions. As Constantin Goschler puts it, the German authorities "expected restitution to come to an end at some point."[64] The Jews, on the other hand, were quite open about the unfinished nature of the settlements. "One hundred billion Deutsche marks, so far paid under implementation of the BEG, is not an insignificant amount, especially in terms of what it means for individuals," Saul Kagan, longtime head of the Claims Conference, told an interviewer years later. "It certainly is meaningful. Is it adequate? Nothing is adequate in relation to the totality of what people suffered," he added.[65] And so as more than one observer has noted, however satisfied the negotiators may have been when the various settlements were concluded, the incomplete character of the agreements meant trouble for the future.

Global Developments

Contemplating the new momentum given to the Holocaust-era restitution, some have identified a unique coming together of factors in the mid- and late 1990s. This conjunction, says Regula Ludi, "opened a window of opportunity for survivors and their lawyers to take on the corporate world."[66] What was this conjunction? Internationally, I will argue, it was defined most importantly by the end of the Cold War, while at the same time reinforced by other developments. But although there is a consensus on this point, commentators define the impact of this epochal change variously, and it is important to see it as operating in several different ways.

First, its legal impact. As we have seen, the last chapter in the story of reparations with the defeated German Reich was not supposed to be written until a final peace settlement was concluded—a settlement that was persistently put off because of the Cold War. However, with the crumbling of Soviet power at the end of the 1980s and the fall of the Berlin Wall, a Treaty on the Final Settlement with Respect to Germany, popularly known as the Two Plus Four Agreement, was negotiated in 1990 between the Federal Republic of Germany and the DDR (the "two") and the occupying powers of Germany, the United States, Britain, France, and the Soviet Union (the "four"), effectively bringing about this long-deferred resolution. Thereafter, there would be one fully sovereign German state, which bound itself to certain limitations, most importantly with respect to nuclear, biological and chemical weapons, the country's armed forces, and its borders with Poland. As to persisting claims for restitution that had been deferred to a final settlement, while the treaty was silent on the matter and indeed made no reference to the Holocaust, the Germans undertook to discharge their remaining responsibilities with respect to the crimes of the Hitlerian era. West German leaders had already made positive commitments to the Americans about the resolution of claims against the former DDR and also for the continuance of the federal restitution policy.[67] With the Two Plus Four Agreement in place, German courts began to ponder how it affected commitments to restitution. In the end, the German Federal Constitutional Court settled the issue, proclaiming the Two Plus Four Agreement tantamount to a peace settlement, hence opening the door to previously rejected claims, both in Germany and, most importantly for our story, in American courts. The end of the Cold War, thereby, cleared the path to American litigation and a new chapter in Holocaust-era restitution.[68]

The end of the Cold War in Europe also helped define a new receptivity to the concept of restitution for the crimes of the Third Reich. For many, the global conflict of East and West had muted the stigmatization of Nazi Germany and had provided some absolution, not only to the West German state, but to many agencies and institutions that might have taken some responsibility for postwar restitution to the victims of Nazism. Specifically with regard to industry in West Germany, the confrontation with the Soviet bloc had cast into suspicion one of the familiar themes of East German historiography, namely the supportive link between Nazism and big business. Historian Gerald Feldman, who dug deeply into company records as they confronted their Nazi past in the late 1990s, described how business willingness to acknowledge past wrongs was utterly dependent on the collapse of Communism. "It is inconceivable that German corporations prior to the 1990s would have gone around looking for, let alone publicly announcing," the documentary revelations that he and his fellow researchers uncovered.[69] "The historical discussion, insofar as there was one, was framed by Cold War–generated ideological fantasies, one side making unprovable, and the more we learn, absurd claims about business as the promoter of National Socialism and dominant force in the Nazi regime, while critics of the left position often labored with might and main to disprove easily disprovable arguments but did not really do much to uncover the actual relationship between business and Nazi regime in the various stages of the 'Third Reich's' hyperactive twelve-year history. The situation was also one in which most German companies could batten down the hatches and, with some notable exceptions, keep their archival sources on the Nazi period closed—insofar as they had archives in the first place."[70]

The lifting of the Iron Curtain also made available new documentary sources to solve old puzzles. Freshly opened archives from the former Soviet Union or Soviet-dominated countries of Central and Eastern Europe yielded evidence on suppliers and funders of concentration camps, slave labor, insurers of SS facilities, gold shipments, and even dormant bank accounts. Research blossomed. As Feldman observed, the boom in Holocaust scholarship "is not the product of some alleged 'Holocaust industry,' but rather the result of extraordinary new research opportunities."[71] Sometimes, there were unexpected discoveries. Information on the secretive world of Swiss banking, for example, surfaced in Moscow when investigators for the Volcker Committee uncovered crucial archives, carried off to the Soviet Union by Russian soldiers at the end of the war.[72] New materials, as so often is the case, prompted fresh questions that in turn quickened the hunt for more documents. When the United States Holocaust Memorial Museum decided in the mid-1990s to microfilm captured German documents from collections in Moscow, it did not even bother to consider newly available files from the Reich Economics Ministry or the Four Year Plan as being relevant to Nazi genocide. But just a few years later, historian Harold James pointed out, "such themes were central" and the documents were much in demand.[73]

The end of the Soviet bloc also prompted new demands to reckon with past wrongs. Successor states emerged out of the wreckage of the Soviet Union, pressing fresh reparation claims that played a major role in the campaigns for slave and forced labor restitution, for example. Those discussions eventually included representatives of Belarus, the Baltic states, the Czech Republic, and Ukraine, who sat alongside those from Russia and Poland. And within states, particularly where nationalisms had been suppressed, groups emerged that were "determined to gain control of their own pasts."[74] In Switzerland, there were calls to re-examine the country's long-standing neutrality. In Austria, an amnesia facilitated by postwar confrontations began to wear off. NATO and the European Union now thought about expanding eastward, and with this there were calls to harmonize the settlements of the Second World War.[75] Commentators have noted how the bitter warfare in the former Yugoslavia in the 1990s forced Europeans and others to confront memories of genocide even as they contemplated its continuing manifestation. Similarly, the mass slaughters in Somalia, Rwanda, Eastern Zaïre, Liberia, and Angola underscored the Holocaust-like failures of humanitarian intervention and the threats posed by such conflicts to international peace and security. "Terms like 'ethnic cleansing,' a contemporary version of Nazi euphemisms for murder, hold up the greater Holocaust as the measure of lesser ones," noted the University of Pennsylvania historian and restitution authority Jonathan Steinberg. "Indeed, the term 'Holocaust' itself has become part of the speech of many victims and groups who wrap their claims in the shrouds left outside Auschwitz and Sobibor."[76] Such developments inevitably called forth new kinds of memory politics that fed restitution claims, calls not only to resolve current conflicts but also to clear the books of accumulated moral and political debts.

These changes meshed with others that were indirectly tied to the promotion of restitution, notably the increasing global orientation of business, its consumers, and also its critics. Just as executives constantly sought to raise their sights in the 1990s and to think globally, so human rights activists and interest groups moved internationally to confront companies for wrongs committed in the past. Often highlighted in media events, these challenges to previously invincible concentrations of corporate power spread globally via print and electronic media and broke through barriers previously guarded by state and commercial interests. Sometimes led by nongovernmental organizations, functioning as "transnational moral entrepreneurs," human rights activists scored some extraordinary successes.[77] In a famous instance in the mid-1990s, which taught lessons around the world, the sporting goods manufacturer Nike was called to account for its use of child labor in Southeast Asia. Activists pursued a related path with the Swiss banks, now possible because they had a significant American presence and a significant dependence on American capital. Helen Junz, an experienced international economist and a member of the Bergier Commission in Switzerland, noted how much more vulnerable those banks were in the 1990s than in the early 1960s, when they managed to fend off demands to look into dormant accounts. "With globalization, any would-be player on the international scene had to become global. Growth-oriented financial institutions could no longer be satisfied with a branch or agency in the United States. Network building and mergers or acquisitions were *de rigueur*, in all of which the large Swiss banks were set to participate and all of which required the fiat of the U.S. federal and state regulators. This meant that for the first time in the postwar period, the weight of leverage lay with those outside Switzerland."[78]

By the mid-1990s, global networks were abuzz with human rights concerns, part of a human rights consciousness that has contributed to the "emergence of a moral cosmopolitanism."[79] Analysts who have looked into this phenomenon, an essential part of the restitution story, have identified an inescapable link with conceptions of the Holocaust, increasingly seen in the 1990s as "a kind of gold standard against which to judge cases of injustice."[80] Social scientists Ariel Colonomos and John Torpey referred, not long ago, to "the emergence of the Holocaust as the central experience of contemporary history and historical consciousness."[81] From having been marginalized, Holocaust memory has become widely shared in Europe, or at least Western Europe; from having been barely present in the history of the Second World War, it has become the central focus for many Europeans' understanding of that conflict.[82] Different explanations have been offered as to why this recent consciousness of the Holocaust should have emerged when it did. The end of the Cold War's demonization of Communism played a role. Charles Maier accents a retreat from "transformative, future-oriented politics," seeing the substitution, instead, of a near-obsessive focus upon the past—past wrongs, past catastrophes, and past sufferings for which the Holocaust emerges with paradigmatic standing.[83] Some prefer a psychological explanation, seeing the Holocaust as a trauma, guilty memories of which have persisted even if repressed, and which are bursting through to full consciousness now that Cold War confrontations have passed.[84] Still others have pointed to the voices of an aging generation of survivors, for whom this particular juncture has become a last opportunity to assert, on a large, public stage, their previously repressed accounts of their ordeals. And finally, also given the aging of survivors of the Holocaust—said to be dying at the rate of 10 percent a year—the question of reparation to individuals has increasingly taken on a sense of urgency.[85] Claimants made the obvious case that restitution was a case of now or never, and this appeal echoed particularly, although not exclusively, in Eastern Europe, where many survivors lived in poverty, alone, uncared for, and in need of medical and material assistance.

Once underway, rumination on the Holocaust seems to have led inexorably to the question of restitution, a final reckoning with which had been deliberately postponed in the early 1950s. "The cold war's chemistry [had] acted as the great neutralizer of the substrate of nationalism and particularistic memories bound up with it," notes Dan Diner.[86] Along with many other settlings of accounts prompted by the fall of the Soviet empire was the removing of obstacles to the resolution of Holocaust-era claims from Eastern Europe. Similarly, survivors living in the West now began to assert claims in former Soviet-dominated countries. Stuart Eizenstat, who was to play such an important role in the American restitution campaigns of the late 1990s, began his work in this area in 1995 when, as the ambassador to the European Union in Brussels, he was asked by Richard Holbrooke, assistant secretary of state for European Affairs in the Clinton administration, to become the American government's special envoy for property restitution in Central and Eastern Europe.[87] To be sure, there were no obvious boundaries separating Holocaust-related claims from other claims, notably those for property nationalized under Communism. Indeed, this is an important point: restitution claims fed on one another, stimulated by sometimes competing memories of wartime victimization.[88] With the restoration of former private ownership rights came a new surge of transgenerational memory, in this case of previously ignored suffering and dispossession.

Restitution snowballed: proceeding "from restored property formerly socialized, it rolled on. Its momentum spread to subsume Aryanized possessions and hidden bank accounts." In a region that had scarcely been familiar with the Holocaust as a publicly acknowledged event, Holocaust restitution "radiated out in a kind of universal wave, a swell from the former Eastern European people's democracies to swamp countries in the West, especially those that had been staunchly neutral during the war."[89] Responding to various kinds of pressure, governments in some twenty-four different countries established national commissions to examine questions of Holocaust-era assets and the wartime conduct of official agencies.[90] And with these inquiries came increasingly forceful calls for the opening of archives long closed to public inspection. The United States government led the effort in this regard, declassifying millions of pages of material and indexing a huge volume of relevant documents in the National Archives.[91] Summing up this international process of what he calls "reparations politics," John Torpey declared that "the concern in contemporary politics and intellectual life with 'coming to terms with the past' has become pervasive," with the truth commission as the "leading institutional innovation designed to address past wrongdoing."[92]

American Developments

Were there specifically American answers to the question, *why now?* On the occasion of the settlement that launched the German Foundation in July 2000, Stuart Eizenstat gave the official view, explaining why the United States government decided to take such a prominent role in what was, after all, an effort to seek restitution from Europeans. His accent was understandably that of the Clinton administration, and he referred both to friendly American relations with Germany and to support of Holocaust victims, among them many American citizens. But Eizenstat also alluded to wider obligations "to provide justice to victims of the Holocaust and Nazi era, to Jews and non-Jews alike, wherever they lived."[93] Holocaust restitution carried with it a distinct flavor of human rights, a theme that was a rhetorical accompaniment of American foreign policy during the Clinton presidency.[94]

Those commitments repeatedly framed the issue in the public discourse of American officials, whether in the testimony at the Senate Banking Committee in April 1996 that first launched the Swiss banks affair as a priority matter for the Clinton administration, or in State Department initiatives to document the related questions of what happened to gold taken from Holocaust victims, or for that matter in Eizenstat's allusions to his own personal background as a Jew whose childhood was spent in Atlanta, Georgia. "I lost relatives of my own in the Holocaust," he told a reporter, "and I have strong identification with the Jewish community. I felt if the U.S. government wanted to initiate a historic effort to do justice, however belated, in this area and I was being asked to take a leadership role, I could not turn down the opportunity."[95] Growing up, he recounted in his memoir on the subject, he had very little contact with the wartime destruction of European Jews. But then came a gradual change, part of the recent transformation of American society. "The growth of my own consciousness about the Holocaust roughly paralleled its increasing recognition by the general public. Without this heightened public sensibility my work on the restitution of Jewish assets would not have been possible, for the story would have had no context." By the 1990s, Holocaust consciousness was part of the American view of its own wartime past. "For me, this was not just another public policy challenge but a chance to help remove a cloud over the history of the United States, which had sacrificed so greatly to win the war but done so little to prevent civilian genocide and then help its survivors after the conflict."[96] Together with the litigation, begun in 1996, Eizenstat's work for the Clinton administration kept the issue on the boil, notably with his two electrifying reports—the first, in May 1997, on stolen Nazi-era assets transferred to Switzerland and exchanged for hard currency, and the second, a year later, on the Nazis' interaction with other neutral countries through the medium of the Swiss banks.

All this put restitution squarely on the American agenda. In his address to the Cardozo Law School conference on the subject in 1998, Israel Singer alluded to what he saw as the sad prehistory of the restitution campaign—to the persistent efforts of survivors since the postwar period to seek restitution for slave labor, for example, and to the numerous frustrations in battling German industrial giants accused of complicity in persecution and genocide.[97] "We did not invent the wheel," Singer said, "the wheel has been there, but it has been dragging a cart that has been filled with *tsuris* (sorrows), filled with a heavy burden."[98] At this point, it seems clear, individuals really did matter. After decades in which the doors to restitution had been shut, Israel Singer and Edgar Bronfman, working through the World Jewish Congress, seized the opportunity created by international revelations and set the wheels of restitution in motion.

Arguably, the World Jewish Congress (WJC) in the mid-1990s was an organization looking for a mission. Edgar Bronfman and Israel Singer prided themselves on being part of a forceful generation of Jewish leaders—assertive, straightforward, no-nonsense advocates of a previously snubbed and outcast minority. "Having come of age in the American civil rights movement, the campaign to free Soviet Jews, and other Holocaust-related controversies," notes one analyst, "they have an intuitive feel for the power of group solidarity and the extent to which calls for equity resonate deeply with the American public."[99] Bronfman became president of the Congress in 1981, taking over the organization originally founded by Nahum Goldmann, who had worked with Edgar's father, Sam Bronfman, the founder of the Seagram whisky empire and a strong supporter of the organization in the 1950s. Bronfman poured his own money into the impecunious structure and steered it into activist campaigns against Austrian president Kurt Waldheim and on behalf of Soviet Jews. These commitments carried the WJC forward for about a decade and a half. Israel Singer, for his part, was a born activist: involved in the organization from the early 1980s, he was a compelling public speaker with a doctorate in political science who wanted to restore the WJC to global Jewish leadership. In one interpretation, the WJC was in the doldrums in the mid-1990s, without a major issue to promote and perhaps as well without a raison d'être. Holocaust restitution seemed like just the kind of issue that could achieve ambitious objectives for the organization. To one interviewer Singer gave the impression that at this time he was seeking some way to keep that cause, and perhaps the wider consciousness of the Holocaust, alive. "This subject had been on the wane," he said. "The last really impressive event was the creation of the U.S. Holocaust Museum in Washington [in 1993]. We jump-started interest in the subject again one more time. We uncovered one more issue."[100]

Singer's histrionics and Bronfman's pugnacious determination made headway. And the two operated with remarkable synergy: "Where Singer had ideas, Bronfman had clout," was the conclusion of one close observer. Time and again, "it was Israel completing the sentence of Edgar and vice versa," reported Stuart Eizenstat, who watched them in action.[101] For tactical reasons, they minimized the restitution achievements of earlier years in order to fortify their case for action in the late 1990s. Survivors, disenfranchised in the negotiations of the earliest phases of restitution, now found their voice—aided by the WJC, which now promoted their case. Publicity came easily. "Some stories have legs," said Singer's second in command at the Congress, Elan Steinberg. "This one has stilts."[102] Politically astute, Congress leaders reached out for allies, important among whom, as I have noted, was the Republican senator Alfonse D'Amato, then in the news for excoriating President Bill Clinton on the Whitewater scandal. D'Amato provided bipartisan color to the campaign that served it well, particularly when so much support was to come from the Clinton administration. For Clinton, the restitution campaign fit a human rights agenda and offered the added advantage of ingratiating the head of Seagram, one of the most important supporters of the Democratic Party. Not only did the administration back the campaign, the president personally intervened on at least two occasions in 1999, writing to German Chancellor Gerhard Schröder to promote a settlement on slave labor restitution. "I hope we can work this out together," Clinton told the German chancellor as a postscript to one of his letters.[103] Along with personal or political reasons, the Clinton administration saw real advantages in assisting the restitution campaign. Veteran diplomat J. D. Bindenagel, who worked on restitution issues for the State Department and became its envoy on Holocaust issues, observed that in addition to fortifying its posture on human rights and the rule of law, American intervention promoted what were understood to be American policy objectives of justice seeking in such matters as engaging with East European governments on issues related to civil society and the promotion of friendly relations with Germany.[104]

Finally, it is worth repeating what has already been observed, that from the viewpoint of some of the most energetic and determined proponents of the Holocaust-era restitution campaign, the decisive contribution was the beneficent, radiating impact of American law. As we have seen, to the lawyers who championed restitution plaintiffs, this was often decisive. It is important only to add at this point that the climate for the application of a distinctive American legal culture was particularly propitious in the 1990s. Human rights litigation on a global scale had taken a huge leap forward with the New York Second Circuit's landmark case of *Filártiga v. Peña-Irala* in 1980 and the remarkable subsequent willingness of American courts, through the application of the Alien Tort Claims Act of 1789, to assume jurisdiction over human rights abuses committed abroad, against noncitizens.[105] This disposition, together with the facilitation of Holocaust-era class action lawsuits against foreign corporations through powerful discovery processes and restrictive interpretations of statutes of limitation cleared the way for prospective legal contests. "By the 1990s," writes Paul Dubinsky, "U.S. procedural law was extraordinary in its ability to allow plaintiffs with small claims and small means to take on bigger opponents. It was also extraordinary in holding out the possibility of collective justice through adjudication."[106] As one close observer of the American legal scene has noted, "Private law claims have become a new paradigm of redress in the United States."[107] It was possible now, as it had never been in 1945, to seek redress through U.S. courts. The environment seemed right. How these claims were structured and how they represented the history of the Holocaust is the subject to which I now turn.

4

Restitution in Law
and History

Historians are storytellers, among other things, and they like to think of themselves as getting to the bottom of issues, even if they know that the ultimate truth will in the end elude them. Lawyers too tell stories. As the Israeli jurist Leora Bilsky observes, "The courtroom [is] maybe the last public space in our modern society where stories in general and oral stories in particular are still considered to be the privileged way of arriving at the truth."[1] However, along with storytelling, the law has an overriding objective, which is to use legal processes to achieve just outcomes. To do so, storytelling in the legal context is heavily regulated by rules and procedures that have evolved to secure those ends. Hence the point of the comment by the distinguished anthropologist Clifford Geertz: "Whatever it is that the law is after it is not the whole story."[2]

The Holocaust restitution movement of the 1990s highlights these different approaches, casting into relief law and history and highlighting the degree to which the campaign's contentions about wrongdoing were not necessarily what historians would write about the persecution and murder of European Jewry. What happens to storytelling about the Holocaust in a legal context? Practitioners of both law and history would probably agree that they are both seeking the truth about the matter. "The focus must remain on discovering the truth, on revealing and owning up to the past," wrote Abraham Foxman, in a widely circulated article in 1998.[3] But Foxman was worried. He mentioned lawsuits against two American companies, Ford and General Motors, for deeds committed by their German subsidiaries during the war. Was there a problem with the choice of these defendants? Was he uncomfortable with the decision to go after American companies for the doings of their wartime European branches decades ago? There was no indication of this, for Foxman pressed on. He lamented that the Swiss bankers did not pay voluntarily, and that they had to be sued. There was no absolute justice, he said. He was concerned lest Holocaust survivors "be used as political footballs or tickets for financial gain." All fair enough. But what was really his problem?

The nub of the matter seemed to be that, with litigation, the story told about wartime murder of European Jews would be trivialized or distorted: "I fear that all the talk about Holocaust era assets is skewing the Holocaust, making the century's last word on the Holocaust that the Jews died not because they were Jews, but because they had bank accounts, gold, art and property," Foxman wrote. Elie Wiesel has expressed a similar view, explaining why he had not taken up the subject before. "I felt reluctant to define the greatest tragedy in Jewish history in terms of money."[4] For many, as suggested in these views, there was a sense that disputes over restitution would render the Holocaust banal. So what was to be done? It was not quite clear. "We owe it to history and to the six million who died to teach the lessons of the Holocaust to new generations," Foxman commented. Did this mean that he opposed the campaign for restitution? He did not say so, and the reader was left with his unease, his sense that things were somehow on the wrong track. The story was not being told properly, the Holocaust was being "skewed," and the fault seemed to be with the restitution campaign. Was there a real problem here? Or was this just a nervous response to a new chapter of justice seeking for the Holocaust? These questions are the subject of this chapter.

Robbery

At the core of the restitution campaign of the 1990s is a view of the Holocaust: "probably the gravest crime against humanity in recorded history," noted Stuart Eizenstat, but also "history's greatest robbery—robbery of personal effects, art, property, insurance, the right to compensation for labor, and ultimately, dignity."[5] Might the attention to robbery cast murder into the shade? Given the salience of property issues in the movement I am discussing, there are grounds to appreciate concerns about how the restitution campaign has framed the spoliation of Jews in the history of the Holocaust. In the slave labor case against the Siemens industrial concern, one of the plaintiffs maintained that the Holocaust should be viewed as if it were "one gigantic robbery." As a contention, this is often bracketed with the assertion that the Holocaust was the largest theft in history, with losses of Jewish assets estimated at between $143 billion and $215 billion in today's dollars.[6] Elaborating on the theme of theft, a commentator on the Siemens case maintained: "The Nazi SS stole their lives, Swiss banks stole their money, European insurance companies stole their insurance claims, some companies stole their gold fillings, and the Pollack plaintiffs claim the defendants stole their labor."[7] Mass murder, in this view, was simply part of a continuum, with the unifying theme being theft.[8]

Abraham Foxman's worry that the Holocaust would appear out of shape when seen through the optic of restitution has its counterpart in at least one distinguished authority's recent evaluation. At the beginning of his important study of the plunder of Jews in Nazi Germany, historian Götz Aly states that one of his aspirations was to correct impressions created by Eizenstat's negotiations on restitution matters.[9] Aly's concern was not that attention to the robbery of Jews would crowd out mass murder, however. His unhappiness was with what he felt was Eizenstat's mistaken implication that the plunder of German Jews was mainly the work of the leading elements of German industry—"world famous companies like Daimler Benz, Volkswagen, Allianz Insurance, Krupp, the Bertelsmann publishing group, and BMW." Aly sought to redirect attention to ordinary Germans and to the spoliation of Jews that was an inescapable part of everyday life in the Third Reich. The villains in his piece, those ordinary Germans, were far indeed from bourgeois elites who masterminded the victimization of Jews and sought to cover up their greed after the war. "Readers of these pages will encounter not Nazi monsters," writes Aly, "but rather people who are not as different from us as we might like them to be. The culprits here are people striving for prosperity and material security for themselves and their children. They are people dreaming of owning a house with a garden, of buying a car of their own, or of taking a vacation. And they are people not tremendously interested in the potential costs of their short-term welfare to their neighbors or to future generations."[10] As Aly suggests, there is a mistaken view that German businessmen and bank directors were the main beneficiaries of the plundering of Jews. Not so, he argues. Most of the loot went to the state, the German war chest as he puts it, as did the dispossession of entire populations of occupied territories. In turn, the state passed along the benefits to the German population—the welfare or "socialist" side of the National Socialist state. Spectacular profiteering by Nazi satraps doubtless existed, but the real story was in a way much more problematic—the passing on of the stolen property to an entire society, boosting its "domestic consumption and public morale with policies of mass murder and state-organized plunder and terror."[11]

To be sure, Aly's is not the only interpretation of the role of plunder in the Nazi state.[12] But interpretations, in the historians' view, should flow from the evidence and not from general theories of wrongdoing. In an example of the latter, law professor, human rights activist, and Canadian politician Irwin Cotler contends that the confiscation of Jewish property amounted to *"thefticide*—the greatest theft on the occasion of the greatest mass murder in history."[13] Cotler's argument poses an intimate interconnection between plunder and genocide—"crimes committed in anticipation of the Holocaust, accompanying the Holocaust, or in consequence of it." As he puts it, "behind every dormant Swiss account, behind every plundered property, behind every gold dental bridge, behind every unrecovered insurance policy, is the narrative/horror of the Holocaust." To Cotler, this linkage poses a challenge for the law: "The existential character of the evil overtakes the law's capacity to address it, while the law's capacity to address it requires us to banalize the evil."[14] His solution is to have no truck with any assessment of the theft of Jewish property that does not point to mass murder or that fails to identify the culprits. Since such robberies should properly be classified among "Nuremberg crimes," these should be set apart—treated in effect as criminal, not civil offenses, placed beyond statutes of limitation or the operation of property law. According to Cotler, with thefticide, "we are talking about the value of human life itself—of the value and worth of entire European Jewish communities selected for genocide, of the 'what might have been' as well as the 'what was' in existential as well as in property terms."[15]

It is hard to know where to start in untangling some of the assumptions and conclusions in this rhetorically elegant but historically muddled discourse. The main point I would make is that while it is no doubt true that the Nazis singled Jews out for particular victimization from the

start, and that mass murderous objectives directed against them became clear from some time in 1941, the looting of subject peoples, Jews
and non-Jews, was an integral part of the Hitlerian regime throughout
its twelve-year life and applied virtually everywhere the Nazi writ ran.
As historians have well established, Germany largely paid for the war
through the looting, exactions, and financial manipulations of its subject peoples and satellite powers.[16] The confiscation of German Jewish
assets, it is true, led the way. As Aly notes, the latter "served as a model
for use in the countries and regions Germany conquered during World
War II."[17] Moreover, the direct beneficiaries of theft were everywhere.
Focusing on the city of Hamburg, Frank Bajohr determined that such
direct recipients amounted to a good portion of the city's population.
"From 1941–1945, in Hamburg alone the property of thirty thousand
Jews from Hamburg, Germany and Western Europe was publicly auctioned. At least one hundred thousand inhabitants of Hamburg and of
its North German neighboring regions may have acquired items of Jewish property in this period."[18] With war, robbery became European-
wide. The Wehrmacht confiscated millions of tons of food and shipped
whatever the troops could not eat back to the Reich. Those who produced the food often starved. The regime's bureaucrats routinely destroyed currencies to the advantage of the Reich, bled away countries'
industrial and agricultural production, stripped them of their businesses, their buildings, their transportation networks, their citizens' personal belongings, bank accounts, furniture, jewelry, art, and libraries.
Larceny, one might say, was written into the DNA of the Nazi regime. In
addition, one should add the obvious if sometimes forgotten point, that
although the victimization of Jews was greater than that of any other
group, given the scale and intensity of the Nazis' theft, the amounts stolen from non-Jews dwarfed the amounts taken from Jews.[19] And finally,
speaking of Jews, one should not forget the wholesale robbery they suffered at the hands of other occupied and allied societies—the "Aryanization" of businesses, institutions, homes, and apartments, but also,
mainly in Eastern Europe, valuables, household goods, clothing, and
even things that could be stripped from the dead.[20]

One example from Götz Aly: "In the depths of winter in 1943, while
the Wehrmacht was suffering catastrophic defeats on the battlefield, the
soldiers of the Eighteenth Army near Leningrad managed, according to
statistics from the post office, to send more than 3 million packages
home. They were filled with items that had been plundered, bought at

bargain prices, or left over from food rations."[21] This was plunder from the bottom up, an integral part of a continent-wide enterprise disposing of stolen goods, both organized and unorganized, high and low, ideologically focused or, as was more likely the case, without much thought, just out of habit. Except to clarify the origins of the "final solution" and to appreciate the particularly harsh victimization of Jews, it makes no sense to distinguish theft from Jews from theft from others. Nor does one need to invent special categories like "thefticide" with implied necessary linkages to the Holocaust. Nazis stole from Jews before they even contemplated a Holocaust; and they stole from non-Jews for whom there was no Holocaust. The regime rested on theft, among other things, and it is complicated enough to work out restitution for it without constant linkages from one crime to another.

From whom, under these circumstances, should restitution come? From the German state, clearly enough, as the agency, or the successor to the agency, that promoted and in many instances directed the process. But beyond that, where does one stop? As Hannah Arendt observed years ago, "There existed not a single organization or public institution in Germany, at least during the war years, that did *not* become involved in criminal actions and transactions."[22] How is the law to contend with this? When complicity is near universal and when wrongdoing is more often than not a question of degree, to be examined everywhere in a society, how are those to be found liable to be identified and how is the degree of their responsibility to be established?

To questions such as these, plaintiffs' lawyers have a ready answer: In the imperfect world of justice seeking, lawyers choose defendants against whom, for any number of reasons, a case can be mounted and who offer reasonable prospects for recovery. Some maintain that, notwithstanding these apparently arbitrary bases for holding some responsible, justice is served through the process, albeit imperfectly. Gerald Feldman once related that his first exposure to this approach occurred "when a prominent Jewish leader suggested to me at a conference in Vienna that Allianz and the other insurance companies were rich enough to afford to re-do the post-war restitutions under the German compensation legislation in a fairer manner."[23] Feldman was flabbergasted. Quite apart from the politics of the matter, historians seek to put matters of responsibility into perspective, telling as much of the story as they can, irrespective of whether specific aspects of wrongdoing lend themselves to successful litigation. In his massive study of the Allianz Feldman found that a preoccupation with restitution could actually *limit* his inquiry of the company's involvement in the crimes of Nazism. As he discovered, "the central issues involve the political behavior and role of its leaders, their treatment of their Jewish employees, the actions of its leaders during the November 1938 Pogrom, the role of Allianz in Germany's expansion, and its involvement in insuring the facilities and production of places like the Lodz Ghetto and the SS factories in the concentration camps."[24] Much of this, Feldman points out, bore no relationship to restitution at all.

My concern about the litigation process, therefore, involves its implications for the history of the destruction of the European Jews. This is best examined, I think, in the context of the most important legal theory of wrongdoing used in the restitution campaign—"the theme that links the Swiss bank cases, the German slave labor cases, the German bank cases, and the German insurance cases," according to Burt Neuborne—namely, unjust enrichment.[25]

Unjust Enrichment and Related Issues

Unfamiliar to many common law lawyers, the doctrine of unjust enrichment is, in my view, ill suited to the characterization of Holocaust-era wrongdoing and those responsible for those crimes. Conceived for purposes far indeed from genocide and mass murder, this complicated area of law usually deals with far more humdrum matters—the circumstances under which there can be recovery of property to which the defendant is not properly entitled. In the classic statement of the linkage between unjust enrichment and restitution, articulated by the American Law Institute in 1937, "A person who has been unjustly enriched at the expense of another is required to make restitution to the other."[26] But as the experts agree, such restitution need not involve wrongful conduct. As Emily Sherwin, a close student of the subject observes, a claim of unjust enrichment does not require that the defendant be a wrongdoer: "It is enough that the plaintiff lost an expected benefit, or in some cases that the plaintiff simply has a superior moral claim to whatever enrichment the defendant obtained."[27] Moreover, thinking about Holocaust-era restitution as unjust enrichment conflates two kinds of claims, for which the doctrine applies quite differently: with banks, insurance companies, and art restitution the heart of the issue was the claimants' efforts to have their property returned to them, whereas in the case of forced and slave labor—the largest part of the demands for Holocaust-era restitution and even part, as we have seen, of the Swiss banks settlement—the object of the claim was the value of the labor itself, what is classified technically as claims in *quantum meruit*.[28] In the latter situations, as I shall argue, unjust enrichment is a particularly distorted lens through which to view the Holocaust.

Let us descend now from legal abstractions. The key element in Holocaust-related restitution cases is the highly seductive motif of perpetrators becoming fabulously wealthy as a result of theft from persecuted and murdered Jews. And further, this enrichment is widely understood to persist until the present day. In one succinct view, "financial giants worldwide are sitting on billions of dollars in funds made on the backs of World War II victims, which they invested and reinvested many times over during the last century."[29] Gerald Feldman noted "the fantasy about the amount of insurance held by Jews and the value of their policies."[30] Ronald Zweig has written similarly about myths of dizzying levels of wealth on the Hungarian Gold Train, linking these to hoary tales about secret stashes of Jewish valuables.[31] These characterizations have quickened demands for pursuing restitution against particular targets, and the emphasis upon greed as the sole explanation for why it is not forthcoming. "Why Won't Those SOBs Give Me My Money?" was the title of one survivor's article on restitution, referring to "the criminals who run European insurance companies that stole hundreds of millions of dollars from those who died prematurely in the gas chambers, and who used the money to hire stooges to make sure the money is not given back." Why would they not do so? "It is because they would rather keep it."[32]

A caricature? Of course, even if understandable given the circumstances. But the interrelated issue of unjust enrichment is worth examining closely as an accompaniment of the legal presentation of wartime theft from the Jews, for it is an excellent example, it seems to me, of how history can be misshapen to fit the idiom of the law.

The starting point is the enrichment, understood as the logical consequence of the devastation of European Jews. According to the claimants, what happened during the Holocaust was the wrongful transfer of massive amounts of wealth from the victims, resulting in unjust profits to the defendants. No one disputes the first part of this claim. In one of the earliest estimations of Jewish property losses, published in 1944, the

Jewish researcher Nehemiah Robinson calculated that more than $8 billion (in 1944 values) had been lost.[33] In the case of the Swiss banks and the European insurance companies, and speaking more generally about the theft of Jewish-owned property of all kinds, including art, one can trace specific instances of confiscation, instances that occurred, in different ways, tens and hundreds of thousands of times. Recently, looking closely at the nearly five million Jews of Germany, Austria, the Netherlands, France, Poland, and Hungary, the economist Helen Junz, the leading authority on the matter and a member of the Volcker Committee, estimated that Jewish wealth in prewar Europe amounted to over $12 billion in values of the time, of which property losses, due to both theft and destruction, involve as much as $10 billion—although every assessment recognizes that these numbers can only be approximate.[34] Robbery was built into the Nazi regime, going far beyond its antisemitic obsession. "Aryanization was only one part of a vast and rapidly growing system of plunder, expropriation and embezzlement under the Third Reich," observes the historian of Nazi Germany Richard Evans.[35] And of course this spread to collaborationist regimes and even to some bystanders. There is no doubt that there was robbery, on an astronomic scale. Enrichment, however, is another matter.

Unfortunately, identifying those who were unjustly enriched and by how much—no small requirements in law—turns out to be a more complicated and historically problematic exercise than might appear at first glance. Proceeding against such parties required a deft legal hand, picking through patterns of ownership and state control, and working around questions of treaty rights, prior history, and involvement in restitution. Some obvious targets were off limits. Volkswagen, for example, owned during the war by the Nazi Party's Labor Front, might well have been protected because of the doctrine of sovereign immunity, which under some circumstances protects state agencies from American courts.[36] For these reasons, there was no possibility of establishing legal liability for forced laborers who worked for railway companies, the post office, or even companies owned by the SS. Some enterprises had long since ceased to exist. Some had divided into successor companies or had been consolidated through one or more mergers. Others had been nationalized by the East German regime. Some companies got off scot free because they did no business in the United States. Because the various contests, in the end, were settled around negotiating tables rather than in the courts, issues raised by this kind of selectivity were never judicially tested. Nor did the lawyers bother overly much with how their choices affected history. "It is understandable that lawyers concentrate on what is actionable rather than on what is simply awful," Gerald Feldman observed. And then he added, ruefully: "The latter seems to be the province of the historian."[37]

For reasons to which I have already alluded, lawyers for the plaintiffs in the various restitution cases chose unhesitatingly to launch their campaign against the "commanding heights" of the corporate world. No litigation lawyer would have dreamed of doing otherwise. This was the only reasonable way to identify defendants clearly and possibly, at the end of a long road, to reach a lucrative settlement. From the historians' point of view this inevitably involved distortions. The most flagrant among these is the implication that the theft was mainly the work of big industry and the major banks—leaving aside what I have seen to be the far more widespread involvement of "ordinary Germans," indeed virtually an entire society. To historians such as the University of Jena specialist Lutz Niethammer, an advisor to the defendants in the restitution negotiations, the German government shaped the outcome of the forced and slave labor settlement to fit the exigencies of legal liability and the responsibility of major German corporations. Most of the victimized still living today had either worked in agriculture or for a company no longer in existence.[38] And as Niethammer elaborates, "The majority of concentration camp prisoners and almost a third of those forced workers deployed outside farming had not been employed by private enterprises but by *public* agencies and organizations." But these facts were irrelevant to the thrust of restitution as negotiated with the industrial giants in the 1990s. Moreover, present-day German farmers, themselves highly dependent on subsidies as Niethammer notes, did not see themselves as even remotely liable for restitution, nor could the German companies that were no more, nor did the German state, which believed that it had discharged its responsibilities years ago.[39] Nor, in all likelihood, did the present-day German industrial concerns whose leaders thought of the settlement much more as a symbolic statement of German responsibility for the Holocaust than as specifically determined responsibilities of their companies.

Of course, this is not to deny that German corporations during the Hitler era were responsible in some sense for slave and forced labor. They most certainly were. It is rather to point out that the companies that were the subject of litigation and the negotiations for settlement in the 1990s bore only a distant relationship to perpetrators in the Third Reich more than half a century before.[40] The high-profile cases against American parent companies of German subsidiaries provide a particularly vivid example of this problem.

Consider three examples of American companies, Ford, General Motors, and IBM, sued as part of the restitution campaign. Of these, Ford was particularly vulnerable to lawsuit by virtue of its prominence in the United States and because of the high-profile antisemitism of its founder, Henry Ford, a determined Jew hater and a promoter, among other sins, of the anti-Jewish mythology of the *Protocols of the Elders of Zion*. A longtime supporter of Adolf Hitler, Ford had the dubious distinction of being appreciated in *Mein Kampf,* in connection with the Führer's fulminations against the Jews.[41] Ford had pride of place in the restitution story when, in March 1998, it was the object of the first in a series of class actions in the United States having to do with forced labor. Begun in New Jersey, this lawsuit was launched on behalf of a single named plaintiff, Elsa Iwanowa, a non-Jewish woman living in Belgium after the war who had been taken from her home in Russia by German soldiers when she was seventeen years old to do heavy labor in the Cologne plant of the company's Ford Werke AG. Iwanowa and her compatriots, altogether some ten thousand workers at the Cologne factory alone, suffered from excruciating conditions at the site. But there was also the enrichment. The complaint against Ford referred to the "enormous profits from the aggressive use of forced labor under inhuman conditions."[42] Without probing too deeply into the details of the case against Ford, the history was at the least problematic.

Ford responded to the allegations by appointing a large investigating team to look into the matter, which eventually produced more than ninety-eight thousand pages of documentation.[43] At the heart of the issue was the relationship between the present-day Ford Motor Company, headquartered in Dearborn, Michigan, and the German branch that had used forced labor during the war. Inquiring into this issue took researchers down a highly complicated path, which to most onlookers would probably have been deemed inconclusive. "By the time that slave labor was introduced," according to one of the Ford investigation's team members, Simon Reich, "Ford Werke was clearly under the direct control of the Nazi government, though administered through the company headquarters in Cologne. . . . The meetings of the board of directors had already been suspended, and didn't resume until after the war.

Although the American parent company desperately sought to retain control of their German assets, they failed to do so. Ford Werke became an instrument of the Nazi state."[44]

Similar questions about the links between American companies and their German subsidiaries arose with General Motors and IBM, with results that certainly did not sustain the allegations of culpable collaboration between American industrial firms and Nazi Germany. In the case of General Motors the issue was the use of slave labor by its German subsidiary Opel AG. Asked by GM to look into the question, Yale University Professor Henry Ashby Turner warned about anachronism—the "application of attitudes that became widely held among Americans only later."[45] In Turner's view at least, the wartime links between the forced-labor-employing Opel and GM in the United States were practically nonexistent. "Allegations that GM continued to exercise control over Opel even after Hitler declared war on the United States in December 1941 are unfounded. Well before then, all direct contact with the Rüsselsheim headquarters of Opel had been lost. The last American had departed many months earlier, leaving the subsidiary's German lawyer in Berlin as the sole remaining channel of communications. Trans-Atlantic telephone contact with him ceased during the summer of 1941." Opel certainly had no excuses for the exploitation of forced labor during the war. However, in Turner's view at least, "General Motors cannot . . . be held responsible for the fate of those victims at that time. When the use of forced labor began in 1942, the American corporation had lost all control over its subsidiary and was cut off from information about what was happening there."[46]

In the case of IBM, a much-publicized book appearing in February 2001 by the energetic, strident American journalist Edwin Black, *IBM and the Holocaust: The Strategic Alliance between Nazi Germany and America's Most Powerful Corporation,* claimed that the company significantly facilitated the enslavement of workers and slaughter of European Jews through its German subsidiary Dehomag (Deutsche Hollerith Maschinen Gesellschaft). IBM did so, claimed Black, and did so knowingly, through the Nazis' supposedly widespread use of the company's pre-computer punch-card Hollerith machines to prepare lists of prospective victims. Published with considerable fanfare, Black's investigation also implicated the company's eccentric chief executive officer from 1915 to 1956, Thomas J. Watson, portrayed as a war profiteer in alliance with Hitler to facilitate the murder of European Jews.[47]

Almost simultaneously with that book's appearance, attorney Michael Hausfeld filed a class action lawsuit in Brooklyn alleging IBM's facilitation of Nazi persecution, genocide, and postwar cover-up and demanding that the company disgorge profits from the sale of Hollerith machines half a century before. "Book, Lawsuit Claim IBM Abetted the Holocaust" headlined a Jewish newspaper in California, reflecting a general view.[48] As with the other allegations against German and American corporations, these contentions were never tested in court: deferring to the wider settlement with German industry and the agreement to secure "legal peace," Hausfeld soon dropped the case against IBM so as to permit the resolution with German industry to go forward. Only the book remained, stoutly defended by Black himself against critical comments and supported by many popular reviewers.[49]

Once again, however, it turns out that the contentions about an American company's involvement in the Holocaust were highly contestable. IBM's crime, according to the allegations, amounted to the leasing, by Dehomag, of IBM tabulating machines to the German government, thereby assisting the murder of European Jews. The *New York Times* reviewer of Black's book observed about this supposed link to the Holocaust that it "threatens to obliterate the moral distinction between the sellers of rope and those who use the rope to hang people."[50] Moreover, Black's claim that the machines greatly facilitated the slaughter of European Jewry did not fare well with Holocaust historians.[51] Most seem to have agreed with Michael Allen, a specialist in the field, who wrote that "traditional means of record-keeping more than sufficed for the destruction of the European Jews."[52] Moreover, it has never been proven that Hollerith machines were used to make deportation lists; in many cases at least the lists were drawn up by hand, and sometimes not even by the Germans. As well, Black's estimation of IBM's chief executive officer at the time as a "corporate scoundrel" was sharply challenged. Thomas Watson's biographer, Kevin Maney, portrayed his subject evenhandedly as an appeaser, an ambitious peacenik, and a maverick champion of his company's interests, but hardly someone complicit with genocide. It is true that the Germans honored him with a decoration in 1937. But they probably did so because he was assuming the presidency of the International Chamber of Commerce and they hoped to get something from him. Watson did pander to Hitler in the 1930s, as did many at the time, but in Maney's view at least, he was a decent if naïve man who warned about the fate of German Jews and even wrote directly to Hitler urging him to apply "the Golden Rule in dealing with these minorities." And he returned the decoration in 1940.[53]

Commenting on the IBM proceedings, a *New York Times* reporter saw a common thread with other Holocaust restitution cases: "Like other lawsuits based on human rights violations, Holocaust litigation often stands on shaky legal ground because evidence is missing or because it focuses on matters that the courts have traditionally left to politicians and diplomats to negotiate on behalf of citizens. But the sensitivity of multinationals to negative publicity and, in some cases, shame about past activity can sometimes give class-action lawyers a strong hand in negotiating settlements."[54] To be clear, my point is not to resolve the issues of wartime control over the German subsidiaries of these American companies or still less to absolve the latter for their associations with Nazi Germany before or during the war. It is rather to contest the historical representation that emerges from "litigating" the Holocaust in each of these cases, attended as they understandably are by negative publicity and shame. In each of the cases referred to here—that of Ford, General Motors, and IBM—there was plenty of each to go around, justified or not. In each, the one-sided picture presented by the plaintiffs misrepresents the past, at least to some degree. In each, the defendants seem to have been chosen because they appeared easy targets rather than exemplary wrongdoers. In each, the lawsuits seem to have raised more questions than they resolved—good news for historians but not so good for companies that value their good name and resist being stigmatized in this way. And finally, in each the pictures presented in the initial, usually highly publicized complaints, are misleading if taken as a fully rounded explanation of the wartime past.

For me, legal commentator Anthony Sebok sums up the situation well: "One of the consequences of 'litigating' the Holocaust is that actions are painted in very stark terms: a company's acts are either illegal or legal, which often translates into their being either intentionally evil or innocent. This area of law is like that: it needs clearly defined states of mind in order to make sense of the past. But the truth is, some of the guilty parties involved in the Holocaust are not so easy to pigeonhole."[55] Historians would wholeheartedly agree. Most find themselves ill at ease in the litigators' environment of intense, high-pressured rush to judgment against particular defendants. Few would accept the characterization of German corporations in the 1990s as "Hitler's willing business partners"—a designation taken from Daniel Goldhagen's controversial book on German complicity in the Holocaust that made similarly sweeping generalizations.[56] Discomfort with such commentary prompted a fine historian like Gerald Feldman, well accustomed to shades of gray even when dealing with the Nazi era, to cringe when he read what sometimes emerged from the plaintiffs' lawyers. "The briefs in some class actions sometimes make me feel that our worst history students have decided to take up law," he complained.[57]

———

When choosing defendants, establishing a link between Holocaust-era perpetrators and present-day companies and institutions may have posed some technical difficulties for the lawyers but no problems of principle or worries about putting matters into historical perspective. Through the well-worn legal fiction of "corporate personality" and through established legal processes that define it, corporate defendants in the 1990s could, to a court's satisfaction in any event, be understood to retain their identities over time and thereby to have participated in the crimes of the Nazi era.[58] Legal fictions, utilized warily by laymen, are of almost second nature to the lawyers and negotiators.[59] Plaintiffs' lawyers pointedly referred to the German corporations and the banks as "tortfeasors," "wrongdoers," or "malefactors." Survivors unhesitatingly demanded that companies give back what "they had stolen" fifty or sixty years before.

To nonlawyers, however, to those of us who are spectators in legal contests to determine responsibility, this identification of past and present could be problematic. Specifically, it is not always obvious that liability can be passed from a group of perpetrators to their organizational successors so many decades later.[60] Time itself was one obstacle. "With the injustices of men, as with the convulsions and disasters of nature," John Stuart Mill once wrote, "the longer they remain unrepaired, the greater become the obstacles to repairing them, arising from the after-growths which would have to be torn up or broken through."[61] Because of such difficulties, some theorists have considered, with Jeremy Waldron, that rights "are capable of 'fading' in their moral importance by virtue of the passage of time and by the sheer persistence of what was originally a wrongful infringement."[62] Waldron contends that, after many years, historic injustices may be *superseded* as a result of the practical difficulties with repairing the past or with unacceptable consequences of holding certain parties responsible for doing so. That is why many prefer a political resolution in lieu of a legal determination of liability, a process in which governments take charge of restitution without necessarily conceding that the present parties are "wrongdoers" or that they are legally obligated to settle the claims.

Among Mill's "aftergrowths"—the obstacles to repair by the defendants in cases such as I am discussing—are the increasing influence of new generations who are either reluctant to accept liability for the decision making of remote predecessors or disinclined to impose this liability on present-day company shareholders. The degree of continuing responsibility for the Nazi era has been, to be sure, a much-debated question in Germany, and by the 1990s this was a widely accepted principle of national life, renewed with the unification agreements at the beginning of the decade. However, the problem of where to draw the line remained. While the responsibility of German society as a whole is widely accepted, in practical terms, banks or companies in the 1990s were often, in a widely held view, scarcely recognizable as the moral successors of their counterparts of the 1930s and 1940s. Company leaders from that era, of course, had long passed from the scene. As we have seen, the companies themselves had sometimes disappeared. Sometimes they had split into fragments, explicitly terminating the liability for past wrongs. Sometimes they had been transformed through their experience under Communism. Sometimes they had cast their lot with others. With Swiss banks, for example, the Volcker Committee noted that since the end of the war there had been more than one hundred mergers among implicated banks that existed in 1945.[63] The structures of public companies also militated against findings of moral responsibility or blameworthiness after a half century—although there may, in some instances, be a case for reparations or the return of assets to claimants.[64]

By the 1990s, captains of German industry were often American-trained, sophisticated, internationally attuned modernists—a far cry from many of their Nazified predecessors of more than half a century before. Many had simply no idea about the history of the companies they directed. Swiss bankers and government officials were less flexibly minded than the Germans, and in most cases unprepared for the legal-political battle with the plaintiffs' attorneys. But as Regula Ludi has noted, "since the late 1990s, the government has essentially embraced the new images of the past that are based on the human rights paradigm."[65] Much has changed in Swiss perceptions of their wartime past and their increasingly multiethnic European environment. Partly as a result of the debates over the banks, "collective memory . . . has become less unambiguous, or rather: instead of one national memory that allegedly embraces the quintessence of past experience, a whole set of narratives now coexist, putting forward different and contradictory interpretations of the past and reflecting a wider variety of perspectives."[66]

Even more problematic, one of the least credible historical arguments made by the plaintiffs was that the present-day companies had enriched themselves, or were "sitting on" great wealth that was generated by the Holocaust. Northwestern University's Peter Hayes, one of the few scholars who have inquired deeply into the issues of unjust enrichment with regard to one importantly implicated industrial concern, reached conclusions quite at odds with those proposed by counsel for the plaintiffs. Looking at Degussa, a chemical corporation that not only used slave labor but was responsible, among other things, for the production and sale of the deadly Zyklon gas used to murder Jews in Auschwitz and for processing gold taken from the victims, he found much that was unjust about the company but very little that entailed enrichment as a result of its exploitation of Jewish and East European workers.[67] Degussa used slave laborers at four known branch locations, and in none of these did the company show any profits. Moreover, in a scenario that was repeated across Germany, Degussa's factories were eventually leveled by Allied aerial bombardment, following which, in 1945, the Russians captured and confiscated the company's cash reserves. In the end, the firm's ruins had to be almost completely written off, since they fell largely into the Soviet occupation zone.[68] Mass murder and mass enslavement, it seems, was far less profitable than the Nazis hoped or intended it to be. Summing up, Hayes notes: "The more I explored Degussa's history under the Nazis, the more I thought the firm had engaged in acts that extinguished or gravely damaged the lives of many and for which it clearly 'owed' at least the survivors something, but that it had not made much money directly from any of these deeds—indeed, it probably, in the aggregate, lost some."[69]

Extrapolating from the case against German industry in which unjust enrichment was at the core, Hayes points out how different were the rhetoric of the law and the findings of his history. The former carried "the implication that the evil of the system lay in its profitability"; the latter told a story that was horrible enough even without the profit-making necessary for a finding of liability in American courts.[70] Going over similar ground focusing on Soviet prisoner of war labor, the German researcher Rolf Keller believes that the use of these workers made no economic sense. Although the German war economy had a voracious appetite for labor, the terrible treatment of these victims and their lack of skills or motivation rendered these workers worse than useless to the German economy.[71] Needless to say, none of these points found a place in the plaintiffs' arguments. As Hayes concluded, the restitution settlements "produced financial obligations for the participating corporations that bear no discernable relationship to what each actually did in Nazi Germany or earned by virtue of doing so, as well as payouts to survivors that seldom approximate adequate compensation for what they lost. In other words, the argument from profits served as a club, not a measuring stick, and it was, at best, partially successful."[72]

To be fair, we do not as yet have conclusive research that would bear out Hayes's generalization that "few enterprises, German or otherwise, grew rich from the Holocaust."[73] Furthermore, a legal case can be made that unjust enrichment does not necessarily require profit making. But at the very least the plaintiffs' empirical arguments seem shaky and their history misleading. There are solid grounds for making this point, for example, with regard to the wartime Daimler Benz—an important firm to examine because Manfred Gentz, the chief financial officer of that company's successor, Daimler Chrysler AG, formed in 1998 from a merger with the Chrysler Corporation, was a vigorous spokesman for German industry during the 1990s settlement negotiations and became chairman of the German industry fund that was instrumental in financing the settlement. The British scholar Neil Gregor studied Daimler's wartime use of forced labor and was unsparing in his description of the cruel conditions that took such a toll upon such workers. However, as he pointed out, what really enhanced production at Daimler Benz was its skilled labor force and not its forced workers.[74] This is what made money for the company. Decision makers at this and other corporations did not turn to involuntary labor because it would raise their profits. As Gregor suggests, this recourse was part of the barbarization of the "Third Reich" and a way of keeping afloat in the latter part of the war.[75]

Moreover, even without conclusive findings across German industry, there are ample grounds to fear, as in one recent discussion, that "framing the claim in the language of unjust enrichment will trivialize the defendant's wrongdoing."[76] After all these years, we are still contending with the Holocaust not because of lost value or unfair labor practices but because of lost lives, limitless cruelty, and the targeting of entire categories of individuals. To historians, of course, inapt theories are deplorable, even if they contribute to just resolutions. And not just to historians. I give the last word on this matter to Anthony Sebok, who in my opinion gets it right: "The problem is that [the language of unjust enrichment] buys into a rhetoric and a vocabulary which fundamentally commodifies the wrong because, ultimately, claims in equity for unjust enrichment are about replacing and returning lost property. The claims are not about violations of human rights. The claims are not about the destruction of a culture. And the claims are not about the oppression of a people. They are about returning property that has been wrongfully taken."[77] The law, thereby, gets the history wrong.

Defendants as Bystanders

To historians, it should not be surprising that the restitution contests of the 1990s are part of that decade's intellectual climate. Indeed, many of the historical issues disputed in the clashes between plaintiffs and defendants are precisely those that historians of the subject have turned to during recent years. These turn, I argue, on questions about bystanders to the Holocaust, loosely defined as individuals, companies, institutions, or governments who were neither perpetrators nor collaborators nor victims but who, being present in some sense at the destruction of European Jews and aware of what was happening, did not intervene in any meaningful way in the process of mass murder or, even worse, became part of a vast apparatus of exploitation and persecution. Bystanders, or at least some of them, were, to use a word one hears increasingly, "enablers" of the Holocaust.[78] The defendants of the 1990s, it seems to me, fall generally into this category. Particularly in light of the historical interest in bystanders during the 1990s, it makes sense to examine the restitution campaign in relationship to what historians have thought about their role.

From the margins of interest in the murder of European Jews, the subject of the bystanders has come to wider public attention, and some might even say to the center of the puzzle of how the catastrophe could have happened. "Slowly but surely," observes Regula Ludi, "the behavior of the bystanders . . . has come to be regarded as a decisive factor in the ability of the Nazis to accomplish their murderous goals. Such insights raise new questions about political and moral responsibility during World War II and suggest the need for many nations to rethink their understanding of the Nazi past."[79] New questions and, she might have added, new understandings. This is as good a sketch as any of the historical fallout of the litigation and settlement contests in the period I am discussing.

"Once filed, the lawsuits were used as a public relations platform to mobilize political and public opinion against the defendant companies," writes Owen Pell, a veteran litigator and defense counsel in both Holocaust-related and other human rights issues.[80] Facilitating this process, U.S. rules of procedure permit the presentation of unproven allegations in order to exert maximum pressure on the parties to settle. Repeatedly in the commentary on the restitution campaign, one reads of the frustrated or even angry contentions of the defendants that they had been caricatured through the litigation process and an attendant misshaping of the history of the Holocaust. However judged in the end, one senses among the European defendants a constantly frustrated effort to relay their version of history to their largely American accusers. "Our neutrality was not opportunistic or of recent vintage, formed as a response to the Nazi takeover of Germany," declared Hans Halbheer, honorary secretary of the American Swiss Foundation Advisory Council. "Instead, neutrality has been a condition of our domestic peace and our foreign policy since time immemorial—dating back to 1515."[81] Comforting for those who care about historical representation is the acknowledgment that history *is* important. "A crucial lesson of the Holocaust asset cases is that companies must invest heavily in historical research so that they will have control and an intimate understanding of the facts," adds Pell.[82] The problem for him, and even more for European executives who contended with what was for them an unfamiliar and unsettling legal environment, was how history seemed to fare when caught up in the litigation process.

At the starting point for all these cases, no one doubts, were massive, unprecedented violations of human rights. Defendants never disputed this element in the restitution cases, and all accepted accounts of the persecution of European Jews, the brutalization of Slavic and other occupied peoples, and the violation of every civilized norm in the conduct of war. But for the defendants in practically every one of the lawsuits, the real culprits were the German and collaborationist regimes and not those who, in their characterization, were sucked into the perpetration of the crimes of the Third Reich.

Research on German industrialists under the Nazis seems now to bear this out. As Hayes notes, "the prevailing view now traces executives' liability not to their supposed congruence of purpose with Hitler's government, but to their reflexive adaptability."[83] Generally speaking, historians do not believe that the profit motive, and certainly not the profit motive alone, drove corporate complicity with Nazism. At least as important were status, ideology, and the corporate culture of leading businessmen. "Making money was not the reason the Reich's increasingly counterproductive, cruel, cumbersome, and chaotic program of labor exploitation came into being, and it is neither morally nor historically sound to measure its evil by its lucrativeness," Hayes observes. And he goes on: "Precisely because the 'slave' labor system emerged out of a vortex of macropolitical not microeconomic forces, international law consistently has defined the German state—and thus its citizens collectively—as the primary party responsible for answering to the financial claims of people exploited under Nazism."[84]

That is why German executives in charge of major corporations in the 1990s repeatedly claimed that the German government had made reparation payments on behalf of the *German people,* that individuals had faced criminal charges for wrongdoing after the war—and that it was impossible and wrong, beyond that, and many years later, to assign liability to individual corporations just because they found themselves in circumstances of legal vulnerability. German industrialists, like most others in that country, believed that the government should assume responsibility for restitution, as indeed it had done over many years. "We are determined that justice is done," insisted Herbert Hansmeyer, a member of the board of the Allianz insurance company at a speech in 1998. Nevertheless, he told his listeners, "the lawsuit came as a surprise to us." As he explained, "the majority of cases were included in postwar compensation programs and treaties among the nations involved in the war. It was our understanding that these programs—initiated after World War II by the Allied governments and continued to this day by the Federal Republic of Germany had, in fact, settled all claims."[85] Count Otto Lambsdorff, the distinguished lawyer, longtime member of the Bundestag, and representative of the German chancellor who worked closely with Eizenstat to secure agreement with German industry, seems to have been instrumental in persuading the German government to join in the funding of the German Foundation that became the agency for restitution.[86] Obviously choosing his words with care, he made it clear that whatever the legal liability, moral responsibility lay heavily on the German government: "I have always defended the decision to finance three-quarters of the Foundation by the public sector. It was not only the direct employment of forced labor in the public sector that brought us to that conclusion, but also the fact that a large part of the labor force was recruited—or, to be more accurate, in many cases apprehended—by the German police and army and subject to draconian and racist laws in order to replace German workers employed in Hitler's armies. This put the bulk of the moral responsibility on the German government that represented Germany in succession to the Third Reich."[87]

"We know that there can never be moral closure," Lambsdorff conceded.[88] Still, participants suffered from the continuing climate of recrimination that was never entirely absent from the negotiations and the legal proceedings. "I'm the last person not to want justice for Holocaust victims," protested Amihud Ben-Porat, the Israeli lawyer for the Generali insurance company. "But there were many groundless, vicious accusations made against Generali in Israel by persons who didn't always verify facts."[89] Reacting to what he felt was a gross injustice, defense attorney Kenneth Bialkin commented on how he and his fellow lawyers defending insurance companies were treated by the plaintiffs. "I went to some of those early meetings with some of these executives from Generali and other companies, many of whom weren't even born when the war ended, and some of my colleagues were addressing them as though it was 1943."[90] A former head of the Conference of Presidents of Major American Jewish Organizations, Bialkin was bitterly attacked for taking on the defense of Generali, part of an intense debate over whether Jewish lawyers ought to have done so.[91] Bialkin stood his ground. "The more I got into it, the more I felt that Generali and others were being pressed and tarred with the anathema of the Holocaust and asked to pay money which they didn't owe in amounts which bore no relationship to what was fair," he said. "I saw there was a kind of terror in the community. All you had to do was to accuse someone of some peripheral involvement in World War II and they bring their attitude toward the Holocaust to anyone who is so accused."[92]

A good illustration of Bialkin's point about "peripheral involvement in World War II" and related problems in the legal assessment of bystanders appeared in the legal responses to accusations about slave labor. Attorneys for the German companies argued that the latter had no choice during the war and had been dragooned into wrongdoing by the

Nazi regime. Critically, and in a crucial argument familiar to the story of bystanders, the industries' lawyers insisted that the claims against them "arise out of a *war*, not a run-of-the-mill private dispute."[93] They sought to have the case thrown out of court on grounds of nonjusticiability—in layman's terms, because it had to do with war making, that is, interstate relations, held to be out of bounds in civil courts in the United States. Lawyer Stephen Whinston identifies the crucial point: "Since wars are fought between nations, claims arising out of wars can only be resolved by such nations."[94] In rebuttal, lawyers for the plaintiffs made a complicated case that the wrongdoing did *not* arise out of the war, but instead was part and parcel of a quite separate undertaking, the Nazis' genocidal design for the Jews. The destruction of the Jews, as Whinston notes, "was unrelated to the armed hostilities of World War II and stemmed from a genocidal motivation."[95] Unintentionally, the lawyers found themselves in detailed disputation on one of the most difficult questions of Holocaust historiography—the relationship between the Nazis' genocidal antisemitism and Hitler's imperial war of conquest.[96] Happily, final resolution of these issues was eventually supplanted by settlement negotiations around the bargaining table and the lawyers no longer had to worry about whether the Holocaust "arose" out of the war or not. For history, it was probably just as well.[97]

Claimants and History

As we have seen, in peace settlements following the cessation of hostilities, states were traditionally in charge. Challenging this system in the 1990s litigation, claimants typically pursued settlements outside governmental authority and without institutional support for their efforts except, in some circumstances, in the case of the Claims Conference. In one exception to this practice, at the very beginning of the Holocaust-era restitution campaign, the United States government took action with respect to Hugo Princz, a Holocaust survivor whose forty-year quest for reparation involved unusual circumstances. A young American citizen living in Slovakia at the beginning of the war, Princz was turned over to the Nazis by local townspeople in 1942, following the United States declaration of war against Germany. Deported to Auschwitz with his family, he managed, miraculously, to survive. After the war, Princz found himself ineligible for reparations because he was not stateless but rather an American citizen for whom there had been no provisions for restitution. To rectify this, Princz took the German government to court, but was blocked because of sovereign immunity—the rule that foreign governments cannot be sued in American courts. He later tried, unsuccessfully, to sue the German companies for whom he had been forced to work. At that point the United States took on Princz's claim, acting on his behalf with the Germans. Following President Bill Clinton's raising the matter with German Chancellor Helmut Kohl in 1995, the issue was resolved through a special American agreement with Germany. Princz and eleven other deportees in related circumstances shared an award of $2.1 million, after a settlement signed with Germany on Capitol Hill. Princz also received undisclosed amounts from Bayer, Messerschmidt-Boelkow-Blohm, BASF, and Hoechst, for his unpaid service as a slave laborer during the war.[98] An individual (in this case, thanks to the eventual assistance of the United States government) achieved some reparation in circumstances that had not been contemplated by the diplomats or international lawyers in the postwar period.

The radical departure of the restitution campaign against the Swiss banks, the German corporations, and insurance was that the United States did not espouse the claims of the plaintiffs as in the Princz case, and the quest for restitution proceeded outside the interstate framework, with the role of the United States government being limited to the encouragement of negotiations and mediation. With respect to the German companies, the American government facilitated talks among representatives of the plaintiffs as well as company representatives, the Claims Conference, several foreign governments, plus Germany and the United States. In all these efforts, there were masses of claimants, represented by private attorneys who had to be satisfied. Moreover, the claimants came from all over the world and were citizens of many different countries.[99] Managing them credibly, and in conformity with the strict requirements of the Federal Rules of Procedure on class actions, was no mean challenge.

In this new environment, the claimants as a collectivity were far more at the center of attention than ever before. Depending on the stage of the restitution process, whether the lawsuits or the settlements, contacting and informing them about the process was the task of the lawyers, the courts, or in the case of insurance, the ICHEIC machinery agreed to by the insurers. In all, more than two million claimants from around the world appeared on the scene—Jews and non-Jews, victims and their heirs, those who had been in camps, forced laborers, or those who claimed accounts or policies.[100] Reaching out to survivors and communicating with them became a fundamental part of the restitution culture—an overlooked and underresearched part of the process that deserves serious inquiry in materials generated by the various participants in the litigation and negotiation process. Of course, no one knew how many survivors there were at the time and there was no template for engaging with them. In the Swiss banks settlement, the notices prescribed in the rules went out around the globe, and an astounding 584,000 questionnaires were returned.[101] ICHEIC developed perhaps the most sophisticated process to communicate with claimants. Its staff produced packets of information and claim forms available in twenty languages. It established a Web site and a twenty-four-hour call center with toll-free numbers in New York and extensive language capabilities. It launched a global press campaign to inform survivors wherever they lived. Anticipating approximately 20,000 claims, in the end ICHEIC received more than 100,000, coming from more than thirty countries, in more than twenty different languages.[102] Similar outreach efforts had to be made on behalf of each of the various class action lawsuits, and these often required follow-up communications and interaction with survivors.

Repeatedly, in the course of the campaign, Holocaust survivors told their stories. Survivors spoke before groups of lawyers, press conferences, public meetings, government officials, congressional committees, regulatory bodies, and the courts. Sometimes they were deeply and movingly gratified by the opportunity to speak, valuing the "small measure of justice" they were seeking or satisfied for the recognition that they had finally received. Sometimes, too, they spoke about their sheer, unalloyed need for restitution money to alleviate their adverse circumstances. Sometimes they were angry, convinced that it had taken far too long for their cause to be recognized. And sometimes, too, they put the emphasis on getting the record straight. Roman Kent, chairman of the American Gathering of Holocaust Survivors and treasurer of the Claims Conference, had no illusions about the process. "With time, I . . . realized that the basis for these negotiations on the part of the Germans, as well as the great majority of class action lawyers, was not founded on moral and humanitarian purposes. It was strictly business. For the Germans it was legal closure; for the lawyers who had filed the class action lawsuits against the German companies, it was millions of dollars in fees." Still, Kent believed restitution was worth pursuing:

> In spite of this I saw the prospect of utilizing the opportunity at hand to bring some relief to needy survivors in Eastern European countries as well as Jewish Holocaust survivors throughout the world. In addition, from a historical point of view, there was something more important to be gained. The negotiations would bring official exposure and acknowledgment of the evil acts perpetrated by Germans against mankind. They would prove the direct, large-scale involvement of German industry at large. Thus the negotiations would show beyond a shadow of a doubt that not only Hitler and the Nazis were responsible for the atrocities, but the totality of the German nation was also responsible.[103]

The survivors were often frustrated, seeing the settlements as a mere pittance, or unhappy with how the aggregation of plaintiffs in class action lawsuits distorted their own experience during the Holocaust or their preferences with regard to settlements. Purists contest whether such flaws in class actions might diminish or undermine the justice seeking capacity of the law. As one critic, Richard Faulk, observes, "To the extent aggregation systems fail to completely appreciate an individual's grievances, and to the extent such systems unduly influence defendants to resolve disputes economically, rather than on their merits, such systems deny justice and pervert the fundamental goals of civilized jurisprudence. The potential for perversion will be exponentially enhanced if demonstrably defective devices, such as American class actions, are given extraterritorial dignity or, even worse, grafted on to rigid international systems that are culturally incapable of preventing abuse."[104]

Claimants were rarely satisfied with settlements, although they disagreed with them for many different reasons. Intending to address the rights and the needs of Holocaust survivors, distribution involved tremendous difficulties and disputes, some of which remain unresolved to this day. Stuart Eizenstat refers to a "three month torment" of deciding how to divide the money provided by German industry on the slave and forced labor issues. "The process brought out the worst in everyone," he observed, as the claimants' representatives sought to divide the pie.[105] Debate persists, centering notably on accountability and institutional matters, challenges to the role of the Claims Conference and the administration of settlement claims, the desperate circumstances of some aged Holocaust survivors, and the right balance between material support for survivors and programs for the Jewish world.[106] There were also disputes about process matters, application deadlines, and standards of proof. What I would like to do here is not to review these disagreements but rather to comment briefly on how some settlement distribution decisions shaped and reflected the historical understanding of the Holocaust that lay behind the restitution campaign and the way in which this played itself out in a particularly American context.

Putting the settlements into the widest context, one should heed historian Regula Ludi's insight that postwar victim reparations "transformed the fact of victimization into normative ideas of victimhood." By this she means that since the end of the Second World War social attitudes toward victims—"public sympathy and respect" for those targeted by the Nazi regime—underwent considerable shifts and changes. In Europe, immediately after the war, she points out, "undeserved suffering was . . . associated with weakness and passivity"; by contrast, resistance fighters were given heroic standing.[107] Variations appeared in various countries based on their own traditions, antipathies, and wartime experiences. In the Holocaust-era restitution campaign of the 1990s, the American understanding of the murder of European Jews set the tone for the definition of victims entitled to restitution, and it is likely that this is how most onlookers understood the process that was being worked out in the courts and around bargaining tables.

Generalizations about claimants are difficult. It is often not appreciated that, for the greatest part of the restitution campaign, having to do with forced and slave laborers, the numbers of non-Jewish victims predominated, receiving more than three-quarters of the funds.[108] Similarly, the Swiss bank settlement included not only Jews but also Jehovah's Witnesses, Sinti and Roma, as well as homosexuals and the disabled.[109] In the settlement with German industry, there were bitter debates between representatives of the Jewish survivors of the Holocaust and East European forced workers, behind which were layers of animosity and utterly different ways of understanding the history of the Second World War. To be divided was some 10 billion deutsche marks, to be paid to claimants for unremunerated labor, in working conditions ranging from a few who were relatively comfortable to some, mostly Jews, who were intended to be worked to death. Of perhaps 12 million people who worked in that capacity, there were estimated to be between 1.2 million and 1.5 million survivors, including those who had worked in agriculture and who were generally acknowledged to have suffered the least. "Everybody agreed that the other side deserved something, but nobody could agree on how much," observe John Authers and Richard Wolffe.[110] The East Europeans rested their case on the devastation in the conquered territories; the Jews stressed the racially motivated persecution and the fact that so many of them were worked to death. Melvyn Weiss, representing Jewish survivors, denounced the East European claimants as "a bunch of anti-Semites." "Go file your own suit," he is supposed to have told them in an effort to beat back their case for greater restitution.[111] On the other side, there were accusations based on need: the Jews had received various forms of reparation to that point, but the East Europeans, with their postwar past under Communism, had not.

Eizenstat describes the exceedingly complex, highly contentious bargaining process by which he and Count Lambsdorff worked out a settlement and eventually secured agreement. The upshot was to distinguish between two classes of workers: slave and forced laborers. The former, survivors of camps and ghettos and destined to be worked to death, would each receive $7,500, and the latter, who had worked in somewhat better although extremely variable conditions, would receive approximately $2,500 apiece. Of the former, Jews were the majority, and of the latter most were East European Slavs, although there were many of the other group on each side.[112]

The disputes were hardly limited to the quarrels between plaintiffs and defendants or between Holocaust victims and others. Among Jews, there were sharp divisions between those who claimed survivor status by virtue of having escaped persecution and murder through emigration, flight, and hiding and those who suffered in camps, ghettos, or forests. While all were victimized, some claimed to have suffered more than others, and this unhappy issue played out in complicated ways when the survivor designation translated into restitution. Notably, the United States–based Holocaust Survivors Foundation–USA (HSF-USA) contested the survivor standing of Jews in the former Soviet Union, arguing that they had managed to flee eastward out of the hands of the Germans and had, therefore, not been directly persecuted by the Nazis as had so many others. Similarly, there were passionate arguments over whether restitution should be based on verifiable claims or whether it should be driven by need—or put otherwise, on suffering at the time of the crime or present-day poverty.[113]

Decisions on such matters in the Swiss banks affair fell to Special Master Judah Gribetz, a respected, high-ranking former New York civil servant and attorney charged by Judge Korman with developing a comprehensive plan of allocation and distribution of the settlement proceeds—including humanitarian funds, specially designated for elderly survivors in need. In a Solomonic resolution, Gribetz recommended that 75 percent of what eventually would be $205 million in humanitarian funds would go to survivors in the former Soviet Union, 13 percent to Israel, and the balance to the rest of the world. HSF-USA received 4 percent. Gribetz accepted the survivor status of the former-Soviet-Union claimants and made the further case that they were most in need, not only due to their circumstances in countries of the former Soviet Union but also due to their not having received reparations in previous years. Representing the HSF, Florida attorney Samuel Dubbin protested bitterly, making the point that many Holocaust survivors in the United States were desperately poor and that they were five times more likely than nonsurvivors to be living below the poverty line in that country. Dubbin unsuccessfully made the case for a population-based formula, under which humanitarian distributions would be allocated according to the percentage of survivors in each country—under which the American survivors would have received 25 percent of the total.[114] Needless to say, it was impossible to please everyone. Michael Bazyler is certainly correct when he observes that "the distribution of money will always produce discord, especially when the payouts are the consequence of a tragedy, man-made or natural. . . . The real questions of how to serve justice and concurrently balance the claims of memory, responsibility, and group survival will inevitably produce competing visions."[115]

Were these distribution decisions faithful to the historical experience of Nazi-era criminality? Did the outcomes of these momentous disputes confirm or validate Holocaust memory as so many had hoped? An obvious but underappreciated point was the great diversity of the historical events associated with these instances of historic wrongs. Take just one example, the case of "forced and slave labor." As Peter Hayes observes, these categories cover an extraordinarily wide spectrum of circumstances, for both Jews and non-Jews: "Considerable differences arise concerning everything from daily treatment and nourishment to ultimate chances for survival depending on whether the laborer was a Jew; male or female; a civilian, prisoner of war, or a ghetto or camp inmate; could or could not speak German; came from Western or Eastern

Europe; and whether he or she had to toil in Germany or the occupied East, in agriculture or industry, directly for the SS or the Wehrmacht, in a state-owned or private enterprise, a large or small one, and in construction or mining or on an assembly line."[116] To the extent that this process highlighted the vast scope and diversity of forced and slave labor, it was therefore helpful to history. And, while a blunt instrument indeed, the broad distinction between "forced" and "slave" laborers did make historical sense, and was a point worth making.

It is therefore appropriate that when the claimants finally spoke, they spoke with many different voices, and that their terrible experiences were not easy to categorize or to enlist in one or another distribution scheme. While undoubtedly painful for those who sought a resolution that would achieve universal support, this outcome is nevertheless in keeping with our understanding of the Holocaust. By now, the destruction of European Jews is slipping from justice seeking into history, a realm that lives with complexity and ambiguity and is becoming more and more the province of the historians rather than the advocates of individuals seeking restitution for themselves and their fellows according to some common formula. Justice seeking is inevitably drawing to an end and with it will come a diminishing of disagreements that may have been, as some feel, inescapable. Meanwhile, the effort to understand the Holocaust in all its complexity continues.

5

Evaluating Some Measure of Justice

Any serious assessment of the Holocaust restitution campaign of the 1990s must acknowledge that its achievements were incomplete. It should always be remembered that, of the millions ravaged by the Nazi Holocaust, only a small proportion have received any kind of restitution. According to one calculation, less than 20 percent of the assets stolen from Jews during the Nazi era has been returned to individuals, their heirs, or Jewish institutions.[1] Stuart Eizenstat's book on the subject was aptly entitled *Imperfect Justice*. "We have to live with the unhappy realization that we cannot possibly fully compensate everyone for the massive injustices perpetrated against them during the war," he wrote.[2] He might have added that even when there was payment, it could never adequately compensate for the terrible events of more than sixty years ago. Moreover, to some degree all sides in the contests over Holocaust-era restitution come away feeling the results were inadequate.

Some claimants, of course, never got anywhere. In England, eighty-year-old Joe Marks is one of apparently several hundred descendants of Holocaust survivors who think they have been unjustly denied restitution. In Marks's case, he continues to seek a Swiss bank account he believes was opened by his uncle, the late Elaia Sczejnman. Marks has no evidence for this, except what he remembers his mother, Brucha, reporting many years ago. Any documentary record that might have existed, he says, was lost when a rocket destroyed their home in England during the war. Joe Marks wrote to Pope John Paul II, among many others, seeking intervention. "I will pray for you," the pontiff replied. As for Joe Marks, he insists he will never give up. "Nothing hurts me more [than] that people are not being paid their money," he says.[3]

More successful in the outcomes for which he fought, Roman Kent, a survivor of Auschwitz who spent more than two years negotiating with German corporations and the German government as one of the leaders of the Claims Conference, seemed ambivalent about all that had been accomplished. Unvarnished in his criticism of the lawyers associated with the class action lawsuits, he referred to them as rapacious and irresponsible. Unsparing in his denunciation of German industrial leaders, he had a contemptuous reply to their claim that they could not afford what was being demanded: "We will make a donation for you."[4] Obviously stung by accusations that it was "all about money," he insisted, in a forceful reply, that Holocaust survivors had the right to finish their lives in relative comfort. But in the final analysis, Kent, like so many others, seems to have felt his struggle for restitution worthwhile because of the "small form of justice" that was realized. How was that to be interpreted? Upon hearing some generous words by German president Johannes Rau, Kent referred, like so many other survivors, to history: "After all, in the long run, the monetary settlement, so reluctantly given by the German government and German industry, will become a footnote in history. However, the meaningful words of President Rau and those inscribed by the Bundestag will live forever as a moral victory. Thus, with such admission of guilt on behalf of the entire German population, *history had now been accurately documented.*"[5]

It is on this documenting of history—an aspiration widely shared—that I have my own ambivalence about the restitution campaign. From the perspective of defendants in some of the contests over reparation claims, New York attorney Owen C. Pell agrees. "History is often very complicated and does not lend itself to sound bites," he says. "Historical reparation claims do not easily fit the mold of typical tort or contract claims, and do not usually survive the motion-to-dismiss phase. As the Holocaust asset cases proved, however, these claims can take on a life of their own and can generate huge settlements on claims that probably would have failed if litigated to final judgment. The lesson of these cases is that, more than other types of litigation, they must be addressed on multiple fronts and with a keen eye to the historical record."[6] To conclude this short volume, I would like to turn in more detail to the relationship of this historical record to what was achieved, to what this meant, and to what it might lead in the future.

Evaluating the Achievement

Few people, just over a decade ago, would have imagined transfers of billions of dollars at the end of the twentieth century to Holocaust survivors. As we have seen, settlements accompanying these "floodgates of litigation" on Holocaust-era restitution have involved payments amounting to perhaps $8 billion to survivors of Nazi persecution and their heirs, although to be sure, except for a handful of cases the amounts received by individuals were small, at most a few thousand dollars. Champions of the Holocaust restitution efforts of the second half of the 1990s consider these results as extraordinary and see the campaign as an historic achievement.[7] Michael Bazyler refers to the settling of the "financial books of the Holocaust," with both the accounting and the leadership in the process coming from the United States.[8] For the litigators, the sense of triumph is palpable. "To me and those whom I represented," writes the plaintiffs' attorney Melvyn Weiss, "the settlement primarily represents the malefactors' acknowledgment of their wrongdoing both during and after World War II, and their profit-motivated complicity with the Nazi regime."[9] To be sure, others contributed to the end result, including the American government and organized and unorganized Holocaust survivors, led by some outstanding individuals. Together, all those who have promoted Holocaust-era restitution have reason to believe that they have effected a historic change.

Analysts differ on the specific nature and significance of the accomplishment, however. Virtually everyone recognizes that, for some survivors living in difficult material circumstances—in Eastern Europe and the former Soviet Union, but also elsewhere, including the United States and Israel—settlements have provided badly needed financial assistance, however inadequate, to sometimes indigent pensioners. But one must always keep in mind the limited impact historically. Historian Ronald Zweig makes the valuable point that this achievement needs to be seen in the context of more than five decades of German and other restitution, and that however significant what has been accomplished recently, this involves no more than about 5 percent of what had been dispensed in the preceding period.[10] And obviously, because of the catastrophic loss of life in the Holocaust as well as the passage of so much time since those events, restitution has reached only a small proportion of those who suffered during the Nazi era. To take just one example: about 90 percent of those who toiled as forced and slave laborers perished before payments of even token amounts were made through the settlement with German industry.[11] And of course, most Jews who endured the Holocaust never had Swiss bank accounts, insurance policies, or valuable works of art. Those who did not escape were murdered, often together with their families, and in material terms at least, the proceeds of restitution were not really about them.

That is why, when it comes to restitution, it is the moral and historical claims for the rectification of historic wrongs that make the most persuasive case for historic achievement. How can these be evaluated? Legal scholars contend that the litigation that drove the recent settlements shifted the focus of restitution "from state-centered to societal- and individual-centered rights and obligations."[12] Rudolf Dolzer, a professor of law at the University of Bonn, even refers to the privatizing of peacemaking.[13] This development, I believe, involves a momentous shift in the direction of public international law in recent times. At the end of the Second World War, as we have seen, it was *governments* that shaped restitution: dispensed according to international agreements, adjusted to serve geopolitical priorities, and prioritized as part of relations among victorious allies—and affected, before long, by the advent of the Cold War. And so when it came to restitution, the general guidelines and principles, adequate or inadequate, generous or mean-spirited, were in the hands of states. During the war itself and immediately afterward the Allies made formal commitments to restitution, although they failed to grasp or articulate the full significance of the genocide of European Jews. Later, West Germany, led by Konrad Adenauer, moved reluctantly and incompletely, but nevertheless decisively, to provide restitution in the 1950s and 1960s and did so through bilateral and multilateral agreements. In particular, the German treaty with the State of Israel in 1953 was a major milestone along that path. So was the involvement of a novel nongovernmental organization, the Claims Conference, operating at the margins of interstate activity. At that time, it should be added, prioritizing was the key to dealing with an unprecedented challenge. With Europe in ruins, and millions homeless, hungry, disoriented, and without resources, support for the formerly persecuted meant social welfare, not compensation for great wrongs.

In the Holocaust-era restitution claims advanced in the mid-1990s individuals, groups of claimants, and their lawyers registered dissatisfaction with the results of this state-driven process and the manner in which it evolved in postwar decades. What happened in the United States was that groups of claimants identified the inadequacy of postwar arrangements, whether with regard to the Swiss or German industry or insurance or the international art market. Using American courts, and taking advantage of both a new climate of opinion and the receptivity of the American legal system, Holocaust survivors and their lawyers sought to reopen previously settled compensation arrangements— or the absence of compensation for particular groups or particular circumstances of loss. In each of these cases governments and corporate entities were caught off guard and scrambled to contend with individual and collective claims in civil courts and in the public arena. In each, recourse to litigation provided a means to stimulate public interest and amplify concerns about persisting historic wrongs. And in each as well, the thirst for more just settlements was part of a wider global effort to provide redress for grave violations of human rights and historic wrongs.[14]

Was the realization of these claims through negotiation and through litigation the moral achievement that its supporters claimed? The answer is yes, if one sees Holocaust-era wrongs as a continuing injustice that needs remedy.[15] "The idea of undoing harm is extremely elusive," writes the social scientist Jon Elster, in obvious understatement.[16] When it comes to Swiss banks, insurance, or even the forced and slave labor of the Nazi regime, the progressive realization of the significance of the Holocaust and the growing concern more completely to rectify violations of international human rights have altered perceptions of what is owing to victims of historic injustice. These alterations prompted a revisiting of the reparations agreements of the 1950s and 1960s and the identification of new categories of wrongdoing for which there were calls for restitution. But I agree with those who contend that this can be overinterpreted: the new approaches of the 1990s did not mean that only now did the world have to face the Nazi past—or that only now did people identify "malefactors" and determine they should pay.[17] Rather, rectifying injustices of the Holocaust era turns out to be a continuous process and not a one-time-only political, legal, and moral exercise. It is not surprising that undoing great historic harm takes time, operates differently in different countries, and impacts people differently—which is to say it is subject to historical evolution, a process that is likely to continue, both with the Holocaust and with other historic wrongs.

About the Money

"It's not about the money," one hears over and over in polemics about Holocaust-era restitution. "I have lost count of the number of times in the course of my work at the Claims Conference when I have sat at negotiations, a meeting, or a briefing and started with the words 'It's not about the money,'" writes Gideon Taylor, who then adds that such protestations quickly segue into questions about cost.[18] "It's not about money," Israel Singer told a law school audience about Holocaust-era restitution in 1998. "What we are doing today is re-humanizing those individuals posthumously and saying that the grand theft that took place in fifteen countries was not permissible. That re-humanization, that re-breathing of life into those people, into those dry bones—is what our activity is all about. It is not about money."[19]

However, money cannot be avoided—whatever one's perspective. For those asked to pay, and notably for European companies for which both the amounts and the mechanisms of high-pressure American litigation were unfamiliar, money could not help but be a major preoccupation. Even when speaking about restitution strictly defined—restoring personal bank accounts, insurance policies, art, or other property—money is an inescapable part of the discussion when what was taken away no longer exists or cannot be found or cannot be restored and its value must be estimated. And similarly from the claimants' camp, seeking justice for human suffering and gross violations of human rights, claims in civil proceedings necessarily involved monetary calculations. Most obviously, claimants sought to undo "unjust enrichment," referring to the great profits that allegedly accompanied Nazi crimes. "World War II was big business, and for fifty years German industry had been able to keep and reinvest massive amounts of seized assets and profits accrued from slave labor," explained the counsel for Milberg Weiss.[20] For forced and slave laborers, the conditions under which they worked were not only inhuman, they were *unpaid*.

To be sure, calculations of what is owed speak much more to the conventions of civil litigation and negotiations for settlement than to the nightmarish cruelty under which innocent people were victimized.

Peter Hayes probably speaks for most economic historians when he detects in the plaintiffs' case "an apparently irresistible inducement for these lawyers to hype the wages of criminality in order to magnify its just deserts."[21] But however ill-founded historically, such notions became an inseparable part of thinking about restitution in the 1990s. Moreover, as settlement negotiations proceeded, discussions frequently turned to questions of need—of which there was plenty among Holocaust survivors, as Jewish aid workers understood all too well. Tens of thousands of survivors of Nazi persecution live in difficult circumstances in various parts of the globe, with insufficient resources even for basic necessities— often in Eastern Europe where they had sometimes never received restitution, but also in the West, in Europe, in North and South America, and in Israel. Thus the claim that "it's not about the money" was not entirely true. The real issue is how thinking about money affected the restitution process discussed here.

Ironically, the restitution initiated by the reparations agreement between Germany and Israel signed in 1953, hugely controversial at the time and pressed forward in the teeth of bitter opposition within the Jewish state, was unambiguously about money. Israeli journalist and historian Tom Segev underscores the practical, precise accounting that prompted most Israelis to support what might have been considered an unacceptable settling of accounts: "The money Israel received was explicitly allocated to cover the cost of absorbing and rehabilitating the survivors of the Holocaust. Israel's opening position was based on the assumption that the cost of absorbing a single refugee was $3,000. Some 500,000 were absorbed, for a total of $1.5 billion. This agreement depicted Israel not as the homeland of the Jewish people, the realization of the Zionist dream, but rather as a state accepting immigrants for money."[22] Notwithstanding their hesitations and second thoughts, and the violent opposition of some leaders, most Israelis agreed.

Nearly half a century later, no one wanted the material side of restitution to be emblematic of the campaign. Particularly given the passage of time, it was felt, monetary claims might be seen to trivialize the wrongs committed. Necessarily, however, thoughts turned to money as negotiations for settlements intensified and pressure upon both sides reached sometimes acrimonious levels. Ronald Zweig has noted how the valuation of the Hungarian Gold Train inflated powerfully in the controversy over the plundered assets of Hungarian Jewry, eventually reaching a fantastic $5 billion. "Fantasies can become 'facts' with a weight and seriousness all their own," he notes. In this case, fantasy drew upon two particularly dangerous myths—"the fantasy that all Jews were wealthy, and an unrealistic belief in the possibility of seizing prosperity and economic well being from one ethnic community and transferring it to another."[23] And to these one might add another: when it comes to the Holocaust we have become used to great magnitudes—unthinkable numbers tracked, persecuted, and murdered, most of all, but also great piles of personal effects taken from victims. It is perhaps understandable that when it comes to wealth associated with the Jews, or what was taken from them, we should think as well in highly inflated terms—amounts that escape the imagination, amounts beyond calculation.[24]

Given the disagreeable associations with monetary settlements, the most compelling argument probably made on their behalf was that payments were *just*, and that the injustice of the Holocaust cried out for a just resolution. This perspective addresses the dilemma of restitution: While there is some discomfort with the payments, there is even more discomfort with foregoing them, with allowing the issue to drop.[25] Michael Ignatieff expressed the dilemma and his sense of its unhappy resolution, observing that while there could be no satisfactory remedy for what had been suffered, it was impossible, at the same time, to ignore the call that the perpetrators must be made to pay.[26] Legal theorist Adrian Vermeule refers to compensatory cash payments as "rough justice." "Rough justice is indefensible," he writes. "It seems attractive only when compared with no justice—when it is recognized that the status quo of inaction is also a proposal, and one that may fare even worse, according to the same criteria that would condemn the relevant reparations proposals." "It is not so much that 'we should do what we can,'" he contends, "it is rather that we can at least do better than we have."[27]

Aware of the rough edges of "rough justice," Gideon Taylor muses on the Claims Conference founders' insistence, more than half a century ago, on the word "material" in naming the Conference on Jewish *Material* Claims Against Germany. Why their addition to an already cumbersome name? "They wanted to emphasize that negotiations regarding material compensation would never replace the moral challenges posed by the Holocaust," he notes. "Perhaps the reality is that Holocaust compensation and restitution is not about the money and it is about the money. It may on occasion cloud the important lessons of the Holocaust, yet it can also be a vehicle for educating a wider public. At the end of the day, it has helped many hundreds of thousands of Holocaust survivors around the world to live out the remainder of their lives with a little more dignity than they might otherwise have had. It ultimately represents a measure of justice—no more, no less."[28]

For Stuart Eizenstat, "the moral dimension of our work often got clouded in the fog of rhetoric, recrimination, and threats of sanctions."[29] This is undoubtedly true, and to the sources of this acrimony one must add the lawyers' fees, which have been the object of controversy. "$52 Million for Lawyers' Fees in Nazi-Era Slave Labor Suits," headlined the *New York Times* in June 2001, carrying an implicit message, to many at least, that the class action lawyers were engaged in some unjust enrichment of their own. The *Times* went on to report that "eleven lawyers were awarded more than $1 million each and that payments to the lawyers would come soon, while those to survivors had been held up by various disputes." In the settlement of the Hungarian Gold Train lawsuit in 2005, conflict erupted over the relatively small $25.5 million settlement. The law firms involved claimed $3.85 million for their work, an amount that Roman Kent deemed "outrageous—scandalous—taking advantage of survivors."[30] "There are widely held views that, somehow, the lawyers in these cases made out like bandits at the expense of Holocaust victims," said Eizenstat, who protested that this was not the case.[31] "The legal fees [that the lawyers] will receive are far less than would normally be received for such a large settlement and represent only about one percent of the total Foundation sum," he told a plenary meeting in the settlement with German industry.[32]

While the "fog of rhetoric" surrounding these cases gradually lifted, unease over legal fees has persisted and has withstood the lawyers' response that they worked hard for their money, that their expenses were huge, and that the litigation was protracted. There was some confusion over claims made about fees because some lawyers who worked pro bono in the case against Swiss banks subsequently earned millions of dollars in the distribution negotiations and in subsequent litigation.[33] Responding to protests, defenders of the process insisted that the litigators' contribution had been essential, and that they had been working on a contingency basis, expecting payment of a percentage of the award only if they succeeded and only with the approval of the court.[34] According to Burt Neuborne, himself to become a target of allegations over fees, payment to all lawyers in the Swiss case—approximately $6 million, or 0.05 percent of the total—was actually quite modest, and amounted to "the lowest fee structure in history for comparable levels of success."[35] Still, more than seven years after agreement was reached, lawyers were still disputing each other's fees, with the disputes seemingly carrying on disagreements among the attorneys about how the settlement should be administered.[36]

Standing back from the issue, the defenders seem to be correct in their insistence that the lawyers' fees were not out of line with what is usually charged in class action settlements. A Cornell University study of that issue in 2003 concluded that 21.9 percent of a settlement was the mean for lawyers' fees in class actions, significantly more than the Holocaust-era payments.[37] On the other hand, both the high dollar amounts paid and the manner in which they were set has left a continuing bad taste in some quarters.[38] Stuart Eizenstat may have it right when he attributes much of the problem to the hothouse legal environment in which these proceedings took place. "The Holocaust cases were part of the broader excesses of the class-action system the United States uses to resolve mass injury cases, which is spinning out of control and exerting a drag on the U.S. economy," he writes. "There is a crying need for reform, but this is no reason for special indictment of the Holocaust settlements."[39] Finally, a case can be made that much of the argument over fees is really about something deeper—the bitter opposition, within the survivor community, to a Jewish establishment with commemorative and communal priorities rather than those of individual victims. Lawyers, in some instances at least, seem to have been caught in the crossfire.[40]

Disagreeable as these quarrels have been, there were even worse instances of public embarrassment. While some lawyers associated with restitution worked pro bono or donated their fees to charitable causes, others crossed clear lines into unethical or illegal conduct on related matters, inescapably reflecting on the way Holocaust litigation was settled. The most egregious case was that of Edward Fagan, who filed the first case against the Swiss banks in 1996 and was deeply involved in the German industry litigation and the subsequent distribution negotiations as well. Described as a master of self-promotion, Fagan was a flamboyant personal injury lawyer turned self-styled "human rights" specialist— with little or no experience in the class action field. Fagan assembled huge numbers of Holocaust claimants and jostled and fought with other lawyers before becoming embroiled with his own clients, some of whom accused him of mishandling Holocaust-related lawsuits. The target of intense criticisms on ABC's prime-time television program *20/20*, Fagan was harshly sanctioned by a New York judge, Shirley Wohl Kram, and most recently was disbarred for wrongdoing in a multibillion-dollar Holocaust-related lawsuit.[41]

Even more serious was the case of Melvyn Weiss of Milberg Weiss, the proud, feared, and awe-inspiring dean of class action lawyers in the United States and a lead counsel in both the Swiss banks and German industry cases. After years of investigation by the Department of Justice, Weiss found himself indicted in Los Angeles in September 2007 for having secretly and illegally paid kickbacks to individuals to enlist them as clients in class action cases as well as having committed perjury, bribery, and fraud along the way.[42] Assessed by his peers as a brilliant and hard-driving counsel, a master of the class action lawsuit, but also as a ruthless, manipulative, and intimidating backroom dealmaker, the seventy-two-year-old Weiss was a force to be reckoned with in the restitution world—used to calling the shots himself and outside the ambit of World Jewish Congress decision makers. Working pro bono on the Swiss banks negotiations, Weiss pushed the envelope of the lawsuit. "This case will never be settled unless the amount starts with a *B*," he said at an early point, proposing $9 billion. "How tight can we squeeze their balls, and how much can we get from them?" he asked.[43] Pleading guilty in March 2008, Weiss was sentenced in a Los Angeles court to thirty months in prison.[44] His career was in tatters. None of this, to be sure, related directly to the Holocaust litigation, but Weiss's misconduct, which shook the legal community, could not help but prompt some reflection on the processes that brought about its resolution.[45]

And there were other cases of misconduct as well—a string of persons associated with the restitution campaign of the 1990s who turned out to have been involved in shady dealing, personal dishonesty, or other improprieties. In June 2000 Chuck Quackenbush, the photogenic California insurance commissioner who was the scourge of European insurers accused of defrauding Holocaust survivors, resigned his position in the face of imputations of mismanagement, soliciting campaign donations from insurers, and misappropriating funds.[46] In August 2003, a U.S. district court in the District of Columbia disbarred Neal Sher, a former Nazi war crimes prosecutor who had been chief of staff for the International Commission on Holocaust Era Insurance Claims, a year after he left that post amidst charges of "unauthorized reimbursements of [commission] travel expenses."[47] In late 2006, New York state comptroller Alan Hevesi, a key figure in the mobilization against the Swiss banks ten years before, faced charges of having improperly benefited from his control of the state's $154 million pension fund and misuse of state employees, leading to a conviction and his resignation in disgrace. According to the *New York Times*, he "pleaded guilty to a single felony charge after arranging a deal with prosecutors that will spare him prison time."[48]

During much of the litigation and settlement discussed in this book, the Israelis were represented internationally by Avraham Hirchson, a founder of the March of the Living and a Likud member of the Knesset since 1981.[49] Known as an advocate for victims of Nazism and a close ally of Israel Singer, Hirchson was a board member of the Special Swiss Committee for Needy Holocaust Survivors, chaired the Knesset Committee on Restitution, and was later Israel's finance minister in the government of Ehud Olmert. Under investigation by the Israeli police for a variety of suspicious financial transactions, Hirchson came to the attention of Israeli media when he was caught by Polish police boarding a plane from Poland for Israel in 1997 with $250,000 in cash stuffed in his suitcases. When this came to light ten years later, Hirchson's reputation collapsed. According to an editorial in the *Jerusalem Post*, "It's an open secret for anyone in the loop that chaos and confusion reign supreme at Israel's Finance Ministry these days, following serious allegations of corruption against Finance Minister Avraham Hirchson leaked to the public by the police."[50] In the spring of 2008, the Israeli authorities indicted Hirchson on charges of embezzlement, fraud, breach of trust, and money laundering in connection with his actions as head of a trade union between 1998 and 2005.[51] Resolution of the matter is pending.

Even at the most senior level of the Holocaust restitution movement, wrongdoing or alleged wrongdoing tainted the leadership that had so forcefully campaigned on behalf of transparency and morality. While not formally accused of any offenses, Alfonse D'Amato, the three-term "Senator Pothole" and Republican powerbroker who worked closely with Edgar Bronfman and Israel Singer in the campaign against the Swiss banks, lost his bid for reelection to the United States Senate in 1998.[52] Described as "the master of (barely) plausible deniability," the colorful D'Amato has had numerous brushes with the authorities, displaying what one investigative journalist has called a "legendary ability to beat a succession of raps."[53] And finally, most embarrassingly of all for the World Jewish Congress, Israel Singer himself ran into an ethical buzz saw in 2006, amid accusations of improperly funneling $1.2 million through a Swiss bank account to personal accounts in London and New York. After being obliged to surrender his financial responsibilities within the World Jewish Congress, an investigation by the New York State attorney general's office concluded that Singer had violated his fiduciary responsibilities and had diverted Congress money to personal use—although it found no evidence of a criminal offense. Not long thereafter, amid new accusations against Singer, Edgar Bronfman fired the thirty-year World Jewish Congress veteran from his post as its chairman, marking "an all-time low in the history of the organization," according to the Israeli newspaper *Haaretz*.[54]

It is hard to know what to make of this cascade of dysfunction, impropriety, and illegality among some major players in the Holocaust restitution movement. In addition to the insalubrious culture of class actions already noted, the reason for it may simply relate to the unhealthy confluence of big rewards and moral posturing that accompanies much restitution seeking in the public arena. It must be said that the wrongdoing discussed here does not seem to have impinged directly on any Holocaust-related litigation, and although there has been a regular drumbeat of accusations in Israel about the mistreatment of Holocaust survivors in that country and the alleged sins of the Claims Conference in particular, none of this seems to be connected with the American-led restitution campaign discussed here.[55] Moreover, as has been pointed out by those familiar with the various walks of life from which these cases arise, it is sadly possible that these are not rare instances of political and administrative impropriety. "None of these personal and professional incidents would be more than curiosities or gossip," observes Marilyn Henry, "except that the efforts to recover Nazi-era assets are not finished. You have to wonder what kind of shadow they will cast, especially when many governments resist new claims and many survivors distrust the players, believing that they will be deceived or victimized." The problem, she concludes, is that "an endeavor cloaked in the sanctity of the Shoah and claims made on moral grounds call for advocates of the highest stature, not mere mortals who cannot stifle the urge to misbehave."[56]

History, Memory, and Restitution

If not just about money and if about justice, how can restitution for Holocaust-era wrongdoing be achieved when the perpetrators are

almost all gone and we are now more than half a century on? How is
that justice to be understood? And how should it be realized? The first
part of a response is to recognize that these questions only arise because
the Holocaust restitution movement made significant achievements in
the settlement of outstanding claims. A look back puts this into perspective. What was breathtaking about the restitution claims was of course
that they reached back more than half a century. "In the history of
American litigation," Michael Bazyler notes, "no class of cases has ever
appeared in which so much time had passed between the wrongful act
and the filing of the lawsuit."[57] This kind of reaching backward was
once unthinkable. In the mid-1960s, former slave laborers sought to sue
the I.G. Farben corporation for what they suffered under Hitler. Only
twenty-odd years after the war the United States Court of Appeals for
the District of Columbia deployed its legal idiom to declare that the
crimes of Nazism were just too remote to be reached by civil courts. In
its view, "The span between the doing of the damage and the application of the claimed assuagement is too vague. The time is too long. The
identity of the alleged tort feasors is too indefinite. The procedure
sought—adjudication of some two hundred thousand claims for multi-
farious damages inflicted twenty to thirty years ago in a European area
by a government then in power—is too complicated, too costly, to justify
undertaking by a court without legislative provision of the means
wherewith to proceed."[58] Remarkably, the courts began to think otherwise thirty years later. Proponents of Holocaust-era litigation owe it to
the evolution of class action lawsuits, to the plaintiffs' initiative in the
mid-1990s, and to the wisdom and capabilities of Judge Edward Korman in the precedent-setting Swiss banks case that the way was opened
for restitution described here.

On how justice should be understood, claimants in Holocaust restitution matters seem as close to unanimity as one can expect for such an
extraordinarily diverse group, scattered internationally and of so many
backgrounds, nationalities, and wartime experiences: what matters to
them is what they describe, in different ways, as the public recognition
of their own and their family's and their people's terrible ordeals. Born
in Krakow in 1945 to Holocaust survivors, Eva Hoffman notes that "the
first task after great wrongs have been committed is to name those
wrongs *as* wrongs."[59] To their frustration, many Holocaust survivors
have felt that the losses that they experienced had never properly been
understood and never been recognized as part of their victimization.

Now, many years later, what victims want is an acknowledgment of what still remains unacknowledged—or what they fear will be unacknowledged. Si Frumkin, liberated from Dachau and a longtime human rights activist, has a typical articulation. Fifty years after the end of the war, what he wants is to see the combined lists of insurance policyholders from the wartime period: "Hitler took away my father's name and gave him a number. The insurance companies took it away again. It isn't on any revealed lists and they pretend that he never existed. I want them to acknowledge that he lived, that he died, and that the way he died matters to his son and to the grandchildren he never knew."[60]

Why should it matter if insurance executives in Europe "acknowledge" these essential facts about victimization so long ago? The reason has to do, I believe, with most survivors' notions of justice. If probed, most survivors' response seems to be that successful outcomes of restitution struggles create and solidify a collective understanding, sometimes referred to as the history or memory of terrible events that happened to them. Often, they add, their wider goal is to see that such things never happen again. Survivors urgently want this collective understanding authoritatively established, with no detail deliberately left unreported, for each detail adds something deemed essential to the integrity of the whole. With this urgency often goes a sense of the fragility of such histories or memories—a fear that what exists in this regard may be lost or denied or forgotten unless properly respected, attended to, and constantly recalled. "A chief function of reparations movements," writes the legal philosopher Christopher Kutz, "is to create and hallow a particular set of memories, to restore to collective consciousness events otherwise obscured by official histories and 'common sense' as defined by dominant groups."[61] Memories, the theorist Tzvetan Todorov points out, are never the integral reconstitution of the past; memories are highly selective, the result of picking and choosing, in which selections are made "by agents who remember with a particular goal in view."[62] Often, this goal is central to an individual's or a people's consciousness. Referring to such cases, Charles Maier refers to the "sacralization of memory," pointing out that its objective is "the retrieval and reliving of a moment of transcendent victimhood [that] is a people's choice."[63]

This observation points to another way of understanding this thirst for justice, so many years after the event, which is to see in it the survivors' quest to take charge of defining memory, or as the Swiss scholar Regula Ludi says, "placing victims of injustice on centre stage"—humiliated by their experience of victimization and silenced as they once may have been, ignored as they often were, and diminished in numbers and increasingly frail as they now may be. And, it needs to be underscored, these perspectives are not peculiar to victims of the Holocaust. Those who have endured great injustice and suffered great wrongs often share a powerful sense that what they experienced must not be forgotten but must be cultivated both in remembrance of those who did not survive and as a warning to future generations.

This is perhaps the point at which to draw an important distinction between history and memory, noting that it is the latter, and not the former, that justice seeking for the Holocaust seems to entail. Following the French historian Henry Rousso, I believe that memory, either individual or collective, involves the apprehension of the past with a view to a *particular* perspective: an individual remembers a thing or event by making intelligible now, a fragment of the past; a collectivity "remembers" a particular part of the past that is deemed important to that collectivity in the present. "Memory," says Rousso, "is a mental representation of the past, but it has only a partial rapport with that past. It can be defined as the *presence* of the *present of the past,* a reconstructed or reconstituted presence that organizes itself in the psyche of individuals round a complex maze of images, words, and sensations."[64] History, by contrast, is an analytical exercise: it draws upon testimony as well as other evidence in order to interpret, recount, assess, and explain. It investigates "individuals, facts, practices, and deep-rooted tendencies that contemporaries perhaps neither perceived nor understood."[65] Unlike memory, which registers a particular meaning of the past and what individuals or groups have experienced, history requires analysis and invites comparison; it seeks an objective assessment that theoretically speaks to everyone.

Memory and history differ in their engagement with the past. Memory lives in individuals and groups; based on experiences, it links with identity in that it constitutes a vision of how the individual or the group is constituted or has come to be in the present. Memory, says Rousso, "is a bearer of affect"; "it is part of our existential experience." History, by contrast, operates at arm's length. It lives in the books and articles that historians write. It derives from conscious reconstruction, it strives for objectivity and it seeks truth. "History is an approach that puts the past at a distance," Rousso continues, "it is an effort destined to create and help us understand the weight and complexity of past events."[66] Along with other historians, Rousso is uncomfortable with the idea that history should engage in a prosecution of the past. "Historians are no longer in their proper element once they don courtroom robes." As the British historian Richard Evans puts it, maintaining this distinction is "to reassert history's primary purposes of explaining and understanding the past, rather than judging it."[67]

While it is true that, under the pressure of the American-led campaign, some two dozen historical commissions were struck by various governments to examine various aspects of different countries' wartime behavior, and numerous German and even some American corporations hired historians to assess their wartime behavior, the litigation and the negotiations involved in settling restitution claims themselves did not generally break new historical ground.[68] Nor was this really their objective. Rather, the justice seeking of the restitution campaign was an effort, prompted by legal proceedings, to clarify and promote a moral contention with the Nazis' assault on innocent victims. It was a way, in Jeremy Waldron's words, "of bringing to imaginative life the full implications of principles to which we are already in theory committed."[69] The goal of the campaign was to insist that victims cannot be ignored and that the wrongs that they have suffered had to be addressed, however imperfectly, one way or another. Consistent with the Anglo-American adversarial legal system, it utilized processes "designed to resolve disputes, as opposed to determining the ultimate truth."[70] It drew upon that part of the past that documents what had been suffered, rather than what had brought that suffering about. As such, it pertained to memory— something perhaps recognized in the German Foundation, "Remembrance, Responsibility, and the Future," that emerged from negotiations with German corporations. Many commentators also seemed to feel that the promotion of remembrance, seen as an outcome marking successful litigation, entailed a transcendence of the legal argumentation that got them started. "In the eyes of the public," writes one legal scholar, "the tedious technicality of questions of statute of limitations, *forum non conveniens,* contract or tort, individual responsibility, international treaty law and political question doctrine was adequately replaced by a Foundation that would not only be able to provide speedy compensation (as compared to lengthy process before the courts) but, more importantly, provide an allegedly more dignified forum through which to remember and to honor this dark past."[71]

Remembered and—it should be noted—*honored*. It is not, I believe, that the survivors crave the limelight; nor is it that they are unappreciative of the deference that is regularly extended to them at meetings and public hearings having to do with the Holocaust. It is rather that claimants have been seeking, through the honor accorded them, what is in fact impossible in the real world we inhabit: to undo the persistent scandal of their victimization, the persistent humiliation associated with the degraded circumstances under which they were persecuted and murdered, and the sense of abandonment that followed them even into the postwar period. Justice seeking through restitution is part of an often quixotic attempt to restore honor and respect, and this may explain why, as John Authers and Richard Wolffe note at the end of their impressive book on the subject, the victims themselves "do not share the same sense of success [about the outcomes] that exists among the lawyers, companies, and governments who waged those fights."[72] The reason, it seems to me, is sadly evident: try as they might, and successful though they have been in various settlements, they could not undo what has happened, nor be entirely confident that their catastrophe has been fully understood or absorbed into people's consciousness, nor accept that the restitution of the 1990s was anything more than some measure of justice.

Conclusion: Looking to the Future

In his influential book *The Guilt of Nations*, historian Elazar Barkan calls attention to the wave of restitution cases around the world in recent years, suggesting that this testifies to "a new globalism." In this view, restitution "embodies the increasing importance of morality and the growing democratization of political life." And in this context, although restitution in the future will doubtless take on the color of local circumstances, German reparation for the Holocaust has become "a precedent and a model for future restitution cases."[73] Is the Holocaust restitution campaign examined here applicable to other historic wrongs? Since the Holocaust has become emblematic of genocidal attacks on entire populations, with assessments of its importance paradoxically increasing rather than decreasing with the passage of time, can one predict that the related restitution of the 1990s will similarly become a model for a new wave of justice seeking? Some contend that a new attention to reparation and restitution to individuals has become part of the transformative legacy of the Second World War for international law, and if so it seems reasonable that the recent American-led campaign will help define that transformation. Certainly some wanted this to happen. According to Neuborne, "Plaintiffs hoped, by asserting international law claims as well as local law claims, to develop a parallel set of international norms designed to eliminate the possibility of profit from knowingly cooperating in the commission of crimes against humanity by finding all such 'profits' to be merely held in constructive trust for the victims."[74] How realistic is this aspiration?

Michael Bazyler identifies specific claims that he believes have already been influenced by the strategies and techniques of Holocaust-era restitution—claims having to do with slavery in the United States, the Armenian genocide of 1915, and prisoner of war and civilian maltreatment by the Japanese during the Second World War. Each of these has been tested, some inconclusively and some unsuccessfully, before American courts, and sometimes with the same lawyers involved in Holocaust cases.[75] To be sure, each case is different. Restitution for slavery and for Armenian victims involve even greater spans of time than those for the Holocaust, and therefore pose special difficulties both with respect to chronology and questions about who the claimants would be. In many cases, claims go beyond individuals and involve arguments that should be extended to an entire people—a theme that certainly appeared in the Holocaust-era restitution campaign described here.[76] In the wings there is a list of other cases that await development and are, according to Bazyler, "claiming inspiration for the American litigation model represented by the Holocaust restitution movement."[77]

Thanks to the examples of Holocaust restitution these claims may encourage U.S. courts to exercise extraterritorial jurisdiction, engage theories of unjust enrichment, or draw upon precedents based on statutes of limitation and sovereign immunity. Optimistically, Bazyler believes that Holocaust restitution cases "can serve as a template for a new era of financial relief and recognition for the victims of present war crimes and crimes against humanity, without the fifty-year delay for justice." He also argues for the existence of a deterrent effect. "As a result of the victories achieved by victims of the Holocaust in courts of the United States, individuals and corporations presently engaged in human rights abuses are on notice: eventually you will be held responsible for your misdeeds."[78] Stuart Eizenstat—no great friend of the aggressive legal maneuvers in the Holocaust-related cases—is more guarded in his expectations. While he sees the application of human rights laws as help-ful in its application to multinational corporations, he acknowledges that the track record of Holocaust-era legal decisions is not entirely pos-itive. In his 2004 book on the subject, Eizenstat implies that champions of restitution should draw lessons from the diplomatic side of these pro-ceedings rather than viewing these as a legal breakthrough.[79] Contest-ing some of the congratulatory rhetoric of his colleagues on the plain-tiffs' side, Burt Neuborne agrees. "The sad fact is that American courts have too often turned their backs on Holocaust victims," he argues. Neuborne complains about court decisions that have barred the way to victory in particular cases and regrets that settlements that were achieved were not more generous to the dwindling numbers of survivors.[80] In ad-dition, Neuborne condemns the attraction of unscrupulous attorneys to great prizes in restitution. "I worry about an explosion of these kinds of suits," he said in 1998, and "that a lot of people will see a potential for what they think is a fast buck."[81]

There is a case to be made that the Holocaust restitution campaign arose in highly unusual circumstances, unlikely to be replicated and un-likely therefore to affect other campaigns for justice for historic wrongs. Frequently overlooked because of the heat of the negotiations, it must be noted that the European countries were almost all, from the very be-ginning, anxious to put the crimes of the Nazis behind them—even if this involved specific restitution to which individual defendants may not have been philosophically, morally, or in their view legally committed.[82] One should recall as well the favorable political climate under which this campaign was launched and succeeded, something particularly evi-dent to Eizenstat, for example, whose diplomatic efforts were so signifi-cantly assisted by the backing of the Clinton administration. The value of presidential support became particularly evident when it effectively evaporated under George W. Bush. "Bereft of a senior-level special envoy on Holocaust-era issues," Eizenstat testifies, "and without the en-gagement of the Bush White House, much of the political and diplo-matic pressure that led to landmark Holocaust restitution agreements on slave and forced labor, Swiss and French bank accounts, payment of insurance policies, and the return of confiscated property and Nazi-looted art to their owners has dissipated. Together with an American legal system that moves at a snail's pace, these factors have caused mo-mentum to be lost in several areas, at a time when Holocaust survivors are passing away at a rate of 10 percent per year."[83] And so we return to the obvious: the time was right for the Holocaust restitution movement—and it may not be so for other claims for restitution for historic wrongs.

There is also reason to doubt whether the application of a *lex americana* defined in the 1990s can persist into the new millennium. Burt Neuborne has argued powerfully on its behalf, and those who believe in the beneficent international impact of American law have urged its continuing application.[84] But the decline of American influence during the second Bush administration and a global restiveness before claims of American hegemony may tell a different story. So, too, may the widespread belief that America abandoned some of its commitment to the rule of law in pursuit of the "Global War on Terror." As several commentators report, European reactions to American restitution proceedings range from puzzlement to outright indignation.[85] Moreover, calls for tort reform in the United States could shift the balance in favor of corporations and against the rights of victims in class action lawsuits.[86] And finally, one should not draw too much comfort from the public claims by Jewish leaders that their efforts were, in part at least, on behalf of a Jewish collectivity—the Jewish people. "No credible legal theory could be mustered for why such a collective entity is a proper plaintiff in a U.S. court," writes the legal authority Paul Dubinsky. Even with liberal rules allowing parties to join the plaintiffs' case in civil suits, "U.S. procedural law does not embrace the remedial aspirations of groups that lack legal personality."[87]

"Historical claims . . . generally cannot be based upon the remedial paradigm of individual perpetrator, individual victim, and proven quantifiable losses," the international legal specialist Dinah Shelton contends.[88] On the basis of what I have examined here, I believe that she is right. Although attorneys in the Holocaust restitution campaign moved legal mountains to apply their theories and to conform to procedures designed for more garden-variety civil wrongs, these failed adequately to address the awesome historic violence of the Holocaust or the ocean of wrongdoing that it caused. Sensing this at the beginning, some Holocaust survivors wanted no part of the process. This is, I believe, the sentiment that motivated the declaration with which I began this book. For the layman, the poor fit between claims and the means of resolution is underscored when successors to Holocaust-era perpetrators are labeled "tort feasors," "wrongdoers," "malefactors," or "Hitler's willing business partners," responsible for "injuries," and who had to "disgorge" their profits, suggest "remedies," or offer "relief" to their victims.

However, this misfit did not mean that nothing was accomplished. "Significantly," Shelton observes, "nearly all instances of reparations for historical injustices, whether in the form of an apology, in land or money, have come about through negotiations or in the political process."[89] To me, this is the principal practical lesson of the Holocaust restitution campaign. Notwithstanding the fragility of legal claims and difficulties of the consequent litigation, the major categories of Holocaust-era restitution since the mid-1990s have been resolved through bargaining, diplomacy, negotiation, and sometimes government intervention, with governments often at the ringside seats, as in the case of the Swiss banks and insurance, or deeply involved in the process itself, as with German industry. Even in the case of art, public pressure, in the form of general ideas about appropriate resolutions of highly complex legal matters and about the public interest, will probably shape the way that these disputes are resolved. This is, I believe, as it should be, for restitution for historic wrongs concerns the deepest impulses and commitments of a society, matters too important to be left entirely to the lawyers.[90]

———

However the Holocaust restitution movement will speak to other victims of historic wrongs, it seems plain now, as we gain some perspective on the campaign, that it achieved what was so frequently claimed on its behalf—*some measure of justice*. Looking back, it was perhaps naïve to tell his critics, as Edgar Bronfman did in 1997: "It's the moral issue that's exciting people, not the money. The issue is the truth. The issue is morality."[91] Bronfman's description of what moved people was not entirely accurate, and his claims about what was at issue were at the very least incomplete. To some degree, as we have argued here, it *was* about money. And truth, what most people understood as an accurate, balanced, and full account of the historical record, did not always fare well in the restitution process, intended as it is to resolve disputes rather than to write history. Morality, or at least morality as an ideal, was even less attainable, as participants in a necessarily gritty process were almost all ready to acknowledge. Eventually, quests for Holocaust-era restitution were resolved around bargaining tables, and this necessarily involved give and take, compromise, and solutions that never completely satisfied.

Among the claims for restitution examined in this book, one of the least convincing to me is that no one should rest until every known instance of injustice during the Holocaust has been rectified. For the more I have studied the wrongs inflicted upon the victims the less, it seems clear, that there can ever be anything like adequate restitution. What I think we can say is that restitution is more about the present than about the past: it speaks to the survivors who are still among us and who have in some cases been mistreated in the reparations process; to the society at large for which such issues may be said to matter; to a legal process that should not ignore great wrongs even as it processes any manner of far more trivial matters; to a legal system that applies to Holocaust-era claims rules intended for utterly different circumstances; and to a world in which injustice and wrongdoing are still too common—but for which, at the very least, we should have mechanisms available, when the carnage ends, to seek some measure of justice.

Notes

Introduction

1. Leon Wieseltier, "Assets," *The New Republic*, November 8, 1999, 98. Among many others, Edgar Bronfman, president of the World Jewish Congress, about his meeting with Georg Krayer, president of the Swiss Bankers Association in September 1995: "It's not the money, it's the principle." See Itamar Levin, *The Last Deposit: Swiss Banks and Holocaust Victims' Accounts*, trans. Natasha Dornberg (Westport, Conn.: Praeger, 1999), 113.

2. Wieseltier, "Assets."

3. Michael J. Bazyler, *Holocaust Justice: The Battle for Restitution in America's Courts* (New York: New York University Press, 2003), xii.

4. Ibid. Still, for perspective: the settlement with the major tobacco companies in 1998 for Medicaid costs associated with smoking-related diseases, the largest civil settlement in U.S. history, was for $206 billion.

5. Michael J. Bazyler and Kearston G. Everitt, *2004 ACLU International Civil Liberties Report*, December 10, 2004, available at http://www.aclu.org/iclr/bazyler.pdf, 1, last accessed April 29, 2008; Daniel Kadden, "Holocaust Restitution and the Claims Conference: Controversies over Organizational Accountability," *Jewish Currents*, July 2006, available at http://www.jewishcurrents.org/2006-july-kadden.htm, last accessed April 25, 2008.

6. Michael R. Marrus, "History and the Holocaust in the Courtroom," in Ronald Smelser, ed., *Lessons and Legacies IV: The Holocaust and Justice* (Evanston, Ill.: Northwestern University Press, 2002), 215–39.

7. "Responsibility of States for Internationally Wrongful Acts, adopted by the International Law Commission at Its Fifty-third Session" (2001) (extract from the Report of the International Law Commission on the Work of Its Fifty-third Session, Official Records of the General Assembly, Fifty-sixth Session, Supplement No. 10 [A/56/10], chp.Iv.E.1), November 2001, available at http://www.ilsa.org/jessup/jessup06/basic mats2/DASR.pdf, last accessed April 27, 2008. For a discussion of this topic see Dinah Shelton, *Remedies in International Law* (2nd ed., Oxford: Oxford University Press, 2004), and idem, "Righting Wrongs: Reparations in the Articles on State Responsibility," *American Journal of International Law* 96 (2002): 835.

8. Sumner Wells, "New Hope for the Jewish People," *The Nation*, May 5, 1945, quoted in Regula Ludi, "The Vectors of Postwar Victim Reparations: Relief, Redress and Memory Politics," *Journal of Contemporary History* 41 (2006): 428. As Wells put it, "No

recompense can be offered to the dead. The efforts today to right the wrongs which have been committed will be of all too little to avail to the bereft, the orphans, to the home-less, and to the wanderers on the face of the earth. But such measure of recompense as can be offered surely constitutes the moral obligation of the free people of the earth as soon as their victory is won." This is consistent with Regula Ludi's view, with which I agree, that "the various terms in use are all, in different ways, deficient and tend to give the wrong impression: that gross human rights violations can be compensated for" (ibid., 427–28). Another terminological candidate is "redress." See Ilaria Bottigliero, *Redress for Victims of Crimes under International Law* (Leiden and Boston: Martinus Nijhoff, 2004), esp. 4–6. While I accept the virtues of this term "as one that extends conceptually beyond narrowly defined notions of remedy, compensation, restitution, recovery, reha-bilitation, apologies, etc." (4), I prefer not to break new ground in what is most com-monly designated as "restitution."

9. *Black's Law Dictionary* (4th ed., rev., St. Paul, Minn.: West, 1968), 1477.

10. Stuart Eizenstat, *Imperfect Justice: Looted Assets, Slave Labor, and the Unfinished Business of World War II* (New York: Public Affairs, 2003), 17.

11. Abraham Foxman, "The Dangers of Holocaust Restitution," *Wall Street Journal*, December 4, 1998.

12. Elli Wohlgelernter, "Compensation Issue Clouds Holocaust Message—Expert," *Jerusalem Post*, January 19, 2001. This line of argument seems to echo Hannah Arendt's implication, in her comments on the Eichmann trial, that only criminal proceedings were appropriate for symbolic representations of the Holocaust, a crime of universal significance. In criminal proceedings, she wrote, "the wrongdoer is brought to justice be-cause his act has disturbed and gravely endangered the community as a whole, and not because, as in civil suits, damage has been done to individuals who are entitled to repa-ration." "Politically and legally," she went on, "these were 'crimes' different not only in degree of seriousness but in essence." Hannah Arendt, *Eichmann in Jerusalem: A Report on the Banality of Evil* (New York: Viking, 1965), 261, 267.

13. Quoted in Richard Z. Chesnoff, *Pack of Thieves: How Hitler and Europe Plundered the Jews and Committed the Greatest Theft in History* (New York: Doubleday, 1999), 279.

14. Raul Hilberg, interview by Eva Schweitzer in the *Berliner Zeitung*, September 4, 2000, posted on Norman G. Finkelstein's Web site, http://www.normanfinkelstein .com/article.php?pg=3&ar=202, last accessed April 28, 2008.

15. Charles Krauthammer, "The Holocaust Scandal," *Washington Post*, December 4, 1998. Cf. Richard Cohen, "The Money Matters," *Washington Post*, December 8, 1998.

16. Christopher Hitchens, "Dead Souls," *The Nation*, September 18, 2000.

17. Yair Sheleg, "The Finkelstein Polemic," *Haaretz Magazine*, March 30, 2001.

18. Gabriel Schoenfeld, "Holocaust Reparations—A Growing Scandal," *Commentary*, September 2000, 25–34.

19. Norman G. Finkelstein, *The Holocaust Industry: Reflections on the Exploitation of Jewish Suffering* (2nd ed., New York: Verso, 2003), 8. To the dismay of many of his colleagues, Raul Hilberg contributed a promotional blurb to a second edition of Finkelstein's book, maintaining that "his conclusions are trustworthy" and that he "has come up with the right results. I am by no means the only one who, in the coming months or years, will totally agree with Finkelstein's breakthrough." For some critical re-views, see Omer Bartov, "A Tale of Two Holocausts," *New York Times*, August 6, 2000;

Andrew Ross, "'The Holocaust Industry' by Norman G. Finkelstein," salon.com, August 30, 2000, available at http://archive.salon.com/books/review/2000/08/30/ finkelstein/, last accessed October 27, 2008; Paul Bogdanor, "The Finkelstein Phenomenon: Reflections on the Exploitation of Anti-Jewish Bigotry—The Holocaust Industry: Reflections on the Exploitation of Jewish Suffering," *Judaism* 51 (Fall 2002): 504–7.

20. Stuart Eizenstat, letter in "Holocaust Reparations: Gabriel Schoenfeld & Critics," *Commentary*, January 2001, 10.

21. Michael J. Bazyler, letter in ibid., 13.

22. Michael Ignatieff, "Blood Money," *New York Times*, September 10, 2000.

23. Burt Neuborne, letter, *The Nation*, October 23, 2000.

24. See, among other works, Mark Osiel, *Mass Atrocity, Collective Memory and the Law* (New Brunswick, N.J.: Transaction Publishers, 1997); Jean-Michel Chaumont, *La Concurrence des victimes: Génocide, identité, reconnaissance* (Paris: La Découverte, 1997); Martha Minow, *Between Vengeance and Forgiveness: Facing History after Genocide and Mass Violence* (Boston: Beacon Press, 1998); Roy L. Brooks, ed., *When Sorry Isn't Enough: The Controversy over Apologies and Reparations for Human Injustice* (New York: New York University Press, 1999); Michael Ignatieff, *Human Rights as Politics and Idolatry* (Princeton, N.J.: Princeton University Press, 2001); Elazar Barkin, *The Guilt of Nations: Restitution and Negotiating Historical Injustices* (New York: Norton, 2000); Janna Thompson, *Taking Responsibility for the Past: Reparation and Historical Justice* (Cambridge: Polity, 2002); Sandrine Lefranc, *Politiques du pardon* (Paris: Presses universitaires de France, 2002); Carol A. L. Prager and Trudy Govier, eds., *Dilemmas of Reconciliation: Cases and Concepts* (Waterloo, Ont.: Wilfred Laurier University Press, 2003); John Torpey, ed., *Politics and the Past: On Repairing Historical Injustices* (Lanham, Md.: Rowman & Littlefield, 2003); John Elster, *Closing the Books: Transitional Justice in Historical Perspective* (Cambridge: Cambridge University Press, 2004); John Torpey, *Making Whole What Has Been Smashed: On Reparations Politics* (Cambridge, Mass.: Harvard University Press, 2006); Mark Gibney, Rhoda E. Howard-Hassmann, Jean-Marc Coicaud, and Niklaus Steiner, eds., *The Age of Apology: Facing Up to the Past* (Philadelphia: University of Pennsylvania Press, 2008).

25. Geraldine Norman, "From Russia, with Caution," *The Guardian*, January 26, 2008.

Chapter 1. Restitution in the 1990s

1. Particularly useful on the subject of the Swiss banks is the official Web site of the Swiss Banks Settlement: *In re Holocaust Victim Assets Litigation*, United States District Court for the Eastern District of New York, Judge Edward R. Korman Presiding (CV-96-4849), available at http://www.swissbankclaims.com/, last accessed September 24, 2008.

2. See the comments by Shari C. Reig, "The Swiss Banks Holocaust Settlement" (2007), available at http://www.redress.org/PeacePalace/HolcaustSettlementSR.pdf, last accessed June 10, 2008.

3. Regula Ludi, "The Swiss Case," Centre for European Studies Working Paper Series No. 80, *Historians as Trouble-Shooters: Officially Commissioned Surveys of Holocaust Legacies in France and Switzerland* (n.d.), available at http://www.ciaonet.org/wps/lur02/lur02 .pdf, last accessed April 29, 2008.

4. Itamar Levin, *The Last Deposit: Swiss Banks and Holocaust Victims' Accounts*, trans. Natasha Dornberg (Westport, Conn.: Praeger, 1999), 99–104. See also Ronald W. Zweig, *German Reparations and the Jewish World: A History of the Claims Conference* (2nd ed., London: Frank Cass, 2001), 4–5.

5. Hans J. Halbheer, "To Our American Friends: Switzerland in the Second World War," American Swiss Foundation, available at http://www.americanswiss.org/content/, last accessed June 9, 2008.

6. Peter Gumbel, "Secret Legacies," *Wall Street Journal*, June 21, 1995; Nathaniel C. Nash, "Swiss Raise Hopes of Tracing Lost War Deposits," *New York Times*, August 3, 1995.

7. Johanna McGeary, "Echoes of the Holocaust," *Time*, February 24, 1997.

8. "Israeli Media Attitudes toward the Shoah: An Interview with Yair Sheleg," Jerusalem Center for Public Affairs (2003), available at http://www.jcpa.org/phas/phas-sheleg.htm, last accessed April 29, 2008. According to Itamar Levin, Singer, whose wife's family came from Switzerland, first became interested in the Swiss issue in 1993 while working for the World Jewish Restitution Organization, which he had helped to found the previous year, under the umbrella of the World Jewish Congress, to seek restitution of Jewish properties from all European countries except Germany and Austria (Levin, *Last Deposit*, 96). According to another report, Singer's first encounter with the issue came the next year when he read Paul Erdman's novel *The Swiss Account*, with its allusion to Allen Dulles's intelligence-gathering activity in wartime Switzerland and a U.S. intelligence operation to track down Nazi gold in that country. See McGeary, "Echoes of the Holocaust."

9. Avi Beker, "Introduction: Unmasking National Myths," in Avi Beker, ed., *The Plunder of Jewish Property during the Holocaust: Confronting European History* (Houndmills, Basingstoke: Palgrave, 2001), 10. Cf. Isabel Vincent, *Hitler's Silent Partners: Swiss Banks, Nazi Gold, and the Pursuit of Justice* (Toronto: Knopf, 1997), 232–33 and passim.

10. The estimate of the number of claimants comes from the calculations of Peter van der Auweraert, "Holocaust Reparations Claims Fifty Years After: The Swiss Banks Litigation," *Nordic Journal of International Law* 71 (2002): 561 and n.13.

11. On "patriotic memories" see Pierre Lagrou, *The Legacy of Nazi Occupation: Patriotic Memory and National Recovery in Western Europe, 1945–1965* (Cambridge: Cambridge University Press, 2000).

12. Stuart E. Eizenstat, *Imperfect Justice: Looted Assets, Slave Labor, and the Unfinished Business of World War II* (New York: Public Affairs, 2003), 48; Regula Ludi, "Waging War on Wartime Memory: Recent Swiss Debates on the Legacy of the Holocaust and the Nazi Era," *Jewish Social Studies* 10 (2004): 134. According to Ludi, Villiger's apology "signaled a change in official images of the past, which no longer relied exclusively on recollections of resistance and achievements of military defense" (ibid.). See also Nathaniel Nash, "Swiss Raise Hopes of Tracing Lost War Deposits," *New York Times*, August 3, 1995.

13. United States Congress, Senate Committee on Banking, Housing, and Urban Affairs, *Hearings before the U.S. Senate Committee on Banking, Housing, and Urban Affairs* (Washington, D.C.: U.S. G.P.O. 1996), April 23, 1996.

14. Vincent, *Hitler's Silent Partners*, 239–40.

15. Alfonse M. D'Amato to Alan Greenspan, February 5, 1998, available at http://www.senate.gov/comm/banking_housing_and_urban_affairs/general/corresp/0205fed.htm, last accessed April 30, 2008. New York governor George E. Pataki similarly

threw his weight behind this effort. According to his press release: "Before these two institutions are given the chance to launch a new era in their respective histories, they must convince New York's bank regulators and the Federal Reserve's Board of Governors that they're doing everything in their power to rectify a great injustice from the past." "Governor Pataki Joins Senator D'Amato to Oppose Swiss Banks Merger," March 24, 1998, available at http://www.claims.state.ny.us/pr980324.htm, last accessed May 13, 2008.

16. John Authers and Richard Wolffe, *The Victim's Fortune: Inside the Epic Battle over the Debts of the Holocaust* (New York: Perennial, 2002), 16 and passim; and McGeary, "Echoes of the Holocaust."

17. Quoted in Tom Bower, *Nazi Gold: The Full Story of the Fifty-Year Swiss-Nazi Conspiracy to Steal Billions from Europe's Jews and Holocaust Survivors* (New York: HarperCollins, 1997), 310.

18. Vincent, *Hitler's Silent Partners*, 180.

19. Michael J. Bazyler, *Holocaust Justice: The Battle for Restitution in America's Courts* (New York: New York University Press, 2003), 31.

20. Auweraert, "Holocaust Reparations Claims," 568; Anthony J. Sebok, "Mass Restitution Litigation in the United States," in David Dyzenhaus and Mayo Moran, eds., *Calling Power to Account: Law, Reparations, and the Chinese Canadian Head Tax Case* (Toronto: University of Toronto Press, 2005), 359; Rudolf Dolzer, "The Settlement of War-Related Claims: Does International Law Recognize a Victim's Private Right of Action? Lessons after 1945," *Berkeley Journal of International Law* 20 (2002): 298.

21. Authers and Wolffe, *Victim's Fortune,* 14–20; Greg Bradsher, "Research, Restitution, and Remembrance: The Federal Government and Holocaust-Era Assets," lecture at B'nai Israel Synagogue, April 20, 2001, available at http://www.archives.gov/research/holocaust/articles-and-papers/federal-government-and-holocaust-assets-1996-2001.html, last accessed July 22, 2008; David Rohde, "Judge Weighs Fate of Suit Filed by Jews against Swiss," *New York Times,* August 1, 1997.

22. Independent Committee of Eminent Persons, *Report on Dormant Accounts of Victims of Nazi Persecution in Swiss Banks,* December 1999, 1–2, available at http://www.crt-ii.org/ICEP/ICEP_Report_ToC.pdf, last accessed April 30, 2008; and *In re Holocaust Victim Assets Litigation,* 105 F.Supp.2d, 151.

23. See the Web site of the Independent Commission of Experts (ICE)–Second World War, available at http://www.uek.ch/en/index.htm, last accessed April 30, 2008.

24. See especially Jane Schapiro, *Inside a Class Action: The Holocaust and the Swiss Banks* (Madison: University of Wisconsin Press, 2003).

25. Eizenstat, *Imperfect Justice,* 231.

26. "A Distinguished Public Servant," *New York Times,* January 19, 1999.

27. Julia Collins, "Taking on the Unfinished Business of the Twentieth Century," *Harvard Law Bulletin,* Summer 1999, available at http://www.law.harvard.edu/news/bulletin/backissues/summer99/index.html, last accessed May 21, 2008.

28. For descriptions, see Authers and Wolffe, *Victim's Fortune,* 94–99; Susan Orenstein, "Gold Warriors: The Inside Story of the Historic $1.25 Billion Settlement between Holocaust Victims and the Swiss Banks," *American Lawyer* (September 1998): 63–64; Eizenstat, *Imperfect Justice,* 168–70.

29. Richard Z. Chesnoff, *Pack of Thieves: How Hitler and Europe Plundered the Jews and Committed the Greatest Theft in History* (New York: Doubleday, 1999), 271.

30. The Swiss government was not a party to the agreement, which was concluded with the Credit Suisse and the Union Bank of Switzerland, the largest and most important of the Swiss banks. The other defendant, the Swiss Bank Corporation, had been allowed to merge in 1998 with the Union Bank of Switzerland.

31. Shari C. Reig, "The Swiss Banks Holocaust Settlement," paper presented at the Conference on Reparations for Victims of Genocide, Crimes against Humanity and War Crimes: Systems in Place and Systems in the Making, the Peace Palace, The Hague, the Netherlands, March 1–2, 2007, available at http://www.redress.org/Peace Palace/HolcaustSettlementSR.pdf, last accessed April 30, 2008. Shari Reig was the Deputy Special Master for the administration of the distribution of the settlement under Judah Gribetz.

32. *In re Holocaust Victim Assets Litigation*, 302F.Supp.2d 59 (E.D.N.Y., 2004); Edward Korman, "Rewriting the Holocaust History of the Swiss Banks: A Growing Scandal," in Michael J. Bazyler and Roger P. Alford, eds., *Holocaust Restitution: Perspectives on the Litigation and Its Legacy* (New York: New York University Press, 2006), 115–32, especially 117; Burt Neuborne, "A Tale of Two Cities: Administering the Holocaust Settlements in Brooklyn and Berlin," in Bazyler and Alford, *Holocaust Restitution*, 77. See also William Glaberson, "Judge Accuses Swiss Banks of Stonewalling," *New York Times*, February 21, 2004.

33. Eizenstat, *Imperfect Justice*, 177. Eizenstat cites Korman's own view of the ultimate resolution: "As crucial as Judge Korman was to the settlement, even he admitted that the courts are too cumbersome for the efficient dispatch of cases with this kind of diplomatic and political weight: 'This should have been done as a government-to-government agreement. Litigation was the least desirable way to deal with it.'" Ibid.

34. Authers and Wolffe, *Victim's Fortune*, 105.

35. Michael J. Bazyler and Amber L. Fitzgerald, "Trading with the Enemy: Holocaust Restitution, the United States Government, and American Industry," *Brooklyn Journal of International Law* 28 (2003): 699, n.48.

36. See the description in Authers and Wolffe, *Victim's Fortune*, 32–36.

37. *In re Holocaust Victim Assets Litigation*, 105F.Supp.2d, 139, 152 (E.D.N.Y., 2000); *In re Holocaust Victim Assets Litigation*, 302F.Supp.2d, 39 (E.D.N.Y., 2004).

38. Bazyler, *Holocaust Justice*, chap. 4.

39. Mark Spoerer, *Zwangsarbeit unter dem Hakenkreuz* (Stuttgart: Deutsche Verlags-Anstalt, 2001); Ulrich Herbert, *Hitler's Foreign Workers* (Cambridge: Cambridge University Press, 1997).

40. "Final Compensation Pending for Former Nazi Forced Laborers," *Deutsche Welle*, October 27, 2007, available at http://www.redress.org/PeacePalace/HolcaustSettlement SR.pdf, last accessed May 5, 2008).

41. Ulrich Herbert, "Forced Laborers in the Third Reich: An Overview," *International Labor and Working Class History* 58 (2000): 193.

42. Benjamin B. Ferencz's classic account is: *Less than Slaves: Jewish Forced Labor and the Quest for Compensation* (Cambridge, Mass.: Harvard University Press, 1979). On this point see 17–30 and passim. See also Christopher R. Browning, *Nazi Policy, Jewish Workers, German Killers* (New York: Cambridge University Press, 2000).

43. "Of the hundreds of German firms that used concentration camp inmates, the number that paid anything to camp survivors could be counted on the fingers of one hand. Less than 15,000 Jews received any share of the combined total of under $13 million

paid by the few German companies. Even the severe hardship cases of those who had survived work for I.G. Farben at Auschwitz got no more than $1,700 each. Krupp's Jewish slaves and those who toiled for Siemens had to settle for $825. The AEG/Telefunken slaves each received no more than $500, and the Jews who worked for Rheinmetall received even less." Ferencz, *Less than Slaves,* 188. See also Herbert, "Forced Laborers in the Third Reich," 207–15.

44. See Keith Bradsher, "Suit Charges Ford Profited by Nazi-Era Forced Labor," *New York Times,* March 5, 1998.

45. John Authers, "Making Good Again: German Compensation for Forced and Slave Laborers," in Pablo De Greiff, ed., *The Handbook of Reparations* (Oxford: Oxford University Press, 2006), 431.

46. Bazyler, *Holocaust Justice,* chap. 2; Anthony J. Sebok, "Unsettling the Holocaust (Part I)," August 28, 2000, available at http://writ.news.findlaw.com/sebok/20000828 .html, last accessed September 18, 2008.

47. Sebok, "Mass Restitution," 364.

48. "Statement by President Johannes Rau on the Agreement on the Level of Foundation Funding for the Compensation of the Victims of Forced Labor," December 19, 1999, German Embassy, Washington, D.C., available at http://www.germany.info/ relaunch/politics/speeches/121799.html, last accessed July 22, 2008.

49. Bazyler, *Holocaust Justice,* 110.

50. Ibid., 113. Generali was the insurance company for which Franz Kafka worked briefly in Prague. Sander L. Gilman, *Franz Kafka* (London: Reaktion Books, 2005), 42; Authers and Wolffe, *The Victim's Fortune,* 108–9.

51. See Lawrence S. Eagleburger and M. Diane Koken, *Finding Claimants and Paying Them: The Creation and Workings of the International Commission on Holocaust Era Insurance Claims* (2007), available at http://www.icheic.org/pdf/ICHEIC%20Legacy%20Document.pdf, last accessed May 6, 2007.

52. Lawrence Kill and Linda Gerstel, "Holocaust-Era Insurance Claims: Legislative, Judicial, and Executive Remedies," in Bazyler and Alford, *Holocaust Restitution,* 241.

53. See the official ICHEIC Web site, The International Commission on Holocaust Era Insurance Claims, available at http://www.icheic.org/, last accessed September 24, 2008.

54. See Bazyler, *Holocaust Justice,* 162–66.

55. *American Insurance Association v. Garamendi,* 539 U.S. 396 (2003).

56. See Sidney Zabludoff, "ICHEIC: Excellent Concept but Inept Implementation," in Bazyler and Alford, *Holocaust Restitution,* 260–67; Charles E. Boyle, "Holocaust Insurance Claims Panel Faces Recriminations over Delays," *Insurance Journal,* February 11, 2002, available at http://www.insurancejournal.com/magazines/west/2002/02/ 11/features/21936.htm, last accessed June 6, 2008; and "Holocaust and Insurance: Too Late, Too Slow, Too Expensive," *Economist,* August 2, 2003. But cf. the positive evaluation by Roman Kent in his statement to the U.S. Senate Foreign Relations Subcommittee on International Operations and Organizations, Democracy and Human Rights, Hearing on "Holocaust Era Insurance Restitution after ICHEIC," May 6, 2008, available at http://www.senate.gov/~foreign/testimony/2008/KentTestimony080506p.pdf, last accessed June 30, 2008.

57. Authers and Wolffe, *Victim's Fortune,* 265.

58. Eagleburger and Koken, *Finding Claimants and Paying Them*, 20.

59. Ibid., 49–50, and Eagleburger's transmittal letter of June 18, 2000, available at http://www.icheic.org/pdf/Chairman%20Eagleburger%20Cover%20Letter.pdf, last accessed June 6, 2007. See also International Commission on Holocaust Era Insurance Claims (ICHEIC), *Lessons Learned: A Report on Best Practices, June 2007*, available at http://www.icheic.org/pdf/ICHEIC%20Best%20Practices%20Paper.pdf, last accessed May 6, 2008.

60. "ICHEIC Announces Successful Completion of Holocaust Era Insurance Claims Process (March 20, 2007)," ICHEIC Final Press Release, available at http://www.icheic.org/pdf/FINAL%20ICHEIC%20PRESS%20RELEASE%203-20-07.pdf, last accessed June 6, 2008.

61. Stuart Eizenstat provides a useful definition appropriate for this context: "Class action suits are specifically recognized in the Federal Rules of Civil Procedure and by most states of the Union. These suits permit a few individuals to bring a case on behalf of hundreds, thousands, or even millions of others who have supposedly suffered similar injuries and who can recover if the suit is successful, even though they may know nothing about the case or even about the potential injury. Class actions are often legal platforms to raise politically sensitive issues. The principal attraction is that large numbers of people may have legitimate claims—often small ones individually—and could never gain redress any other way. The suits are an increasingly effective way to hold companies publicly responsible for mass injuries." Eizenstat, *Imperfect Justice*, 75–76.

62. Charles E. Boyle, "Holocaust Insurance Claims Panel Faces Recriminations over Delays," *Insurance Journal*, February 11, 2002, available at http://www.insurancejournal.com/magazines/west/2002/02/11/features/21936.htm, last accessed June 6, 2008.

63. Morris A. Ratner, "Factors Impacting the Selection and Positioning of Human Rights Class Actions in United States Courts: A Practical Overview," *New York University Annual Survey of American Law* 58 (2003): 623–50; Authers and Wolffe, *Victim's Fortune*, 39–40.

64. Ratner, "Selection and Positioning of Human Rights Class Actions," 623.

65. Ibid., 626. As Ratner freely admits, "Often, the parties most directly responsible for torture, genocide, mass conversion of assets, and other international law violations are not susceptible to suit in a United States court." Reasonably enough, he notes, "corporations doing business in the United States . . . are the easiest entities to bring to justice in United States courts." Ibid., 629. Ratner further notes that the defendants must often be chosen *before* a careful investigation of the facts: "Although the advice to conduct historical research prior to filing seems relatively obvious and mundane, lawyers often file prior to having completed a factual investigation, such that the complaint must be revised and the class must be redefined during the course of the litigation. Although not ideal, this is sometimes unavoidable, either because information is not readily available or because the plaintiffs are aged or infirm and need quick relief. Any research, especially interviews of potential witnesses, must be conducted within applicable ethical constraints." Ibid., 625, n.5.

66. Ibid., 646–47.

67. Ibid., 648.

68. Hannah Arendt, *Eichmann in Jerusalem: A Report on the Banality of Evil* (New York: Viking, 1965), 292.

69. Authers and Wolffe, *Victim's Fortune,* 382.

70. Robert A. Swift, "Holocaust Litigation and Human Rights Jurisprudence," in Bazyler and Alford, *Holocaust Restitution,* 53.

71. Burt Neuborne, "Holocaust Reparations Litigation: Lessons for the Slavery Reparations Movement," *New York University Annual Survey of American Law* 58 (2003): 619; Joel Siegel, "Getting His Due," *New York Magazine,* October 2, 2006.

72. See Richard O. Falk, "Armageddon through Aggregation? The Use and Abuse of Class Actions in International Dispute Resolution," *Michigan State University/Detroit College of Law Journal of International Law* 10 (2001): 205–38.

73. Eizenstat, *Imperfect Justice,* 226, 340–42.

74. Ibid., 75.

75. Ibid., 366.

76. Drew Cullen, "IBM Escapes Holocaust Suit," *The Register,* March 30, 2001; Robert Lenzner and Emily Lambert, "Mr. Class Action," *Forbes,* February 16, 2004.

77. Eizenstat, *Imperfect Justice,* 116–18.

78. Ibid., 118–19.

79. Ibid., 153.

80. Ibid., 77; Barry Meier, "An Avenger's Path," *New York Times,* September 8, 2000; "Metro Views: An Endeavor Cloaked in Sanctity," *Jerusalem Post,* February 4, 2008.

81. Orenstein, "Gold Warriors," 64.

82. Barry Meier, "Jewish Groups Fight for Spoils of Swiss Case," *New York Times,* November 29, 1998.

83. This seems likely to have been the reason behind Simon Wiesenthal's warning "against too harsh an attitude toward" the Swiss. See David Rohde, "Judge Weighs Fate of Suit Filed by Jews against Swiss," *New York Times,* August 1, 1997, cited in a report from Agence France-Press, July 31, 1997.

84. Bazyler, *Holocaust Justice,* 137.

85. John Authers, "Stories: The Road to Restitution," FT.com, August 15, 2008, available at http://www.ft.com/cms/s/0/bdc94ee-68d0-11dd-ae5-0000779fd18c.html, accessed September 16, 2008. Speaking of sanctions, Bazyler notes that these threats of boycott were not only opposed by the Swiss, who filed diplomatic protests with Washington, but also the Clinton administration: "All during the movement, the federal government urged the state and local governments not to impose sanctions. The most vocal critic of the sanctions was Stuart Eizenstat, Clinton's 'point man' on the Holocaust restitution issues. Eizenstat argued that the sanctions were counterproductive, but time and time again, he was wrong. The sanctions worked and became a much-used tool in the claims against subsequent defendants in the Holocaust restitution movement. Sanctions were either used or threatened against Austrian and French banks, European insurance companies, and German firms. In each instance, they worked magnificently either to invigorate long-ignored World War II claims or to break impasses over stalled negotiations." Bazyler, *Holocaust Justice,* 22.

86. Eizenstat, *Imperfect Justice,* 140.

87. "Remarks of Stuart E. Eizenstat, Deputy Secretary of the Treasury, Special Representative of the President and Secretary of State for Holocaust Issues, 12th and Concluding Plenary on the German Foundation, Berlin, Germany, July 17, 2000," available at http://germany.usembassy.gov/germany/img/assets/8497/eizenstat071700.pdf, last accessed May 12, 2008. On the subject of fees, see chapter 5.

88. Authers and Wolffe, *Victim's Fortune*, 364.

89. Bazyler, *Holocaust Justice*, xii–xiii, emphasis in original.

90. Melvyn I. Weiss, "A Litigator's Postscript to the Swiss Banks and Holocaust Litigation Settlements: How Justice Was Served," in Bazyler and Alford, *Holocaust Restitution*, 111–12.

91. Burt Neuborne, "Preliminary Reflections on Aspects of Holocaust-Era Litigation in American Courts," *Washington University Law Quarterly* 80 (2002): 831–32.

92. Christopher Hodges, "Multi-Party Actions: A European Approach," *Duke Journal of Comparative and International Law* 11 (2001): 343.

93. Allen C. Guelzo, "Reparations Then and Now," *First Things*, June/July 2002, available at http://www.firstthings.com/article.php3?id_article=2038, last accessed May 13, 2008.

94. Samuel P. Baumgartner, "Human Rights and Civil Litigation in United States Courts: The Holocaust-Era Cases," *University of Washington Law Quarterly* 80 (2002): 842.

95. Vivian Grosswald Curran, "Globalization, Legal Transnationalization and Crimes against Humanity: The Lipietz Case," Legal Studies Research Paper Series, Working Paper No. Year-Number 2008-03, February 2008, 4–5, available at http://papers.ssrn.com/so13/papers.cfm?abstract_id=1087425, last accessed May 13, 2008.

96. Authers and Wolffe, *Victim's Fortune*, 154. On "rough justice," see also Eizenstat, *Imperfect Justice*, 137–38.

97. Gerald D. Feldman, "The Business History of the 'Third Reich' and the Responsibilities of the Historian: Gold, Insurance, 'Aryanization,' and Forced Labor," an Occasional Paper of the Center for German and European Studies at the University of California, Berkeley (January 1999): n.p., republished in a revised version in Norbert Frei, Dirk van Laak, Michael Stolleis, eds., *Geschichte vor Gericht. Historiker, Richter und die Suche nach Gerechtigkeit* (Munich: Beck, 2000),103–29.

98. Samuel P. Baumgartner, "Class Actions and Group Litigation in Switzerland," *Northwestern Journal of International & Business Law* 27 (2007): 316.

99. Baumgartner, "Human Rights and Civil Litigation in United States Courts," 845. For the general context of this perspective, with particular reference to Switzerland, see Wolfgang Wiegand, "The Reception of American Law in Europe," *American Journal of Comparative Law* 39 (1991): 229–48. See also Siobhan Morrissey, "Vive les class actions: Europe Is Showing More Interest in Legal Mechanisms That Have Come under Fire in the United States," *ABA Journal*, September 15, 2005, available at http://abajournal.com/magazine/vive_les_class_actions/, last accessed July 20, 2008.

100. Falk, "Armageddon through Aggregation," 228.

101. Adam Liptak, "Class-Action Firms Extend Reach to Global Rights Cases," *New York Times*, June 3, 2007. See also idem, "Foreign Courts Wary of U.S. Punitive Damages," *New York Times*, March 26, 2008; and John Y. Gotanda, "Charting Developments concerning Punitive Damages: Is the Tide Changing?" *Columbia Journal of Transnational Law* 45 (2007): 507–28.

102. Stuart E. Eizenstat, "The Unfinished Business of the Unfinished Business of World War II," in Bazyler and Alford, *Holocaust Restitution*, 311.

103. Bazyler and Fitzgerald, "Trading with the Enemy," 742–48.

104. See "Plunder and Restitution: Findings and Recommendations of the Presidential Advisory Commission on Holocaust Assets in the United States and Staff Report,"

December 2000, available at http://www.pcha.gov/PlunderRestitution.html/html/ Home_Contents.html, last accessed May 12, 2008.

105. Bazyler and Fitzgerald, "Trading with the Enemy," 749. However, see the replies to his critics by Kenneth Klothen, former executive director of PCHA, in ibid., 797–810.

106. Ralph Blumenthal, "Panel on Nazi Art Theft Fell Short, Experts Say," *New York Times*, March 3, 2003.

107. *Rosner et al. v. United States*, Case No. 01-1859-CIV-SEITZ (S.D.Fla).

108. Ronald W. Zweig, *The Gold Train: The Destruction of the Jews and the Second World War's Most Terrible Robbery* (New York: Allen Lane, 2002). See the official Web site, "The Hungarian Gold Train Settlement, U.S. District Judge Patricia Seitz," available at http://www.hungariangoldtrain.org/index_en.asp, last accessed September 4, 2008. See also Gábor Kádár, *Self-financing Genocide: The Gold Train, the Becher Case and the Wealth of Hungarian Jews* (Budapest: Central European University Press, 2004).

109. See "Justice for 'Gold Train' Victims," *New York Times*, August 9, 2004; "The Hungarian Gold Train Settlement. U.S. District Judge Patricia Seitz," available at http://www.hungariangoldtrain.org/index_en.asp, last accessed September 4, 2008. Eizenstat's judgment is not complimentary: "Instead of acting as we had urged other governments and their companies to act, instead of seeking a neutral examination of the facts found by our presidential commission, the Justice Department moved to dismiss the case on the basis of the statute of limitations, the sovereign immunity of the United States, and the inappropriateness of the federal court system as a proper forum. These were the kinds of defenses made by the foreign governments with whom I dealt." Eizenstat, "Unfinished Business of World War II," 312.

110. Zweig, *Gold Train*, 4.

Chapter 2. Art, Law, and History

1. Jeanette Greenfield, "'The Spoils of War,'" in Elizabeth Simpson, ed., *The Spoils of War: World War II and Its Aftermath: The Loss, Reappearance, and Recovery of Cultural Property* (New York: Harry N. Abrams, 1997), 34.

2. Ibid., 38; Michael J. Bazyler and Amber L. Fitzgerald, "Trading with the Enemy: Holocaust Restitution, the American Government, and American Industry," *Brooklyn Journal of International Law* 28 (2002–3): 709.

3. Lynn H. Nicholas, Plenary Session on Nazi-Confiscated Art Issues, Washington Conference on Holocaust-Era Assets (1999), available at http://fcit.usf.edu/HOLOCAUST/resource/assets/heac4.pdf, last accessed June 17, 2008, 449; Hector Feliciano, *The Lost Museum: The Nazi Conspiracy to Steal the World's Greatest Works of Art* (New York: Basic Books, 1997), 23.

4. Jonathan Petropoulos, written comments for House Banking Committee, Hearing of February 10, 2000, available at http://financialservices.house.gov/banking/21000 pet.htm, last accessed June 17, 2008; David Rapp, "Stolen Treasure," *Haaretz*, August 12, 2004. Petropoulos strikes an appropriate note of caution on these data: "This is a vast topic, too much for any one book, or even any one person to cover. Put simply, the Nazis plundered so many objects over such a large geographical area that it requires a collaborative effort to reconstruct this history." Petropoulos, "Art Looting during the

Third Reich: An Overview with Recommendations for Future Research," Washington Conference on Holocaust-Era Assets (1999), available at http://fcit.usf.edu/HOLO CAUST/resource/assets/heac4.pdf, last accessed June 17, 2008, 441.

5. Feliciano, *Lost Museum,* 4–5; Ralph Blumenthal, "New Effort to Recover Nazi Plunder; but Pessimism Grows for Recoveries," *New York Times,* February 27, 2003.

6. Jeanette Greenfield, "The Return of Cultural Property," *Antiquity* 60 (1986): 29. Cf. idem, *The Return of Cultural Treasures* (Cambridge: Cambridge University Press, 1989); Phyllis Mauch Messenger, ed., *The Ethics of Collecting Cultural Property: Whose Culture? Whose Property?* (Albuquerque: University of New Mexico Press, 1989). For a helpful survey, see Lawrence M. Kaye, "Laws in Force at the Dawn of World War II: International Conventions and National Laws," in Simpson, *Spoils of War,* 100–105.

7. "Inter-Allied Declaration against Acts of Dispossession Committed in Territories under Enemy Occupation or Control; Establishment of Inter-Allied Sub-Committee on Acts of Dispossession," United States Department of State, *Foreign Relations of the United States,* 1943, vol. 1, 443–44, available at http://www.ushmm.org/assets/documents/usa/ i-17.pdf, last accessed June 25, 2008.

8. Elazar Barkan, "Collecting Culture: Crimes and Criticism," *American Literary History* 10 (1998): 753.

9. Directive to Commander-in-Chief of United States Forces of Occupation regarding the Military Government of Germany; April 1945 (JCS 1067), available at http://usa.usembassy.de/etexts/ga3-450426.pdf, last accessed June 25, 2008.

10. Jonathan Petropoulos, written comments for House Banking Committee, Hearing of February 10, 2000, available at http://financialservices.house.gov/banking/21000 pet.htm, last accessed June 17, 2008; David Rapp, "Stolen Treasure," *Haaretz,* August 12, 2004.

11. Feliciano estimates that in France some thirteen thousand works, deemed to be of minor aesthetic value, were "put up for auction without much public announcement" after the war. See *Lost Museum,* 218.

12. Oliver Rathkolb, "From 'Legacy of Shame' to the Auction of 'Heirless Art in Vienna': Coming to Terms 'Austrian Style' with Nazi Artistic War Booty," (1999), 485–501, available at http://www.museum-security.org/ww2/Legacy-of-Shame.html, last accessed June 20, 2008.

13. Gideon Taylor, "Testimony, United States House of Representatives, House Committee on International Relations, Subcommittee on Europe & Emerging Threats, Washington, D.C., October 3, 2007," available at http://foreignaffairs.house.gov/110/ tay100307.pdf, last accessed July 7, 2008.

14. Patricia Youngblood Reyhan, "A Chaotic Palette: Conflict of Laws in Litigation between Original Owners and Good-Faith Purchasers of Stolen Art," *Duke Law Journal* 50 (2001): 955.

15. Kelly Diane Walton, "Leave No Stone Unturned: The Search for Art Stolen by the Nazis and the Legal Rules Governing Restitution of Stolen Art," *Fordham Intellectual Property Media & Entertainment Law Journal* 9 (1998–99): 552.

16. Eric Gibson, "De Gustibus: The Delicate Art of Deciding Whose Art It Is," *Wall Street Journal,* July 16, 1999, quoted in Michael J. Bazyler, *Holocaust Justice: The Battle for Restitution in American's Courts* (New York: New York University Press, 2003), 214.

17. Walton, "No Stone Unturned," 615.

18. Judith H. Dobrzynski, "Man in the Middle in the Schiele Case," *New York Times,* January 29, 1998.

19. Nathaniel Popper, "Suit Highlights Failures on Art Restitution," *Forward,* May 13, 2005.

20. Reyhan, "A Chaotic Palette," 955–1043.

21. Dobrzynski, "Man in the Middle in the Schiele Case."

22. See, for example, Owen C. Pell, "The Potential for a Mediation/Arbitration Commission to Resolve Disputes Relating to Artworks Stolen or Looted during World War II," *DePaul-LCA Journal of Art & Entertainment Law* 10 (1999–2000): 27–66; and especially Geoff Edgers, "Holocaust Historians Blast MFA Stance in Legal Dispute," *Boston Globe,* May 28, 2008, describing a sharply contested case in which there are allegations of duress for Oskar Kokoschka's painting *Two Nudes (Lovers)* sold in Vienna in 1939 but in which the defendant, Boston Museum of Fine Arts, claims that the work was sold to a Jewish dealer and had been part of a group of paintings on sale since the 1920s.

23. See the case of Fernand Léger's *Smoke over Rooftops,* apparently painted six times. Mary Abbe, "MIA Sends Nazi 'Loot' Home to Paris," *Minneapolis-St. Paul Star Tribune,* October 30, 2008.

24. See Norman Palmer, *Museums and the Holocaust* (Leicester: Institute of Art and Law, 2000), 80–82.

25. Clifford Geertz, *Local Knowledge: Further Essays in Interpretative Anthropology* (New York: Basic Books, 1983), 173.

26. Stephan J. Schlegelmilch, "Ghosts of the Holocaust: Holocaust Victim Fine Arts Litigation and a Statutory Application of the Discovery Rule," *Case Western Reserve Law Review* 87 (1999–2000): 96.

27. Similarly, provenance disputes can prompt decisions not to lend or not to borrow paintings for exhibition. See, for example, Robin Pogrebin, "Met Won't Show a Grosz at Center of a Dispute," *New York Times,* November 15, 2006.

28. Geoffrey Barker and Gerhard Charles Rump, "Great-Nephew of Original Owner of $104m Picasso Challenges 1949 Sale," *The Telegraph,* June 13, 2004; Anemona Hartocollis, "Judge Refuses to Halt Auction of a Picasso," *New York Times,* November 6, 2006. A related case involving Mendelsohn-Bartholdy descendants led by the same grand-nephew was a high-profile lawsuit against the Museum of Modern Art and the Guggenheim Museum in Manhattan for the restitution of two extraordinarily valuable works by Picasso (*Le Moulin de la Galette,* painted in 1900, and *Boy Leading a Horse,* painted in 1906). See Michael Sontheimer, "European Heirs Demand New York Museums Return Picassos," Spiegelonline, August 20, 2008, available at http://www .spiegel.de/international/germany/0,1518,druck-573090,00.html, last accessed September 22, 2008, and "Die Museen sind auf dem Kriegspfad," Weltonline, available at http://www.welt.de/welt_print/article2361903/Die-Museen-sind-auf-dem-Kriegs pfad.html, last accessed September 22, 2008. After protracted legal maneuverings the parties settled in February 2009, in a secret agreement in which the museums kept the paintings. "In an unusual reprimand," Reuters reported, "U.S. District Judge Jed Rakoff strongly urged both sides to release the terms of the settlement saying the heirs invoked 'the weight of history on their behalf,' and it would be 'extraordinarily unfortunate that

the public would be left without knowing what the truth is.'" "NY Museums Keep Nazi-Looted Picassos in Claim Settlement," *Haaretz,* February 3, 2009. To date, because of the unwillingness of the plaintiffs to disclose the terms of the settlement, the public remains in the dark.

29. Michelle I. Turner, "The Innocent Buyer of Art Looted during World War II," *Vanderbilt Journal of Transnational Law* 32 (1999): 1511–48.

30. Randi Dotinga, "U.S. Lawsuits Pursue Lost Art," *Christian Science Monitor,* July 5, 2005.

31. Bazyler, *Holocaust Justice,* 212. Cf. Detlev F. Vagts, "Restitution for Historic Wrongs: The American Courts and International Law," *American Journal of International Law* 92 (1998): 232–35.

32. To assist this process, California enacted a law extending until 2010 the statute of limitations for Nazi looted art found in museums. A federal judge in 2007 held the statute unconstitutional and the case is now on appeal before the 9th Circuit. Museum Security Network, "Norton Simon Museum Keeps Cranachs—for Now," available at http://msn-list.te.verweg.com/2007-October/008435.html, last accessed September 11, 2008.

33. "Germany Sued over 'Holocaust Art,'" BBC News, June 24, 2004, available at http://news.bbc.co.uk/2/hi/entertainment/3833955.stm, last accessed June 18, 2008.

34. An exception is the class action suit launched by a group of Holocaust survivors against the United States government, seeking restitution for the valuables seized from the so-called Hungarian Gold Train by American troops at the end of the war. This suit, *Rosner et al. v. United States of America,* was resolved in 2005 by a settlement agreement in which the United States agreed to pay $25.5 million into a settlement fund, to be used for educational, historical, and archival purposes as well as social services for Hungarian Jewish survivors. The United States admitted no wrongdoing in the affair. See U.S. District Judge Patricia Seitz, "Hungarian Gold Train Settlement," available at http://www.hungariangoldtrain.org/index_en.asp, last accessed June 24, 2008; and Ronald Zweig, *The Gold Train: The Destruction of the Jews and the Second World War's Most Terrible Robbery* (London: Allen Lane, 2002).

35. See, for example, Robert Schwartz, "The Limits of the Law: A Call for a New Attitude toward Artwork Stolen during World War II," *Columbia Journal of Law & Social Problems* 32 (1998): 1–33; Emily J. Henson, "The Last Prisoners of War: Returning World War II Art to Its Rightful Owners—Can Moral Obligations Be Translated into Legal Duties?" *DePaul Law Review* 51 (2001–2): 1103–58; Benjamin E. Pollock, "Comment: Out of the Night and Fog: Permitting Litigation to Prompt an International Resolution to Nazi-Looted Art Claims," *Houston Law Review* 43 (2006–7): 193–233; Schlegelmilch, "Ghosts of the Holocaust," 87–126.

36. Lynn H. Nicholas, intervention on "Nazi Confiscated Art Issues," Washington Conference on Holocaust-Era Assets, November 30–December 3, 1998, 452, available at http://www.state.gov/www/regions/eur/holocaust/heac4.pdf, last accessed June 25, 2008.

37. Felicia R. Lee, "Seattle Museum to Return Looted Work," *New York Times,* June 16, 1999.

38. Carol Vogel, "Two Museums Go to Court over the Right to Picassos," *New York Times,* December 8, 2007.

39. Gilbert S. Edelson, intervention on "Nazi Confiscated Art Issues," Washington Conference on Holocaust-Era Assets, November 30–December 3, 1998, 541, available at http://www.state.gov/www/regions/eur/holocaust/heac4.pdf, last accessed June 25, 2008.

40. See, most recently, Randy Kennedy, "Museums and Heirs Settle Dispute over Picasso," *New York Times*, February 3, 2009.

41. "To create a monotype, the artist applies oils to a metal plate, rearranging them until satisfied. A paper is placed on the metal plate, and all is then placed into a press, transferring the image to the paper." Howard J. Trienens, *Landscape with Smokestacks: The Case of the Allegedly Plundered Degas* (Evanston, Ill.: Northwestern University Press, 2000), 3.

42. Ibid., 19–21.

43. On the particularly convoluted arguments deployed on the question of whether Illinois law or New York law should have applied in the case, see ibid., 82–83. More generally on the problems of sorting out ownership in related circumstances, see Ashton Hawkins, Richard A. Rothman, and David B. Goldstein, "A Tale of Two Innocents: Creating an Equitable Balance between the Rights of Former Owners and Good Faith Purchasers of Stolen Art," *Fordham Law Review* 64 (1995): 49–96.

44. Bazyler, *Holocaust Justice*, 215–21; Judith Dobrzynski, "Settlement in Dispute over a Painting Looted by Nazis," *New York Times*, August 14, 1998; Trienens, *Landscape with Smokestacks*.

45. David Rapp, "Stolen Treasure," *Haaretz*, August 12, 2004.

46. Marilyn Henry, "Recovering Looted Art: A Rich Man's Game," *Jerusalem Post*, April 3, 1998. I am grateful to Marilyn Henry for providing me with the context for this reference. Michael Bazyler suggests that for the plaintiffs in the case of the Degas monotype it was indeed worth it: "According to Nick Goodman, after paying the costs of litigation, the Gutmann heirs were 'at least able to break even. Overall, I'm pleased with the result. The painting was brought back to the family, it is now hanging in a beautiful museum, and most importantly, we significantly raised public awareness of this issue.'" Bazyler, *Holocaust Justice*, 221. Goodman also told the *New York Times:* "I've never seen the painting. I'm looking forward to holding it for the first and probably last time."

47. Trienens, *Landscape with Smokestacks*, 101; Dobrzynski, "Settlement in Dispute over a Painting Looted by Nazis."

48. For a detailed explanation of the federal involvement, see Howard N. Spiegler, "Portrait of Wally: The U.S. Government's Role in Recovering Holocaust Art," in Michael J. Bazyler and Roger P. Alford, *Holocaust Restitution: Perspectives on the Litigation and Its Legacy* (New York: New York University Press, 2006), 280–87.

49. "Freezing the Schiele Paintings," *New York Times*, January 9, 1998; Judith H. Dobrzynski, "Strategy in Schiele Art Case Questioned," *New York Times*, October 12, 1999; "Free 'Portrait of Wally'!" CultureGrrl, Lee Rosenbaum's Cultural Commentary, March 28, 2007, available at http://www.artsjournal.com/culturegrrl/2007/03/free_portrait_of_wally.html, last accessed June 24, 2008.

50. Celestine Bohlen, "Judge Revives Case of Nazi-Looted Art," *New York Times*, April 27, 2002.

51. "Write in your newspaper that we are not Nazi-lovers," Mrs. Leopold added, "and we have nothing taken away from Jews." Judith H. Dobrzynski, "More Paintings by Schiele Face Ownership Questions," *New York Times*, January 15, 1998. On Leopold,

see Jean-Michel Stoullig, "Rudolf Leopold, the Man Who 'Rediscovered' Schiele," *European Jewish Press*, February 22, 2006, available at http://www.ejpress.org/article/6138, last accessed July 17, 2007.

52. Martha Lufkin, "U.S. Lawsuit to Confiscate Schiele's Portrait of Wally Suspended," *The Art Newspaper*, July 1, 2008.

53. Statement by Glenn D. Lowry, Director of the Museum of Modern Art, New York, to the Committee on Banking and Financial Services, United States House of Representatives, February 10, 2000, available at http://financialservices.house.gov/banking/2100010w.htm, last accessed June 19, 2008. Cf. Testimony before the House Banking and Financial Services Committee by Glenn D. Lowry, Director, the Museum of Modern Art, New York, Washington, February 12, 1998, available at http://www.house.gov/financialservices/banking/212989low.htm, last accessed June 19, 2008.

54. Judith H. Dobrzynski, "Austria Refuses to Cede Klimt Paintings," *New York Times*, July 1, 1999.

55. Paul Jandl, "Goldene Adele: Rekordpreis für Klimt-Gemälde," *Neue Züricher Zeitung*, June 20, 2006; Carol Vogel, "Lauder Pays $135 Million, a Record, for a Klimt Portrait," *New York Times*, June 19, 2006; Christopher Benfey, "Perils of Adele: Ronald S. Lauder Buys a Klimt," Slate, June 20, 2006, available at http://www.slate.com/id/2144092/, last accessed June 26, 2008.

56. Report of Professor Jonathan Petropoulos, Claremont McKenna College, July 14, 2005, available at http://www.bslaw.com/altmann/Klimt/Petropoulos.pdf, last accessed June 19, 2008, 11–13.

57. Ibid., 21.

58. Hubertus Czernin, *Die Fälschung: Der Fall Bloch-Bauer und das Werk Gustav Klimts* (Vienna: Czernin Verlag, 1999). Czernin's revelations were further supported by the Report of Professor Jonathan Petropoulos, Claremont McKenna College, July 14, 2005, available at http://www.bslaw.com/altmann/Klimt/Petropoulos.pdf, last accessed June 19, 2008.

59. Bazyler, *Holocaust Justice*, 246–47.

60. Supreme Court of the United States, *Republic of Austria et al. v. Altmann*, June 7, 2004, available at http://www.law.cornell.edu/supct/html/03-13.ZS.html, last accessed June 19, 2008.

61. The Austrian arbitration panel awarded five of the Klimt paintings to the Bloch-Bauer heirs but not the sixth, an unfinished 1918 portrait of Amalie Zuckerhandl. Amalie was a Christian convert to Judaism, married in 1895 to a Viennese urologist and friend of the Bloch-Bauers, Otto Zuckerhandl. Together with her daughter, Amalie was deported to Theresienstadt in 1942 and eventually murdered in Belzec. Amalie apparently sold the painting to her friend Ferdinand Bloch-Bauer some time in the 1920s, and while the work eventually left his collection between 1939 and 1942, it is by no means clear precisely how it did so or to whom it was sold, possibly with the assistance of Amalie herself. See Report of Professor Jonathan Petropoulos, Claremont McKenna College, July 14, 2005, available at http://www.bslaw.com/altmann/Klimt/Petropoulos.pdf, last accessed June 19, 2008.

62. These fees would have amounted to virtually all of her assets. For details see E. Randol Schoenberg, "The Recovery from Austria of Five Paintings by Gustav Klimt, an IFAR Evening with the Neue Galerie," July 31, 2006, available at http://www.bslaw.net/news/060731.doc, last accessed June 19, 2008.

63. Ibid.

64. Marilyn Henry, "Stolen Images," *Hadassah Magazine* 87 (May 2008): 30–36.

65. Emily Sharpe and Jason Edward Kaufman, "Lauder Raises $190m Cash as Bloch-Bauer Klimts Come Up for Sale," *The Art Newspaper,* October 8, 2006.

66. Outside the United States, according to one observer, legal processes ignore the substantive in favor of the procedural and the technical: "Domestic laws—in almost all countries—do not directly address the issue and the outcome of most litigation, and therefore turn on domestic legal idiosyncrasies rather than on grounds of substantive legal policies. The majority of works of art that have been returned have been returned as acts of goodwill and diplomacy or to avoid national or museum-world embarrassment." Molly Ann Torsen, "National Reactions to Cultural Property Looting in Nazi Germany: A Window on Individual Effort and International Disarray," *Electronic Journal of Comparative Law* 9 (December 2005), available at http://www.ejcl.org/94/art94-1 .html, last accessed July 11, 2008.

67. Carol Vogel, "$491 Million Sale Shatters Art Auction Record," *New York Times,* November 9, 2006; David Usborne, "Klimt Sales Take Christie's Auction to $491m," *The Independent,* November 10, 2006.

68. Celestine Bohlen, "Lauder's Mix of Restitution and Collecting," *New York Times,* February 27, 2003. These issues are exacerbated, of course, by the fact that Lauder's collection involves precisely that German and Austrian modernist art that was so avidly collected by Viennese Jewish collectors, whose art was ravaged by the Nazis. On this see in particular Sophie Lillie, *Was Einmal War. Handbuch der enteignete Kunstsammlungen Wien* (Vienna: Czernin Verlag, 2003). In the interview for Bohlen's *New York Times* article, Lauder insisted: "As for me, I am going to doubly, triply and quadruply check everything." To his critics, best practice would not only involve checking, but publishing. Candidly, Lauder admitted that provenance had not been a concern when be began collecting in the late 1960s: "I was like everyone else," he said. "It didn't occur to me. It was not a question that people were looking at." Cf. "Lauder Covets the Four Other Klimts," CultureGrrl, July 13, 2006, available at http://www.artsjournal.com/ culturegrrl/2006/07/lauder_covets_the_four_other_k.html, last accessed July 24, 2008; Robin Pogrebin, "Lauder's Openness Is Sought on Artwork," *New York Times,* October 18, 2007.

69. Christopher Benfley, "Perils of Adele: Ronald S. Lauder Buys a Klimt," Slate, June 20, 2006, available at http://www.slate.com/id/2144092/, last accessed July 10, 2008. The critic in the *New York Times* described the painting as "the new marquee attraction for Mr. Lauder's luxe museum, which now, thanks to her, will surely jump high up on the list of New York's must-see sites." Michael Kimmelman, "New Klimt in Town: The Face That Set the Market Buzzing," *New York Times,* July 14, 2006.

70. See Judith Dobrzynski, "Man in the Middle in the Schiele Case," *New York Times,* January 29, 1998; "Outtakes from Ronald Lauder's Interview on 'Charlie Rose,'" CutureGrrl, September 7, 2006, available at http://www.artsjournal.com/culturegrrl/ 2006/09/outtakes_from_ronald_lauders_i.html, last accessed July 14, 2008; Stephanie Strom, "Cosmetics Heir to Lead World Jewish Congress," *New York Times,* June 11, 2007; Robin Pogrebin, "Lauder's Openness Is Sought on Artwork," *New York Times,* October 18, 2007; Ben Harris and Jacob Berkman, "Lauder Downplays Role in Klimt Restitution, Vows to Avoid Conflicts," *The Jewish Standard,* October 26, 2007.

71. Tyler Green, "'This Is Our Mona Lisa,'" *Fortune,* September 28, 2006, available

at http://money.cnn.com/magazines/fortune/fortune_archive/2006/10/02/8387512/ index.htm, last accessed July 29, 2008.

72. Marilyn Henry, *Confronting the Perpetrators: A History of the Claims Conference* (London: Valentine Mitchell, 2007), 163–64.

73. Lynn H. Nicholas, *The Rape of Europa: The Fate of Europe's Treasures in the Third Reich and the Second World War* (New York: Alfred Knopf, 1994), 443.

74. Stuart Eizenstat, *Imperfect Justice: Looted Assets, Slave Labor, and the Unfinished Business of World War II* (New York: Public Affairs, 2003), 189; Nicholas, *Rape of Europa;* Hector Feliciano, *Le Muse Disparu. Le pillage des oeuvres d'art* (Paris: Austral, 1995), appeared in English as *The Lost Museum: The Nazi Conspiracy to Steal the World's Greatest Works of Art;* Konstantine Akinsha and Gregori Kozlov, *Beautiful Loot: The Soviet Plunder of Europe's Art Treasures* (New York: Random House, 1995). Cf. as well Thomas Buomberger, *Raubkunst—Kuntsraub: Die Schweitz und der Handel mit gestohlene Kulturgüter zur Zeit des Zweiten Weltkrieges* (Zurich: Orell Füssli, 1998).

75. Monica S. Dugot, "The Holocaust Claims Processing Office: New York State's Approach to Resolving Holocaust-Era Art Claims," in Bazyler and Alford, *Holocaust Restitution,* 271–79.

76. For an outline of the conference and postings of the major interventions see "International Reports: Presentation of the World Jewish Congress at the Washington Conference, 30 November–3 December 1998," The Central Registry of Information on Looted Cultural Property, 1933–1945, lootedart.com, available at http://www.looted art.com/MGWL332703, last accessed June 24, 2008.

77. J. D. Bindenagel, "Dealing with the Last Vestiges of the Second World War: Research, Remembrance, and Education," delivered at the Organizing Seminar for the Washington Conference on Holocaust-Era Assets, June 30, 1998, available at http://www.ushmm.org/assets/jdspeech.htm, last accessed June 23, 2008.

78. Washington Conference Principles on Nazi-Confiscated Art, December 3, 1998:

Description

On 3 December 1998 the 44 governments participating in the Washington Conference on Holocaust-Era Assets endorsed the following principles for dealing with Nazi-confiscated art.

Principles

In developing a consensus on non-binding principles to assist in resolving issues relating to Nazi-confiscated art, the Conference recognizes that among participating nations there are differing legal systems and that countries act within the context of their own laws.

1. Art that had been confiscated by the Nazis and not subsequently restituted should be identified.

2. Relevant records and archives should be open and accessible to researchers, in accordance with the guidelines of the International Council on Archives.

3. Resources and personnel should be made available to facilitate the identification of all art that had been confiscated by the Nazis and not subsequently restituted.

4. In establishing that a work of art had been confiscated by the Nazis

and not subsequently restituted, consideration should be given to unavoidable gaps or ambiguities in the provenance in light of the passage of time and the circumstances of the Holocaust era.

5. Every effort should be made to publicize art that is found to have been confiscated by the Nazis and not subsequently restituted in order to locate its pre-War owners or their heirs.

6. Efforts should be made to establish a central registry of such information.

7. Pre-War owners and their heirs should be encouraged to come forward and make known their claims to art that was confiscated by the Nazis and not subsequently restituted.

8. If the pre-War owners of art that is found to have been confiscated by the Nazis and not subsequently restituted, or their heirs, can be identified, steps should be taken expeditiously to achieve a just and fair solution, recognizing this may vary according to the facts and circumstances surrounding a specific case.

9. If the pre-War owners of art that is found to have been confiscated by the Nazis, or their heirs, can not be identified, steps should be taken expeditiously to achieve a just and fair solution.

10. Commissions or other bodies established to identify art that was confiscated by the Nazis and to assist in addressing ownership issues should have a balanced membership.

11. Nations are encouraged to develop national processes to implement these principles, particularly as they relate to alternative dispute resolution mechanisms for resolving ownership issues.

Proceedings of the Washington Conference on Holocaust-Era Assets, available at http://www.state.gov/www/regions/eur/holocaust/heac.html, last accessed June 23, 2008.

79. J. Christian Kennedy, "The Role of the United States Government in Art Restitution," Potsdam, Germany, April 23, 2007, U.S. Department of State, available at http://www.state.gov/p/eur/rls/rm/83392.htm, last accessed June 23, 2008.

80. Eizenstat, *Imperfect Justice*, 198–99.

81. See, for example, Bazyler, *Holocaust Justice*, 259.

82. Carol Kino, "Stolen Artworks and the Lawyers Who Reclaim Them," *New York Times*, March 28, 2007.

83. See "Vilnius International Forum on Holocaust-Era Looted Cultural Assets, 3–5 October 2000," lootedart.com, The Central Registry of Information on Looted Cultural Property, 1933–1945, available at http://www.lootedart.com/MGD3S66604, last accessed June 23, 2008.

84. Stuart Eizenstat, "The Unfinished Business of the Unfinished Business of World War II," in Bazyler and Alford, *Holocaust Restitution*, 308.

85. Marilyn Henry, "The Arts: Stolen Images," *Hadassah Magazine* 87 (May 2006). For a review of some important examples, see Jonathan Petropoulos, "Provenance Research as History: Reconstructed Collections and National Socialist Art Looting," *Contemporary Austrian Studies* 14 (2006): 373–81.

86. Michael Franz, "Information, Transparency and Justice: International Provenance Research Colloquium," *International Journal of Cultural Property* 12 (2005): 508.

87. Kennedy, "Role of the United States Government."

88. Palmer, *Museums and the Holocaust.*

89. Alan Riding, "Dutch Agree to Return Seized Art: Nazis' Trove Going to Art Dealer's Heirs," *International Herald Tribune,* February 7, 2006.

90. Ralph Blumenthal, "New Efforts to Recover Nazi Plunder; but Pessimism Grows for Recoveries," *New York Times,* February 27, 2003; Alan Riding, "An Essay: Foot Dragging on the Return of Art Stolen by the Nazis," *New York Times,* May 18, 2004; Molly Ann Torsen, "National Reactions to Individual Effort and International Disarray," *Electronic Journal of Comparative Law* 9 (2005), available at http://www.ejcl.org/94/art94-1.html, last accessed June 24, 2008.

91. Nathaniel Popper, "Suit Highlights Failures on Art Restitution," *Forward,* May 13, 2005.

92. "Plunder and Restitution: Findings and Recommendations of the Presidential Advisory Commission on Holocaust Assets in the United States and Staff Report, December 2000," available at http://www.pcha.gov/PlunderRestitution.html/html/Home_Contents.html, last accessed June 24, 2008; Popper, "Suit Highlights Failures."

93. Eizenstat, "Unfinished Business," 307; Marilyn Henry, "Pressure Russia to Reveal Looted Art's Heritage," *Forward,* September 6, 2006.

94. See Claire Andrieux, "Two Approaches to Compensation in France: Restitution and Repatriation," in Martin Dean, Constantin Goschler, and Philipp Ther, eds., *Robbery and Restitution: The Conflict over Jewish Property in Europe* (New York: Berghahn, 2007), 150.

95. For a recent contention that there should be greater concern for the "public interest," see Norman Rosenthal, "The Time Has Come for a Statute of Limitations," *The Art Newspaper,* November 12, 2008. Sir Norman Rosenthal, from a family that included victims of the Holocaust, was exhibitions secretary of the Royal Academy of Arts from 1977 to 2008. Cf. Jonathan Jones, "Should All Looted Art Be Returned?" Jonathan Jones on Art Blog, January 9, 2009, available at http://www.guardian.co.uk/art anddesign/jonathanjonesblog/2009/jan/09/looted-art-norman-rosenthal, last accessed March 10, 2009; and Robin Cembalest, "Inconvenient Truths," ARTnews, March 2009, available at http://www.artnews.com/issues/article.asp?art_id=2640&current=True, last accessed March 10, 2009.

Chapter 3. Restitution in Historical Perspective

1. Stuart Eizenstat, *Imperfect Justice: Looted Assets, Slave Labor, and the Unfinished Business of World War II* (New York: Public Affairs, 2003), x. Cf. Richard Z. Chesnoff, *Pack of Thieves: How Hitler and Europe Plundered the Jews and Committed the Greatest Theft in History* (New York: Doubleday, 1999), 3: "Why has justice been so long in coming?"

2. This is the title of the introductory chapter of Eizenstat, *Imperfect Justice.*

3. Thane Rosenbaum, "The Holocaust's Defrauded Survivors," *International Herald Tribune,* June 17, 2007.

4. Israel Singer, "Why Now?" *Cardozo Law Review* 20 (1998): 422. Singer went on to give an odd assessment on the historiographical storm raised by Goldhagen's book: "I would like to tell Professor Goldhagen that his colleagues are just plain jealous of him. I know exactly how that feels, to be marginalized by someone who is better [*sic*]." Ibid.

5. Ibid., 423–24.

6. Gulie Ne'eman Arad, ed., "Passing into History: Nazism and the Holocaust beyond Memory," special issue, *History & Memory* 9 (Fall 1997).

7. Peter Novick, *The Holocaust in American Life* (New York: Houghton Mifflin, 1999), 229–30.

8. See Dan Diner, "Restitution and Memory—The Holocaust in European Political Cultures," *New German Critique* 90 (2003): 36–44; Dan Diner and Gotthart Wunberg, eds., *Restitution and Memory: Material Restoration in Europe* (New York: Berghahn, 2007).

9. Nomi Morris, "Bronfman Takes on Swiss Banks," *Macleans,* June 9, 1997.

10. Sumner Wells, "New Hope for the Jewish People," *The Nation*, May 5, 1945, quoted in Regula Ludi, "The Vectors of Postwar Victim Reparations," *Journal of Contemporary History* 41 (2006): 428. For further indication of the importance, in official American postwar planning, of relief, rehabilitation, and resettlement of Jews, as opposed to restitution to individuals, see Ronald Zweig, "Restitution and the Problem of Jewish Displaced Persons in Anglo-American Relations, 1944–1948," *American Jewish History* 78 (1988): 54–78.

11. Zweig, "Restitution and the Problem of Jewish Displaced Persons," 429. On the paucity of international law in this area see Dinah Shelton, "Righting Wrongs: Reparations in the Articles on State Responsibility," *American Journal of International Law* 96 (2002): 835–37.

12. Jacob Robinson, "Transfer of Property in Enemy Occupied Territory," *American Journal of International Law* 39 (1945): 216.

13. Rudolf Dolzer, "The Settlement of War-Related Claims: Does International Law Recognize a Victim's Private Right of Action? Lessons after 1945," *Berkeley Journal of International Law* 20 (2002): 296–97. For an authoritative survey, see Quincy Wright, "War Claims: What of the Future?" *Law and Contemporary Problems* 16 (1951): 543–48.

14. Dolzer, "Settlement of War-Related Claims," 319.

15. Brian Urquhart, "The New American Century?" *New York Review of Books*, August 11, 2005, 42–45.

16. Schalom Adler-Rudel, "Aus der Vorzeit der kollektiven Wiedergutmachung," in Hans Trawner, ed., *In zwei Welten. Siegfried Moses zum 75 Geburtstage* (Tel Aviv: Bitan, 1962), 200–217; Nana Sagi, *German Reparations: A History of the Negotiations* (New York: St. Martin's Press, 1986), 14; Angelika Timm, *Jewish Claims against East Germany: Moral Obligations and Pragmatic Policy* (Budapest: Central European University Press, 1997), 73.

17. Nahum Goldmann, *The Autobiography of Nahum Goldmann: Sixty Years of Jewish Life*, trans. Helen Sebba (New York: Holt, Rinehart and Winston, 1969), 250. See also Norman Bentwich, "Nazi Spoliation and German Restitution: The Work of the United Restitution Office," *Leo Baeck Institute Year Book* 10 (1965): 204–24.

18. Arthur L. Smith, Jr., "A View of U.S. Policy toward Jewish Restitution," *Holocaust and Genocide Studies* 5 (1990): 250. See also Hans Günter Hockerts, "Wiedergutmachung: Ein umstrittener Begriff und ein weites Feld," in Hans Günter Hockerts and Christiane Kuller, *Nach der Verfolgung: Wiedergutmachung nationalsozialistischen Unrechts in Deutschland?* (Göttingen: Wallstein, 2003), 10.

19. Bruno Weil in *American Journal of International Law* 39 (1945): 362–64, reviewing Hugo Marx, *The Case of the German Jews vs. Germany: A Legal Basis for Their Claims* (New York: Egmont Press, 1944); and *American Journal of International Law* 40 (1946): 222, reviewing Nehemiah Robinson, *Indemnification and Reparations: Jewish Aspects* (New York: Institute

of Jewish Affairs, 1944); Siegfried Moses, *Jewish Post-War Claims* (Tel Aviv: Irgun Olej Merkaz Europa, 1944); Louis C. Bial, *Vergeltung und Wiedergutmachung in Deutschland* (Havana: Editorial Lex, 1945); Herbert Dorn, *Problemas de Post-Guerra en el Transcurso de los Tiempos* (Havana: Revista de Derecho Internacional, 1944), 221–27. For other discussions see Kurt Schwerin, "German Compensation for Victims of Nazi Persecution," *Northwestern University Law Review* 67 (1972): 481–89; Ágnes Peresztegi, "Reparation for Holocaust-Era Human Rights Violations," *Jewish Studies Yearbook* 3 (2002–3): 135–46; and Sagi, *German Reparations*, chap. 2.

20. Moses, *Jewish Post-War Claims*, 3.

21. Ibid., 4–5. George Weis, an Austrian Jewish commentator, looked back upon those years: "To me, as to all those Jews from Central Europe, the demand for restitution from those who did us wrong seemed the most natural thing in the world. But I was afraid that this demand might not be so popular with the Governments in exile once they returned to their homelands. . . . Unfortunately, my misgivings proved only too justified." George Weis, "Restitution through the Ages," *Noah Barou Memorial Lecture, 1962* (London: World Jewish Congress, 1962), 3.

22. Nehemiah Robinson, *Indemnification and Reparations: Jewish Aspects* (New York: Institute of Jewish Affairs, 1944), 92, 273.

23. Hiram Motherwell, *The Peace We Are Fighting For* (New York: Harper & Brothers, 1943), 32–33, quoted in Robinson, *Indemnification and Reparations*, 92, n.16.

24. Moses, *Jewish Post-War Claims*, 28.

25. Quoted in Richard M. Buxbaum, "A Legal History of International Reparations," *Issues in Legal Scholarship*, Article 5 (2006), available at http://www.bepress.com/cgi/viewcontent.cgi?article=1079&context=ils, p. 25, last consulted May 15, 2008; Tom Segev, *The Seventh Million: The Israelis and the Holocaust*, trans. Haim Watzman (New York: Hill and Wang, 1993), 197.

26. Ronald W. Zweig, review of Norman Finkelstein, *The Holocaust Industry: Reflections on the Exploitation of Jewish Suffering* (London: Verso, 2000), in *Journal of Israeli History* 20 (2001): 212.

27. Goldmann, *Autobiography*, 251.

28. Benjamin Ferencz, *Less than Slaves: Jewish Forced Labor and the Quest for Compensation* (Cambridge, Mass.: Harvard University Press, 1979), xix.

29. Bruno Weil, *American Journal of International Law* 40 (1946): 227. Weil underscored that the challenge required legal innovation: "Those who try to master the legal consequences of the bloody anti-humanitarian, and anti-legal Hitlerian period only from the standpoint of positive, that is written, international law, must fail in their conclusions. Unprecedented events make it a duty for jurists and writers to produce new creative ideas and new roads to justice and to the conservation of basic human rights based on precedents and the laws of the past." Ibid., 364. This was Nehemiah Robinson's view as well. "Extraordinary circumstances require extraordinary measures," was how he summed it up. Robinson, *Indemnification and Reparations*, 177.

30. The Inter-Allied Declaration is printed in an appendix to Robinson, *Indemnification and Reparations*, 275–78.

31. Constantin Goschler, "German Compensation to Jewish Nazi Victims," in Jeffry M. Diefendorf, ed., *Lessons and Legacies*, vol. 6, *New Currents in Holocaust Research* (Evanston, Ill.: Northwestern University Press, 2004), 373; idem, *Wiedergutmachung: Westdetuschland und die Verfolgten des Nationalsozialismus, 1945–1954* (Munich: Oldenbourg, 1992); and idem,

Schuld und Schulden: Die Politik der Wiedergutmachung für NS-Verfolgte seit 1945 (Göttingen: Wallstein, 2005).

32. Given the tremendous dislocations in defeated Germany and the unprecedented character of the restitution provided to the displaced and battered survivors, some evaluated the work of the occupation and the Länder quite positively. "The scope of the laws themselves is remarkable concerning both the kind and degree of the wrongs to be remedied. However well—or poorly—these laws have worked, they constitute an important and useful precedent in the development of world law." Monroe Karasik, "Problems of Compensation and Restitution in Germany and Austria," *Law and Social Problems* 16 (1951): 468.

33. Goschler, "German Compensation to Jewish Nazi Victims," 381–83. Identifiable property referred to tangible assets within West Germany and West Berlin that had been taken away between 1933 and 1945; nonidentified property referred to "the series of robberies committed by the German treasury, whose booty consisted of huge amounts of Jewish stocks and shares, gold, silver, jewels and jewelry, pieces of art, and household goods." Ibid., 382.

34. Buxbaum, "Legal History of Reparations," 23.

35. Seymour J. Rubin and Abba P. Schwartz, "Refugees and Reparations," *Law and Contemporary Problems* 16 (1951): 390. Seymour Rubin was a former legal adviser of the U.S. State Department, and Abba Schwartz was a former reparations director of the International Refugee Organization.

36. Lothar Merens, *Davidstern unter Hammer und Zirkel: Die jüdischen Gemeinden in der SBZ/DDR und ihre Behandlung durch Partei und Staat 1945–1990* (Hildesheim: Olms, 1997); Angelika Timm, *Hammer, Zirkel, Davidstern: Das gestörte Verhältnis der DDR zu Zionismus und Staat Israel* (Bonn: Bouvier, 1997).

37. See Karen Heilig, "From the Luxembourg Agreement to Today: Representing a People," *Berkeley Journal of International Law* 20 (2002): 177–78. For a recent, critical assessment of restitution conducted by the German authorities in the Federal Republic, see Jürgen Lillteicher, *Raub, Recht und Restitution: Die Rückerstattung jüdischen Eigentums in der frühen Bundesrepublik* (Göttingen: Wallstein, 2007).

38. Jeffrey Herf, *Divided Memory: The Nazi Past in the Two Germanys* (Cambridge, Mass.: Harvard University Press, 1997), 313.

39. Quoted in ibid., 282.

40. Goldmann, *Autobiography*, 260.

41. See Ronald W. Zweig, *German Reparations and the Jewish World: A History of the Claims Conference* (2nd ed., London: Frank Cass, 2001), chap. 2. See also the Web site of the Conference on Jewish Material Claims against Germany, available at http://www.claimscon.org/, last accessed September 24, 2008.

42. Nicholas Balabkins, *West German Reparations to Israel* (New Brunswick, N.J.: Rutgers University Press, 1971), 138. On *shilumim*, see Axel Frohn, "Introduction, the Origins of *Shilumim*," in Axel Frohn, ed., *The Holocaust and Shilumim: The Policy of Wiedergutmachung in the Early 1950s* (Washington, D.C.: German Historical Institute, 1991), 1–2. Ruti Teitel provides a useful summation: "Wiedergutmachung was Germany's term for the reparations, literally meaning 'to make good again,' that is, to return to former conditions. . . . By contrast, rejecting the notion that reparations could ever make anything 'good' again, victims' groups called reparations by a Hebrew term *shilumim*, meaning 'to make amends, to bring about peace.' For the victims, reparations were a matter of economic

necessity, and so, for them, the point of departure in the negotiations was the refugees' cost of resettlement. For the perpetrators and victims alike, reparations were about settling accounts, but each in a different way. Nevertheless, despite completely different understandings of the nature and purposes of the reparations scheme, negotiations over the varying concepts culminated in a political agreement." *Transitional Justice* (New York: Oxford University Press, 2000), 124.

43. The Agreement between the Federal Republic of Germany and the State of Israel and the related protocols may be conveniently found in Sagi, *German Reparations*, appendix 2 and 3, 212–41. See also Balabkins, *West German Reparations to Israel*, passim; Frederick Honig, "The Reparations Agreement between Israel and the Federal Republic of Germany," *American Journal of International Law* 48 (1954): 564–78.

44. "Restitution: Why Did It Take 50 Years or Did It?"; Gideon Taylor, "Testimony, United States House of Representatives, House Committee on International Relations, Subcommittee on Europe & Emerging Threats," Washington, D.C., October 3, 2007, available at http://foreignaffairs.house.gov/110/tay100307.pdf, last accessed July 7, 2008; Press Releases, August 4, 2004, "Germany's Compensation to Former Forced Laborers," available at http://www.germany.info/relaunch/info/press/releases/pr_08 _04_04.htm, last accessed May 20, 2008. Disarmingly, Nahum Goldmann admitted to an important reason for the progressive renegotiation of restitution with Germany: "What was signed in 1952 was no more than a basis for a body of legislation that has been steadily extended and amended during the ensuing years and that proved infinitely more complicated to put into effect than one would ever have expected, primarily because during the negotiations nobody had any idea of the extent of Nazi crimes and the great number of victims entitled to restitution." Goldmann goes on to talk about one specific, striking illustration: "When the concrete negotiations began, I had a series of conversations lasting several months with German Finance Minister Fritz Schaeffer. Schaeffer thought that the total cost to the Federal Republic would be eight billion marks; on the basis of estimates by my own experts I spoke in terms of six billion. Now, in 1968, it seems that the final sum will amount to at least fifty to sixty billion marks, that is, more than eight times what we expected and almost six and one-half times the German estimate. The final total may be even higher. These payments have not of course been confined to Jews, but since the vast majority of victims of National Socialism was Jewish, the bulk of this astronomical sum has gone to them." Goldmann, *Autobiography*, 279–80. For a critical evaluation of the implementation see Christian Pross, *Paying for the Past: The Struggle over Reparations for Surviving Victims of the Nazi Terror*, trans. Belinda Cooper (Baltimore: Johns Hopkins University Press, 1988).

45. Honig, "Reparations Agreement between Israel and the Federal Republic of Germany," 564. See also Schwerin, "German Compensation for Victims of Nazi Persecution," 494.

46. "No similar case is recorded of the voluntary payment of indemnities by a state to its own subjects and foreign subjects on account of crimes and outrages committed by a former government." Bentwich, "Nazi Spoliation and German Restitution," 224. And similarly George L. Mosse: "The Luxembourg Treaty . . . is an accord without precedent. Massacres and genocide took place in the past (if not on such a vast scale), but no compensation has ever been paid to the survivors by a government that was not itself a party to such brutality." Review of Nicholas Balabkins, *West German Reparations to Israel*, in

American Historical Review 77 (1972): 1094. On the historic character of the agreements, see also Balabkins, *West German Reparations to Israel*, 150–54, and Marilyn Henry, *Confronting the Perpetrators: A History of the Claims Conference* (London: Valentine Mitchell, 2007), 2–4.

47. Sagi, *German Reparations*, 4.

48. Goldmann, *Autobiography*, 274–75.

49. Ibid., 277.

50. Segev, *Seventh Million*, 214.

51. Ibid., 220–21.

52. Yossi Sarid, "Israel's Great Debate," *Haaretz*, September 17, 2007, available at http://www.haaretz.com/hasen/pages/ShArt.jhtml?itemNo=904448, last accessed May 20, 2008. According to Sarid, "Sharett's battle during those years is a classic example of diplomacy and leadership, waged without apologies and without deviousness, without self-pity and without feelings of self-sacrifice." Drawing on recently released documents on the debate, Sarid is particularly harsh on then Minister of Labor Golda Meir: "Golda Meir was in favor and against, against and in favor, worrying about such questions as how to receive the money without signing, how to sign without meeting, how to meet without delivering a speech, how to deliver a speech without shaking hands, and a few other tricks meant to soothe one's conscience. Her central theme over more than two years of discussions was 'a German is a German,' and she never wearied of developing variations on this subject. At a session of Mapai's central committee in December 1951 she declared, 'My position is absolutely resistant. In my eyes every German is a future Nazi German. . . . I am no longer prepared to distinguish between good and bad Germans. In my eyes, they are all the same.'"

53. The countries were France, the Netherlands, Belgium, Luxembourg, Greece, Great Britain, Denmark, and Norway, later joined by Italy, Sweden, Switzerland, and Austria. The latter's claims were settled in a separate treaty of 1962. See Susanna Schraftstetter, "The Diplomacy of *Wiedergutmachung:* Memory, the Cold War, and the Western European Victims of Nazism, 1956–1964," *Holocaust and Genocide Studies* 17 (2003): 459–79.

54. See Zweig, *German Reparations*, 188–89.

55. See Timothy W. Guinname, "Financial *Vergangenheitsbewältigung:* The 1953 London Debt Agreement," Center Discussion Paper No. 880, Economic Growth Center, Yale University, January 2004, available at http://www.econ.yale.edu/growth_pdf/cdp880.pdf, last accessed May 21, 2008. Considering its implications, Regula Ludi judges this to have been "one of the most decisive documents of international reparation politics." Among the important claims deferred were those for compensation for slave labor, a matter which was then put off for half a century. See Regula Ludi, "Michael Bazyler's Holocaust Justice," Paper 1, UCLA Center for European and Eurasian Studies (2003), 4, available at http://repositories.cdlib.org/cgi/viewcontent.cgi?article=1002&context=international/cees, last accessed May 21, 2008; Ulrich Herbert, "Forced Laborers in the Third Reich: An Overview," *International Labor and Working-Class History* 58 (2000): 209–10.

56. "German reparations are the biggest reparations program that has ever been implemented. . . . Overall, its economic magnitude is impressive. On September 30, 1965, according to different estimations, Germany had paid more than DM 18 billion (US$4.5 billion), on January 1, 1986, that figure rose to more than DM 59 billion (US$27.5 billion) and in 2000 it was estimated to have reached more than DM 82 billion (US$38.6 billion).

Added together, the different kinds of payments issuing from the BEG, of certain laws outside of the BEG, the Federal Restitution Law, the agreements reached in Luxembourg, the treaties Germany made with twelve Western countries, payments made to individuals who underwent medical experiments and other various payments, the German government has paid approximately US$61.5 billion (€70 billion) in reparations, including US$37.5 billion (€42.5 billion) under federal individual indemnifications laws as of December 2001." Ariel Colonomos and Andrea Armstrong, "German Reparations to the Jews after World War II: A Turning Point in the History of Reparations," in Pablo De Greiff, ed., *The Handbook of Reparations* (New York: Oxford University Press, 2006), 408.

57. Bentwich, "Nazi Spoliation and German Restitution," 224.

58. George L. Mosse, *Confronting History: A Memoir* (Madison: University of Wisconsin Press, 2000), 212.

59. Constantin Goschler, "The Politics of Restitution for Nazi Victims in Germany West and East (1945–2000)," Working Paper OP-3, Center for German and European Studies, University of California, Berkeley, September 25, 2003, 6, available at http://www.ciaonet.org/wps/goc04/, last accessed May 20, 2008. According to Goldmann, in a later interview, he and Adenauer "were not discussing the Holocaust, but chatting about 'Bach, Goethe and God knows.'" Interview with Nahum Goldmann, November 24, 1971, William E. Wiener Oral History Library of the American Jewish Congress, Jacob Blaustein Oral History Project, Center for Jewish History, New York, quoted in ibid. See also Constantin Goschler, *Schuld und Schulden: Die Politik der Wiedergutmachung für NS-Verfolgte seit 1945* (Göttingen: Wallstein, 2005); Goldmann, *Autobiography*, 260–61.

60. Goschler, "German Compensation to Jewish Nazi Victims," 403.

61. "Agreement between the Federal Republic of Germany and the State of Israel," in Sagi, *German Reparations*, 212, emphasis mine.

62. Bentwich, "Nazi Spoliation and German Restitution," 224.

63. Dolzer, "Settlement of War-Related Claims," 327.

64. Goschler, "The Politics of Restitution," 6.

65. Henry, *Confronting the Perpetrators*, 53.

66. Ludi, "Michael Bazyler's Holocaust Justice," 5.

67. Henry, *Confronting the Perpetrators*, 78.

68. Ulrich Herbert, "Nicht entschädigungsfähig. Die Wiedergutmachungsansprüche der Ausländer," in Ulrich Herbert, ed., *Arbeit, Volkstum, Weltanschauung. Über Fremde und Deutsche im 20. Jahrhundert* (Frankfurt: Fischer-Taschenbuch, 1995), 157–92.

69. Gerald Feldman, "Holocaust Assets and German Business History: Beginning or End?" *German Studies Review* 25 (2002): 26.

70. Ibid.

71. Ibid. See Nicholas Weil, "L'Europe se réapproprie l'histoire de ses crimes," *Le Monde*, November 29, 1996.

72. "The Long Fight for Holocaust Compensation," BBC News, January 26, 2000, available at http://news.bbc.co.uk/2/hi/europe/619896.stm, last accessed May 20, 2008.

73. Harold James, *The Deutsche Bank and the Nazi Economic War against the Jews: The Expropriation of Jewish Property* (New York: Cambridge University Press, 2001), 5–6.

74. Jonathan Steinberg, "Compensation Cases and the Nazi Past: Deutsche Bank

and Its Historical Legacy," in Diefendorf, *Lessons and Legacies*, vol. 6, *New Currents in Holocaust Research*, 424.

75. Paul R. Dubinsky, "Justice for the Collective: The Limits of Human Rights Class Action," *Michigan Law Review* 102 (2004): 1169; Pierre d'Argent, "Wrongs of the Past, History of the Future?" *European Journal of International Law* 17 (2006): 282.

76. Steinberg, "Compensation Cases and the Nazi Past," 424.

77. Ethan A. Nadelman, "Global Prohibition Regimes: The Evolution of Norms in International Society," *International Organization* 44 (1990): 479–526; Ariel Colonomos, "The Morality of Belief in the Profits of Virtue," *International Social Science Journal* 57 (2005): 457–67.

78. Helen Junz, "Holocaust-Era Assets: Globalization of the Issue," in Diefendorf, *Lessons and Legacies*, vol. 6, *New Currents in Holocaust Research*, 439–40; Steven R. Ratner, "Corporations and Human Rights: A Theory of Legal Responsibility," *Yale Law Journal* 111 (2001): 443–545. Ronald Zweig notes another element of the Swiss banks' vulnerability—their visibility: "The banks of Zurich and Geneva are an easy target. Unlike the dispersed communal assets of Polish Jewry, or the 'vanished' assets of Hungarian Jewry, the imposing banks of Switzerland, with the imagery of underground vaults of gold, can be seen and photographed." Zweig, *German Reparations*, 5.

79. Goschler, "Politics of Restitution," 16.

80. Jean-Michel Chaumont, *La Concurrence des victimes: Génocide, identité, reconnaissance* (Paris: La Découverte, 1997); John Torpey, "'Making Whole What Has Been Smashed': Reflections on Reparations," *Journal of Modern History* 73 (2001): 338; idem, *Making Whole What Has Been Smashed: On Reparations Politics* (Cambridge, Mass.: Harvard University Press, 2006); Daniel Levy and Natan Sznaider, *The Holocaust and Memory in a Global Age*, trans. Assenka Oksiloff (Philadelphia: Temple University Press, 2006).

81. Ariel Colonomos and John Torpey, "Introduction: World Civility?" *Journal of Human Rights* 3 (2004): 140.

82. For a discussion of this issue and some problems associated with it, see Tony Judt, "The 'Problem of Evil' in Postwar Europe," *New York Review of Books*, February 14, 2008, 33–5.

83. Charles Maier, *The Unmasterable Past: History, Holocaust, and German National Identity* (Cambridge, Mass.: Harvard University Press, 1988), 161; idem, "A Surfeit of Memory? Reflections on History," *History & Memory* 5 (1993): 136–51.

84. Avi Beker, "Introduction: Unmasking National Myths," in Avi Beker, ed., *The Plunder of Jewish Property during the Holocaust: Confronting European History* (Houndmills, Basingstoke: Palgrave, 2001), 19–22; "Restitution Issues Destroy National Myths: An Interview with Avi Beker," Jerusalem Center for Public Affairs (n.d.), available at http://www.jcpa.org/phas/phas-beker.htm, last accessed May 22, 2008.

85. Michael J. Bazyler, *Holocaust Justice: The Battle for Restitution in America's Courts* (New York: New York University Press, 2003), xvii.

86. Diner, "Restitution and Memory," 37.

87. Eizenstat, *Imperfect Justice*, 23–25. According to Eizenstat, Holbrooke understood restitution work idealistically, in the context of American interests: "Property restitution was to be part of a broader U.S. policy to encourage the rule of law, respect for property rights, tolerance toward minorities, and the creation of nonpolitical administrative and judicial practices in the former Communist countries. It was an essential part of what

we called 'civil society,' without which the transition to viable democracy is impossible."
Ibid., 23–24.

88. "Many of the 'wrongs' of Communism for which redress has been sought are not qualitatively (sometimes not even quantitatively) different from policies which were pursued in the first half of the twentieth century by a succession of non-Communist (or, at most, partially Communist) regimes in Central and Eastern Europe. Government takings of private property without payment of compensation, or the imprisonment, torture and execution of 'enemies of the state,' were not an invention of the Soviet-backed administrations installed after World War II." István Pogany, *Righting Wrongs in Eastern Europe* (Manchester: Manchester University Press, 1997), 10.

89. Ibid., 40–41.

90. Helen B. Junz, "Confronting Holocaust History: The Bergier Commission's Research on Switzerland's Past," Post-Holocaust and Anti-Semitism, Jerusalem Center for Public Affairs, no. 8, May 2003, available at http://www.jcpa.org/JCPA/Templates/ShowPage.asp?DRIT=3&DBID=1&LNGID=1&TMID=111&FID=253&PID=0&IID=721&TTL=Confronting_Holocaust_History:_The_Bergier_Commission, last accessed May 23, 2008. Of the commissions, the Bergier Commission for Switzerland seems to have had the widest mandate and the greatest government support in terms of infrastructure and public support. Norway's was the first commission, established in March 1996.

91. "Stolen Assets," Online Newshour, June 2, 1998, available at http://www.pbs.org/newshour/bb/europe/jan-june98/eizenstat_6-2.html, last accessed June 5, 2008; Julia Collins, "Taking on the Unfinished Business of the Twentieth Century," *Harvard Law Bulletin*, Summer 1999, available at http://www.law.harvard.edu/news/bulletin/backissues/summer99/index.html, last accessed May 21, 2008; Greg Bradsher, "Turning History into Justice: Holocaust-Era Assets Records, Research and Restitution, March 1966–March 2001" (2001), available at http://www.archives.gov/research/holocaust/articles-and-papers/turning-history-into-justice.html, last accessed June 10, 2008.

92. Torpey, *Making Whole What Has Been Smashed*, 5. See also Elazar Barkan, *The Guilt of Nations: Restitution and Negotiating Historical Injustices* (New York: Norton, 2000); Janna Thompson, *Taking Responsibility for the Past: Reparation and Historical Justice* (Malden, Mass.: Polity, 2002); Priscilla Hayner, *Unspeakable Truths: Confronting State Terror and Atrocity* (New York: Routledge, 2001).

93. Remarks of Stuart E. Eizenstat, Deputy Secretary of the Treasury, Special Representative of the President and Secretary of State for Holocaust Issues, 12th and Concluding Plenary on the German Foundation, Berlin, Germany, July 17, 2000, available at http://germany.usembassy.gov/germany/img/assets/8497/eizenstat071700.pdf, last accessed May 23, 2008. Eizenstat estimated that there were over 100,000 Holocaust survivors in the United States. See his testimony before the Senate Foreign Relations Committee on April 5, 2000, available at http://usembassy-israel.org.il/publish/press/treasure/archive/2000/april/dt20407.htm, last accessed May 23, 2008.

94. See Yves Dezalay and Bryant Garth, "From the Cold War to Kosovo: The Rise and Renewal of the Field of International Human Rights," *Annual Review of Law and Social Science* 2 (2006): 231–55.

95. Julia Collins, "Stuart Eizenstat: Taking on the Unfinished Business of the Twentieth Century," *Harvard Law Bulletin* (Summer 1999), available at http://www.law.harvard.edu/news/bulletin/backissues/summer99/index.html, last accessed May 26, 2008.

96. Eizenstat, *Imperfect Justice*, 6–8.

97. See Ferencz, *Less than Slaves*, passim. Without evidence, and with some exaggeration, perhaps, Abraham Foxman, a survivor and head of the Anti-Defamation League, offered a view on why "we didn't deal with this issue for fifty years": "Because the trauma of the human tragedy was so tremendous, so enormous, so gargantuan, that nobody wanted to talk about material loss for fear that it will lessen the human tragedy." Quoted in Michael J. Bazyler, "Litigating the Holocaust," *University of Richmond Law Review* 33 (1999): 606.

98. Singer, "Why Now?" 421.

99. Paul R. Dubinsky, "Justice for the Collective: The Limits of the Human Rights Class Action," *Michigan Law Review* 102 (2004): 1161–62.

100. Authers and Wolffe, *Victim's Fortune*, 381.

101. Nathaniel Popper, "Ugly Allegations Fly as Fabled WJC Duo Splits," *Forward*, March 23, 2007.

102. "Restitution: Why Did It Take 50 Years or Did It?"; Frank Bruni, "A Voice for Jews Shows Range and Resonance," *New York Times*, February 16, 1997.

103. Eizenstat, *Imperfect Justice*, 243, 248–49.

104. J. D. Bindenagel, "Justice, Apology, Reconciliation, and the German Foundation: 'Remembrance, Responsibility, and the Future,'" in Elazar Barkan and Alexander Karn, eds., *Taking Wrongs Seriously: Apologies and Reconciliation* (Stanford, Calif.: Stanford University Press, 2006), 295–96.

105. Summarizing the judgment that concerned the successful claim of jurisdiction, in a civil case, over Paraguayan state perpetrators of torture by relatives of a Paraguayan victim, Michael Bazyler notes: "The decision was a ringing endorsement of the principle of universal jurisdiction, that certain human rights violations are so abhorrent to modern society that their perpetrators can be brought to justice anywhere in he world." Bazyler, *Holocaust Justice*, 55. For legal context, see Harold Hongju Koh, "Transnational Public Law Litigation," *Yale Law Journal* 100 (1991): 2350–75.

106. Dubinsky, "Justice for the Collective," 1173.

107. Anthony J. Sebok, "Mass Restitution Litigation in the United States," in David Dyzenhaus and Mayo Moran, eds., *Calling Power to Account: Law, Reparations, and the Chinese Canadian Head Tax Case* (Toronto: University of Toronto Press, 2005), 342.

Chapter 4. Restitution in Law and History

1. Leora Bilsky, *Transformative Justice: Israeli Identity on Trial* (Ann Arbor: University of Michigan Press, 2004), 141.

2. Clifford Geertz, *Local Knowledge: Further Essays in Interpretive Anthropology* (New York: Basic Books, 1983), 173.

3. Abraham Foxman, "The Dangers of Holocaust Restitution," *Wall Street Journal*, December 4, 1998.

4. Elie Wiesel, preface to Stuart E. Eizenstat, *Imperfect Justice: Looted Assets, Slave Labor, and the Unfinished Business of World War II* (New York: Public Affairs, 2003), ix. But Wiesel goes on to say that Eizenstat's book "is not really about money. . . . It is about the ethical value and weight of memory." Ibid., xi.

5. Stuart E. Eizenstat, Remarks at the 12th and Concluding Plenary on the German Foundation, July 17, 2000, Deputy Secretary of the Treasury Stuart E. Eizenstat, U.S.

Diplomatic Mission to Germany, available at http://usa.usembassy.de/etexts/ga7-000717e
.htm, last accessed October 8, 2008, p. 1. Cf. Richard Z. Chesnoff, *Pack of Thieves: How
Hitler and Europe Plundered the Jews and Committed the Greatest Theft in History* (New York:
Doubleday, 1999).

6. Sidney Zabludoff, "Restitution of Holocaust-Era Assets: Promises and Reality,"
Jewish Political Studies Review 19 (Spring 2007): available at http://www.jcpa.org/JCPA/
Templates/ShowPage.asp?DRIT=3&DBID=1&LNGID=1&TMID=111&
FID=253&PID=0&IID=1678&TTL=Restitution_of_Holocaust-Era_Assets:_Promises
_and_Reality, last accessed October 1, 2008. Michael J. Bazyler, *Holocaust Justice: The
Battle for Restitution in America's Courts* (New York: New York University Press, 2003), xi,
estimates the losses at between $230 billion and $320 billion.

7. Justin H. Roy, "Strengthening Human Rights Protection: Why the Holocaust
Slave Labor Claims Should Be Litigated," *The Scholar* 1 (1999): 162.

8. See Jonathan Petropoulos, "The Nazi Kleptocracy: Reflections on Avarice and
the Holocaust," in Dagmar Herzog, ed., *Lessons and Legacies VII* (Evanston, Ill.: Northwestern University Press, 2006), 29–38.

9. Götz Aly, *Hitler's Beneficiaries: Plunder, Racial War, and the Nazi Welfare State*, trans. Jef-
ferson Chase (New York: Metropolitan Books, 2006), 1.

10. Ibid., 4.

11. Ibid., 331–32.

12. For various perspectives on the economic war against the Jews, see Helmut
Genschel, *Der Verdrängung der Juden aus der Wirtschaft im Dritten Reich* (Göttingen: Mus-
terschmidt, 1966); Avraham Barkai, *From Boycott to Annihilation: The Economic Struggle of
German Jews, 1933–1943*, trans. William Templer (Hanover, N.H.: University Press of
New England, 1989); United States Holocaust Memorial Museum, *Confiscation of Jewish
Property in Europe, 1933–1945: New Sources and Perspectives* (Washington, D.C.: Center for
Advanced Holocaust Studies, United States Holocaust Memorial Museum, 2003); Ger-
ald D. Feldman, "The Economics of the 'Final Solution,'" *Australian Journal of Politics and
History* 53 (2007): 57–67; Adam Tooze, *The Wages of Destruction: The Making and Breaking of
the Nazi Economy* (New York: Viking, 2007); and Martin Dean, Constantin Goschler, and
Philipp Ther, eds., *Robbery and Restitution: The Conflict over Jewish Property in Europe* (New
York: Berghahn, 2007).

13. Irwin Cotler, "The Holocaust, Thefticide, and Restitution: A Legal Perspective,"
Cardozo Law Review 20 (1998): 602, emphasis in original.

14. Ibid., 602–3.

15. Ibid., 623.

16. See, for example, Gerhard Weinberg, *A World at Arms: A Global History of World
War II* (New York: Cambridge University Press, 1994), 897.

17. Aly, *Hitler's Beneficiaries*, 184.

18. Frank Bajohr, *"Aryanization" in Hamburg: The Economic Exclusion of Jews and the Confiscation of Their Property in Nazi Germany* (New York: Berghahn, 2002), 291.

19. This is especially evident in the plundering of precious metals, even of gold
taken from private individuals. For a detailed examination of this looting, see Peter
Hayes, *From Cooperation to Complicity: Degussa in the Third Reich* (New York: Cambridge University Press, 2004), chap. 5, and for some calculations, see 175. For a magisterial overview,
see Mark Mazower, *Hitler's Empire: How the Nazis Ruled Europe* (New York: Penguin, 2008).

20. Ibid., 453.

21. Aly, *Hitler's Beneficiaries*, 102. Aly comments further: "To the disappointment of the soldiers, probably because of state restrictions the packages traveling in the other direction were markedly fewer. By then the government was seeking to conceal the extent to which Germans were enriching themselves at the cost of others. According to accounts by the military postmaster general, Karl Ziegler, his department was required 'to burn all records of total statistics compiled for the military postal service.'" Ibid.

22. Hannah Arendt, *Eichmann in Jerusalem: A Report on the Banality of Evil* (New York: Viking, 1965), 159, emphasis mine. Similarly, as she wrote in 1945: "The totalitarian policy has achieved the result of making the existence of each individual in Germany depend either upon committing crimes or upon complicity in crimes." Ron H. Feldman, ed., *Hannah Arendt: The Jew as Pariah: Jewish Identity and Politics in the Modern Age* (New York: Grove Press, 1978), 228.

23. Gerald D. Feldman, "The Historian and Holocaust Restitution: Personal Experiences and Reflections," *Berkeley Journal of International Law* 23 (2005): 352.

24. Ibid., 354.

25. Burt Neuborne, "Preliminary Reflections on Aspects of Holocaust-Era Litigation in American Courts," *Washington University Law Quarterly* 80 (2002): 829. In Neuborne's summary: "The Swiss and German cases were based on classic principles of restitution and unjust enrichment. In each case, a private entity was unjustly enriched by the transfer of identifiable property from a victim of a crime against humanity. The remedy sought by plaintiffs in the Holocaust cases consisted of a simple reversal of the unjust wealth transfer." Neuborne, "A Tale of Two Cities: Administering the Holocaust Settlements in Brooklyn and Berlin," in Michael J. Bazyler and Roger P. Alford, eds., *Holocaust Restitution: Perspectives on the Litigation and Its Legacy* (New York: New York University Press, 2006), 74. See also *Black's Law Dictionary*'s most recent definition of "Restitution": "A body of substantive law in which liability is based not on tort or contract but on the defendant's unjust enrichment." *Black's Law Dictionary* (8th ed., St. Paul, Minn.: Thomson, 2004), 1339.

26. American Law Institute, *Restatement of the Law of Restitution: Quasi-Contracts and Constructive Trusts* (St. Paul, Minn.: American Law Institute Publishers, 1937), 5.

27. Emily Sherwin, "Reparations and Unjust Enrichment," Cornell Law School Legal Studies Research Paper Series, Paper 6 (2004), 9, available at http://papers.ssrn.com/so13/papers.cfm?abstract_id=580802, last accessed June 5, 2008; Peter D. Maddaugh and John D. McCamus, *The Law of Restitution* (Aurora, Ont.: Canada Law Book Inc., 1990), 33; Peter Birks, *Unjust Enrichment* (Oxford: Oxford University Press, 2003), 3–18; Daniel Friedman, "Restitution for Wrongs: The Basis of Liability," in W. R. Cornish, Richard Nolan, Janet O'Sullivan, and Graham Virgo, eds., *Restitution: Past, Present and Future* (Oxford: Hart Publishing, 1998), 133, 152–54.

28. *Quantum meruit* (Latin: as much as is deserved). See Anthony J. Sebok, "A Brief History of Mass Restitution Litigation in the United States," in David Dyzenhaus and Mayo Moran, eds., *Calling Power to Account: Law, Reparations, and the Chinese Canadian Head Tax* (Toronto: University of Toronto Press, 2005), 359. Sebok argues that the basic claims with respect to dormant accounts—and he might have added unpaid insurance policies—were based on replevin, "where the proceeds of the wrongfully taken property had been held . . . in a constructive trust on behalf of their true owners." Ibid.

29. Michael J. Bazyler, "The Holocaust Restitution Movement in Comparative Perspective," *Berkeley Journal of International Law* 20 (2002): 41. Cf. Chesnoff, *Pack of Thieves.*

30. Gerald Feldman, "The Historian and Holocaust Restitution: Personal Experiences and Reflections," address to the 31st Annual Symposium of the Alexander von Humboldt Foundation Prize Fellows, Bamberg, Germany (March 20–22, 2003), 10, available at http://www.bepress.com/cgi/viewcontent.cgi?article=1080&context=ils, last accessed May 29, 2008.

31. See his aptly titled "The Hungarian Gold Train: Fantasies of Wealth and the Madness of Genocide," in Dean, Goschler, and Ther, *Robbery and Restitution*, 211–22.

32. Si Frumkin, "Why Won't Those SOBs Give Me My Money? A Survivor's Perspective," in Bazyler and Alford, *Holocaust Restitution*, 92.

33. Nehemia Robinson, *Indemnification and Reparations: Jewish Aspects* (New York: Institute of Jewish Affairs), 83.

34. Helen B. Junz, "Report on the Pre-War Wealth Position of the Jewish Population in Nazi-Occupied Countries, Germany, and Austria," in Independent Committee of Eminent Persons, *Report on Dormant Accounts of Victims of Nazi Persecution in Swiss Banks* (Bern: Independent Association of Eminent Persons, 1999), Appendix S, 127–206. Cf. Sidney Zabludoff, "Restitution of Holocaust-Era Assets: Promises and Reality," Jerusalem Center for Public Affairs, March 2007, available at http://www.jcpa.org/JCPA/Templates/ShowPage.asp?DRIT=3&DBID=1&LNGID=1&TMID=111&FID=625&PID=1666&IID=1678&TTL=Restitution_of_Holocaust-Era_Assets:_Promises_and_Reality, last accessed October 1, 2008. See also Dean, Goschler, and Ther, *Robbery and Restitution*, 7–8, and passim.

35. Richard J. Evans, *The Third Reich in Power, 1933–1945* (New York: Penguin, 2005), 400.

36. Hans Mommsen with Manfred Grieger, *Das Volkswagenwerk und seine Arbeiter im Dritten Reich* (Dusseldorf: Econ Verlag, 1996); Detlev Vagts and Peter Murray, "Litigating the Nazi Labor Claims: The Path Not Taken," *Harvard International Law Journal* 43 (2002): 510–12.

37. Gerald Feldman, *Allianz and the German Insurance Business, 1933–1945* (New York: Cambridge University Press, 2001), 536.

38. Vagts and Murray, "Litigating the Nazi Labor Claims," 527.

39. Lutz Niethammer, "Converting Wrongs to Rights? Compensating Nazi Forced Labor as a Paradigm," in Dan Diner and Gotthart Wunberg, eds., *Restitution and Memory: Material Restoration in Europe* (New York: Berghahn, 2007), 88.

40. Ibid., 99.

41. Adolf Hitler, *Mein Kampf*, trans. Ralph Manheim (Boston: Houghton Mifflin, 1943), 639. See Keith Sward, *The Legend of Henry Ford* (New York: Rinehart & Co, 1948), 139; Ken Silverstein, "Ford and the Führer," *The Nation*, January 24, 2000.

42. *Iwanowa v. Ford Motor Co.*, 67 F.Supp.2d, 424 (D.N.J., 1999); Keith Bradsher, "International Business: Suit Charges Ford Profited by Nazi-Era Forced Labor," *New York Times*, March 5, 1998; Bazyler, *Holocaust Restitution*, 63.

43. See *Research Findings about Ford-Werke under the Nazi Regime* (Dearborn, Mich.: Ford Motor Company, 2001), available at http://media.ford.com/events/pdf/0_Research_Finding_Complete.pdf, last accessed September 10, 2008. See also Simon Reich, "Ford's Research Efforts in Assessing the Activities of Its Subsidiary in Nazi Germany," in ibid., 6. For a critical view of the use of historians in this context, see Michael

Pinto-Duschinsky, "Selling the Past," *Times Literary Supplement,* October 23, 1998, 16–17. But cf. Gerald D. Feldman, "The Business History of the 'Third Reich' and the Responsibilities of the Historian: Gold, Insurance, 'Aryanization' and Forced Labor," University of California, Berkeley, Center for German and European Studies, *Working Papers,* January 1999, available at http://www.ciaonet.org/wps/feg01/, last accessed May 28, 2008.

44. Simon Reich, "The Ford Motor Company and the Third Reich," *Dimensions* 13 (December 1999), 15–17; idem, "Corporate Social Responsibility and the Issue of Compensation: The Case of Ford and Nazi Germany," in Francis R. Nicosia and Jonathan Huener, eds., *Business and Industry in Nazi Germany* (New York: Berghahn, 2004), 104–28.

45. Henry Ashby Turner, Jr., *General Motors and the Nazis: The Struggle for Control of Opel, Europe's Biggest Carmaker* (New Haven, Conn.: Yale University Press, 2005), 155.

46. Ibid., 158. Turner does, however, have some harsh words for GM on its postwar conduct: "General Motors bears full responsibility . . . for laying claim in 1951 to the Opel dividends put aside for it during the war, another aspect of the corporation's relationship to its German subsidiary that has hitherto escaped notice. That decision appears not to have been made by the top ranks of GM, possibly because the money involved, which amounted to only a twentieth of one percent of GM's net income for that year, seemed too paltry to merit attention at the highest level of management." Ibid. Cf. Reinhold Billstein, Karola Fings, and Anita Kugler, eds., *Working for the Enemy: Ford, General Motors, and Forced Labor in Germany during the Second World War,* trans. Nicholas Levis (New York: Berghahn, 2000).

47. Edwin Black, *IBM and the Holocaust: The Strategic Alliance between Nazi Germany and America's Most Powerful Corporation* (New York: Crown, 2001).

48. "Book, Lawsuit Claim IBM Abetted the Holocaust," *Jewish News Weekly,* February 16, 2001.

49. Michael Berenbaum, "An Enabler of Genocide," *The Jewish Journal,* March 8, 2001; Drew Cullen, "IBM Escapes Holocaust Suit," *The Register,* March 30, 2001. For a discussion of the relations between this case and the ongoing quest for "legal peace" in the negotiations for the settlement of the lawsuits against the German corporations, see John Authers and Richard Wolffe, *The Victim's Fortune: Inside the Epic Battle over the Debts of the Holocaust* (New York: Perennial, 2003), 336–39. See also Edwin Black's Web site, available at http://www.edwinblack.com/, last accessed October 20, 2008.

50. Richard Bernstein, "IBM's Sales to Nazis: Assessing the Culpability," *New York Times,* March 7, 2001.

51. See, for example, the devastating critiques in Peter Hayes, "Did IBM Really Cozy Up to Hitler?" *Business Week,* March 19, 2001; Omer Bartov, "Did Punch Cards Fuel the Holocaust?" *Newsday,* March 25, 2004; and Henry Ashby Turner in *Business History Review* 75 (2001): 636–39. See also Gabriel Schoenfeld, "The Punch-Card Conspiracy," *New York Times,* March 18, 2001.

52. Michael Allen, "Stranger than Science Fiction: Edwin Black, IBM, and the Holocaust," *Technology and Culture* 43 (2002): 153.

53. Black, *IBM and the Holocaust,* 32; Kevin Maney, *The Maverick and His Machine: Thomas Watson, Sr. and the Making of IBM* (Hoboken, N.J.: Wiley, 2003), 218 and passim. Idem, "IBM Founder Wasn't Bad Guy Book Portrays," *USA Today,* February 14, 2001. "On June 6, 1940, Watson packaged up the medal and sent it back to Hitler. In an enclosed note, Watson pointed out that Hitler had lied to him about avoiding war and about developing trade with other nations. The five-sentence letter ended: 'In view of the

present policies of your Government, which are contrary to the causes for which I have been working and for which I received the decoration, I am returning it.'" Idem, *Maverick and His Machine*, 219–20. For Black's view of this matter, see *IBM and the Holocaust*, 217.

54. Barnaby J. Feder, "Lawsuit Says I.B.M. Aided the Nazis in Technology," *New York Times*, February 11, 2001.

55. Anthony J. Sebok, "IBM and the Holocaust: The Book, the Suit, and Where We Go From Here," FindLaw, March 12, 2001, available at http://writ.news.findlaw.com/sebok/20010312.html, last accessed May 29, 2008.

56. Michael J. Bazyler, "Suing Hitler's Willing Business Partners: American Justice and Holocaust Morality," *Jewish Political Studies Review* 16 (2004), available at http://www.jcpa.org/phas/phas-bazyler-f04.htm, last accessed July 2, 2008.

57. Feldman, "Business History of the 'Third Reich' and the Responsibilities of the Historian," 7. In his discussion of how cases such as these should be managed, litigator Morris Ratner offers what might be to historians a hair-raising glimpse into the role of the mass media: "Attorneys coordinating with victims' advocates . . . often utilize litigation as part of an overall strategy that includes media coverage to complement the political activities and grassroots activism. The lawyers' rule in connection with generating media coverage regarding a particular human rights case is fraught with difficulty. First, there are often rules which constrain counsel's ability to make representations to the press regarding a pending litigation matter. Second, counsel should be wary of becoming the target of media attention, which risks the inevitable anti-lawyer, anti-legal fees type of coverage that plagued the Holocaust cases. . . . In the Nazi-era cases, the most effective coverage, in the opinion of the author, resulted from direct contact between media outlets and victims themselves or traditional victims' groups, or from paid advertisements placed by victims' groups." Morris A. Ratner, "Factors Impacting the Selection and Positioning of Human Rights Class Actions in United States Courts: A Practical Overview," *New York University Annual Survey of American Law* 58 (2003): 649.

58. Arthur W. Machen, Jr., "Corporate Personality," *Harvard Law Review* 24 (1911): 347: "A corporation, or indeed any group or succession of men . . . is regarded as a person only by way of metaphor or by a fiction of law." See the excellent discussion in Katrina Wyman, "Is There a Moral Justification for Redressing Historical Injustices?" *Vanderbilt Law Review* 61 (2008): 125–96.

59. "Mass restitution suits are remarkable because they are such extraordinary performances of a legal fiction," notes Antony Sebok, "Brief History of Mass Restitution Litigation in the United States," in Dyzenhaus and Moran, *Calling Power to Account*, 366.

60. Janna Thompson, for example, refers to "a robust tradition in American thought, and indeed in liberal thought in general, that holds that a democratic nation of free individuals ought not to tolerate" "the imposition of moral debts on citizens who were unborn when the wrongs occurred." Janna Thompson, "Repairing the Past: Confronting the Legacies of Slavery, Genocide, & Caste," Proceedings of the Seventh Annual Gilder Lehrman International Center at Yale University, October 27–29, 2005, available at http://www.yale.edu/glc/justice/mccarthy.pdf, last accessed May 30, 2008. Cf. idem, *Taking Responsibility for the Past: Reparation and Historical Justice* (Cambridge: Polity, 2002).

61. J. S. Mill, *Principles of Political Economy* (Fairfield, N.J.: Augustus Kelley, 1987), 220, quoted in John Elster, *Closing the Books: Transitional Justice in Historical Perspective* (New York: Cambridge University Press, 2004), 172.

62. Jeremy Waldron, "Superseding Historic Injustice," *Ethics* 103 (1992): 15.

63. Independent Committee of Eminent Persons, *Report on Dormant Accounts*, 6.

64. For a discussion of this issue and related questions see Sherwin, "Reparations and Unjust Enrichment." "Moral indignation against a corporate entity, when all the individuals who owned or controlled the corporation at the time of the wrong are long dead, is much like moral indignation against a deodand. It may provide some satisfaction, but it is irrational and should not be encouraged by law." Ibid., 30–31. Cf. Larry May, *Sharing Responsibility* (Chicago: University of Chicago Press, 1992); Eric A. Posner and Adrian Vermeule, "Reparations for Slavery and Other Historical Injustices," *Columbia Law Review* 103 (2003): 704; and Adrian Vermeule, "Reparations as Rough Justice," University of Chicago John M. Olin Program in Law & Economics, Working Paper No. 260, September 2005, available at http://ssrn.com/abstract=813086, last accessed June 5, 2008.

65. Regula Ludi, "The Swiss Case," *Center for European Studies Working Paper Series*, no. 80, n.d., 12, available at http://www.ciaonet.org/wps/lur02/lur02.pdf, last accessed May 28, 2008.

66. Idem, "Waging War on Wartime Memory: Recent Swiss Debates on the Legacies of the Holocaust and the Nazi Era," *Jewish Social Studies* 10 (2004): 142.

67. Hayes, *From Cooperation to Complicity*, chap. 7.

68. Idem, "Corporate Profits and the Holocaust: A Dissent from the Monetary Argument," in Bazyler and Alford, *Holocaust Restitution*, 201.

69. Ibid., 202.

70. Idem, "The Ambiguities of Evil and Justice: Degussa, Robert Pross, and the Jewish Slave Laborers at Gleiwitz," in Jonathan Petropoulos and John K. Roth, eds., *Gray Zones: Ambiguity and Compromise in the Holocaust and Its Aftermath* (New York: Berghahn, 2005), 19. According to Hayes, "this is a distortion imposed by a form of 'path dependency' in the American judicial system, where the language of civil suits emphasizes the 'disgorgement' of unjust proceeds from unlawful conspiracies as the principal means of making them good." Ibid.

71. Rolf Keller, "Racism versus Pragmatism: Forced Labor of Soviet Prisoners of War in Germany (1941–1942)," Center for Advanced Holocaust Studies, *Forced and Slave Labor in Nazi-Dominated Europe: Symposium Presentations* (Washington, D.C.: United States Holocaust Memorial Museum, 2004), 109–23.

72. Hayes, "Corporate Profits and the Holocaust," 203.

73. Ibid. See the similar assessment by Harold James, concluding that while the bank incurred a significant "moral liability" from its involvement in "Aryanization," it did not make a large profit. James illustrates how complicated it is to calculate such a profit or loss and concludes that "there is fundamentally no financial way of correcting an injustice perpetrated over fifty years ago." Harold James, *The Deutsche Bank and the Nazi Economic War against the Jews* (New York: Cambridge University Press, 2001), 209.

74. Neil Gregor, *Daimler-Benz and the Third Reich* (New Haven, Conn.: Yale University Press, 1998), 250.

75. Ibid., 216–17. Cf. Stephan Linder, *Inside I.G. Farben: Hoechst in the Third Reich* (New York: Cambridge University Press, 2005); Hans Mommsen and Manfred Grieger, *Das Volkswagenwerk und seine Arbeiter im Dritten Reich* (Düsseldorf: Econ Verlag, 1996).

76. Monica Chowdry and Charles Mitchell, "Responding to Historic Wrongs: Practical and Theoretical Problems," *Oxford Journal of Legal Studies* 27 (2007): 345.

77. Anthony J. Sebok, "Reparations, Unjust Enrichment and the Importance of Knowing the Difference between the Two," *New York University Annual Survey of American Law* 58 (2003): 656. But cf. a critique of this view by Dennis Klimchuk, "Unjust Enrichment and Reparations for Slavery," *Boston University Law Review* 84 (2004): 1257–75.

78. On "enablers," see Bernie M. Farber, "The Nazi Enablers among Us," *National Post*, February 9, 2007; Yossi Klein Halevi, "Iran's German Enablers," Wall Street Journal, September 24, 2007.

79. Regula Ludi, "Waging War on Wartime Memory: Recent Swiss Debates on the Legacies of the Holocaust and the Nazi Era," *Jewish Social Studies* 10 (2004): 116–52. More generally on bystanders, see Victoria J. Barnett, *Bystanders: Conscience and Complicity during the Holocaust* (Westport, Conn.: Praeger, 1999); and David Cesarani and Paul A. Levine, eds., *Bystanders to the Holocaust: A Re-evaluation* (London: Frank Cass, 2002).

80. Owen C. Pell, "Historical Reparation Claims: The Defense Perspective," in Bazyler and Alford, *Holocaust Restitution*, 333.

81. Hans Halbheer, "To Our American Friends: Switzerland in the Second World War," American Swiss Foundation, available at http://www.americanswiss.org/content/, last accessed June 9, 2008.

82. Pell, "Historical Reparation Claims," 331–32.

83. Peter Hayes, "The Ambiguities of Evil and Justice: Degussa, Robert Pross, and the Jewish Slave Laborers at Gleiwitz," in Jonathan Petropoulos and John K. Roth, *Gray Zones: Ambiguity and Compromise in the Holocaust and Its Aftermath* (New York: Berghahn, 2005), 7. See also idem, "Industry under the Swastika," in Harold James and Jakob Tanner, eds., *Enterprise in the Period of Fascism in Europe* (Aldershot, England: Ashgate, 2002), 14–37.

84. Hayes, *From Cooperation to Complicity*, 271.

85. "Herbert Hansmeyer at the Washington Conference on Holocaust-Era Assets 1998," Allianz Group Portal, available at http://www.allianz.com/de/allianz_gruppe/ueber_uns/geschichte/firmenhistorisches_archiv_der_allianz/menu_data/page5.html, last accessed June 5, 2008.

86. Authers and Wolffe, *Victim's Fortune*, 227; Eizenstat, *Imperfect Justice*, 238; "Erklärung des Beauftragten des Bundeskanzlers Dr. Otto Graf Lambsdorff," *Stiftung Erinnerung, Verantwortung und Zukunft: 12. und abschließende Sitzung des Vorbereitenden Ausschusses*, Berlin, July 17, 2000, available at http://germany.usembassy.gov/germany/img/assets/8497/lambsdorff.pdf, last accessed March 31, 2009.

87. Otto Graf Lambsdorff, "The Negotiations on Compensation for Nazi Forced Laborers," in Bazyler and Alford, *Holocaust Restitution*, 173.

88. Ibid., 179.

89. Chesnoff, *Pack of Thieves*, 277.

90. Authers and Wolffe, *Victim's Fortune*, 268.

91. Michael J. Bazyler, "The Gray Zones of Holocaust Restitution: American Justice and Holocaust Morality," in Petropoulos and Roth, eds., *Gray Zones*, 353–54.

92. Authers and Wolffe, *Victim's Fortune*, 267.

93. Memorandum in Support of Defendant's Motion to Dismiss at 33, *Lichtman v. Siemens AG*, No. 98-4252 (D.N.J. filed September 9, 1998), quoted in Stephen Whinston, "Can Lawyers and Judges Be Good Historians? A Critical Examination of the Siemens Slave-Labor Cases," *Berkeley Journal of International Law* 20 (2002): 164, emphasis in original.

94. Ibid.

95. Ibid., 167.

96. See Hannah Arendt's comments in *Eichmann in Jerusalem*, 257, referring to the Nazis' crimes against the Jews as "not only crimes that 'no conception of military necessity could sustain' but crimes that were in fact independent of the war and that announced a policy of systematic murder to be continued in time of peace." For recent, authoritative evaluations, see Christopher R. Browning, with contributions by Jürgen Mattäus, *The Origins of the Final Solution: The Evolution of Nazi Jewish Policy, September 1939– March 1942* (Lincoln: University of Nebraska Press, 2004), 425–33; and Mazower, *Hitler's Empire*, chap. 12.

97. See the discussion in Libby Adler and Peer Zumbassen, "The Forgetfulness of Noblesse: A Critique of the German Foundation Law Compensating Slave and Forced Laborers of the Third Reich," *Harvard Journal on Legislation* 39 (2002): 41–51.

98. Matthew Dorf, "American Holocaust Survivor Wins Fight for Payment," *Jewish News Weekly*, September 22, 1995; Douglas Martin, "Hugo Princz, 78, U.S. Winner of Holocaust Settlement, Dies," *New York Times*, July 31, 2001; Mitchell G. Bard, *Forgotten Victims: The Abandonment of Americans in Hitler's Camps* (Boulder, Colo.: Westview Press, 1994).

99. Ronald J. Bettauer, "The Role of the United States Government in Recent Holocaust Claims Resolution," *Berkeley Journal of International Law* 20 (2002): 1–10.

100. Peter Van Der Auweraert, "Holocaust Reparation Claims Fifty Years After: The Swiss Banks Litigation," *Nordic Journal of International Law* 71 (2002): 560–61, based on his calculations that include Swiss bank claimants and those received as part of the German Foundation settlement. As for the numbers of Holocaust survivors, demographic studies produced different conclusions, ranging from just under 700,000 to just over a million, depending in part on definitions of "survivors." See Bazyler, "Suing Hitler's Willing Business Partners."

101. Burt Neuborne, "A Tale of Two Cities: Administering the Holocaust Settlements in Brooklyn and Berlin," in Bazyler and Alford, *Holocaust Restitution*, 62.

102. Lawrence Eagleburger and M. Diane Koken, with Catherine Lillie, *Finding Claimants and Paying Them: The Creation and Workings of the International Commission on Holocaust Era Insurance Claims* (n.p.: National Association of Insurance Commissioners, 2007), 21–22; International Commission on Holocaust Era Insurance Claims, *Lessons Learned: A Report on Best Practices*, June 2007, 7.

103. Roman Kent, "It's Not about the Money: A Survivor's Perspective on the German Foundation Initiative," in Bazyler and Alford, *Holocaust Restitution*, 206.

104. Richard O. Faulk, "Armageddon through Aggregation? The Use and Abuse of Class Actions in International Dispute Resolution," *Michigan State University, Detroit College of Law, Journal of International Law* 10 (2001): 236. On the complex dynamics of victims' responses to historic wrongs, see Martha Minow, *Between Vengeance and Forgiveness: Facing History after Genocide and Mass Violence* (Boston: Beacon, 1998).

105. Eizenstat, *Imperfect Justice*, 261.

106. Daniel Kadden, "Holocaust Restitution and the Claims Conference: Controversies and Organizational Accountability," *Jewish Currents*, July 2006, available at http://www.jewishcurrents.org/2006-july-kadden.htm, last accessed June 10, 2008.

107. Regula Ludi, "Who Is a Nazi Victim? Constructing Victimhood through Post-War Reparations in France, Germany and Switzerland," UCLA Center for European

and Eurasian Studies, Paper 3 (2005), available at http://repositories.cdlib.org/cgi/
viewcontent.cgi?article=1012&context=international/cees, last accessed June 9, 2008.

108. Eizenstat, Remarks at the 12th and Concluding Plenary on the German Foundation; Burt Neuborne, letter, *The Nation*, October 23, 2000; Peter Hayes, "Forced and Slave
Labor: The State of the Field," in *Forced and Slave Labor*, 1; Bazyler, *Holocaust Justice*, 10.

109. See Holocaust Victim Assets Litigation (Swiss Banks), the official Web site of
the *Swiss Banks Settlement: In re Holocaust Victim Assets Litigation*, United States District
Court for the Eastern District of New York, available at http://www.swissbankclaims
.com/Overview.aspx, last accessed June 9, 2008.

110. Eizenstat, *Imperfect Justice*, 239, according to Professor Lutz Niethammer's calculation. Niethammer also estimated that of these, 200,000 had been slave laborers, slightly
more than half of whom were Jews. But cf. Authers and Wolffe, *Victim's Fortune*, 217, 231.

111. Authers and Wolffe, *Victim's Fortune*, 226, 233.

112. Eizenstat, *Imperfect Justice*, 239, 263–66; Bazyler, *Holocaust Justice*, 81.

113. David A. Lash and Mitchell A. Kamin, "Poor Justice: Holocaust Restitution
and Forgotten, Indigent Survivors," in Bazyler and Alford, *Holocaust Restitution*, 315–21.

114. Stewart Ain, "One-Fourth of Holocaust Survivors in U.S. Living below Poverty
Line," *United Jewish Communities*, November 20, 2003, available at http://www.ujc.org/
page.aspx?id=51886, last accessed November 7, 2008; Adam Liptak, "Ideas & Trends:
For Holocaust Survivors, It's Law versus Morality," *New York Times*, March 14, 2004;
Michael J. Bazyler, "The Gray Zones of Holocaust Restitution: American Justice and
Holocaust Morality," in Petropoulos and Roth, *Gray Zones*, 345.

115. Bazyler, *Holocaust Justice*, 284–85. See also Bazyler, "Suing Hitler's Willing Business Partners." For a good summary of the distribution controversies see Bazyler, *Holocaust Justice*, chap. 6. For Gribetz's perspective and a detailed summary, see Judah Gribetz and Shari C. Reig, "The Swiss Banks Holocaust Settlement," a larger version of a
paper presented by Shari C. Reig at the conference on Reparations for Victims of Genocide, Crimes against Humanity and War Crimes: Systems in Place and Systems in the
Making, the Peace Palace, The Hague, the Netherlands, March 1–2, 2007.

116. Hayes, "Forced and Slave Labor," in *Forced and Slave Labor*, 1.

Chapter 5. Evaluating Some Measure of Justice

1. Sidney Zabludoff, "Restitution of Holocaust-Era Assets: Promises and Reality,"
Jewish Political Studies Review 19 (Spring 2007), available at http://www.jcpa.org/JCPA/
Templates/ShowPage.asp?DRIT=3&DBID=1&LNGID=1&TMID=111&FID=253&
PID=0&IID=1678&TTL=Restitution_of_Holocaust-Era_Assets:_Promises_and_Reality,
last accessed October 1, 2008.

2. Stuart Eizenstat, "The Unfinished Business of the Unfinished Business of World
War II," in Michael J. Bazyler and Roger P. Alford, *Holocaust Restitution: Perspectives on the
Litigation and Its Legacy* (New York: New York University Press, 2006), 307. Here is the
start of an article on this theme: "This is about money. But not exactly. This is about
righting an old wrong. But not entirely. This is about making peace with history. But not
really." Clyde Haberman, "NYC; Putting Price on Holocaust? Not Even Close," *New
York Times*, August 3, 2004.

3. Candice Krieger, "'Give Me Back My Stolen Family Fortune,'" *Jewish Chronicle*,
January 24, 2008.

4. Roman Kent, testimony at Restitution of Holocaust Assets: Hearings before the Committee on Banking and Financial Services, U.S. House of Representatives, One Hundred Sixth Congress, second session, February 9, 10, 2000, 61, available at http://www.archive.org/stream/restitutionofho100unit/restitutionofho100unit_djvu.txt, last accessed June 26, 2008.

5. Roman Kent, "It's Not about the Money: A Survivor's Perspective on the German Foundation Initiative," in Bazyler and Alford, *Holocaust Restitution*, 214, emphasis mine.

6. Owen C. Pell, "Historical Reparation Claims: The Defense Perspective," in Bazyler and Alford, *Holocaust Restitution*, 341–42, emphasis mine.

7. Ronald J. Bettauer, "Keynote Address—The Role of the United States Government in Recent Holocaust Claims Resolution," *Berkeley Journal of International Law* 20 (2002): 1.

8. Michael J. Bazyler, *Holocaust Justice: The Battle for Restitution in America's Courts* (New York: New York University Press, 2003), xi–xii.

9. Melvyn I. Weiss, "A Litigator's Postscript to the Swiss Banks and Holocaust Litigation Settlements: How Justice Was Served," in Bazyler and Alford, *Holocaust Restitution*, 109–10.

10. "Restitution: Why Did It Take 50 Years or Did It? An Interview with Ronald Zweig," Jerusalem Center for Public Affairs, n.d., available at http://www.jcpa.org/phas/phas-zweig.htm, last accessed June 26, 2008. Gideon Taylor, of the Claims Conference, makes a similar point. See Netty C. Gross, "Looking Back in Pride and Anger," *Jerusalem Report*, November 24, 2008, 64.

11. Lutz Niethammer, "Converting Wrongs to Rights? Compensating Nazi Forced Labor as a Paradigm," in Dan Diner and Gotthart Wunberg, eds., *Restitution and Memory: Material Restoration in Europe* (New York: Berghahn, 2007), 83–104; Richard Buxbaum, "German Reparations after the Second World War," *African-American Law and Policy Report* 6 (2004): 36.

12. Richard M. Buxbaum, "A Legal History of International Reparations," *Issues in Legal Scholarship*, Article 5 (2006), available at http://www.bepress.com/cgi/viewcontent.cgi?article=1079&context=ils, last accessed June 26, 2008.

13. Rudolf Dolzer, "The Settlement of War-Related Claims: Does International Law Recognize a Victim's Private Right of Action? Lessons after 1945," *Berkeley Journal of International Law* 20 (2002): 340.

14. Dinah Shelton, "The World of Atonement: Reparations for Historical Injustices," *Netherlands International Law Review* 50 (2003): 289–325; John Torpey, *Making Whole What Has Been Smashed: On Reparations Politics* (Cambridge, Mass.: Harvard University Press, 2006).

15. Dolzer offers a strongly argued negative view, well-informed by hindsight: "The attempt to privatize peacemaking at the end of a lengthy historical process of government-to-government negotiations in order to provide the appropriate satisfaction for specially affected groups is only a second or third best alternative to comprehensive peacemaking by governments at a time near the end of military hostilities. The lessons after the Second World War have indirectly reconfirmed the wisdom behind the classical rules of international law which place peacemaking into the hands of governments and not of individuals. In principle, governments were rightly prepared after 1945 to follow these rules. However, to the extent that these rules were in part modified and revised

by way of adding elements of open-endedness, of permitting delay and of allowing incursions of uncertainty and unilateralism into government-to-government peacemaking, the inadequacy of government-to-government action led to lawsuits by individuals, albeit unsuccessful ones. Thus, the central lesson from the long-belated end of the World War II peacemaking process is that governments must more effectively, promptly and carefully incorporate the legitimate concerns of groups and individuals particularly affected by a war into the inter-governmental process of making peace." Dolzer, "Settlement of War-Related Claims," 340–41.

16. Jon Elster, *Closing the Books: Transitional Justice in Historical Perspective* (Cambridge: Cambridge University Press, 2004), 167.

17. "Restitution: Why Did It Take 50 Years or Did It?"; Marilyn Henry, *Confronting the Perpetrators: A History of the Claims Conference* (Edgware, Middlesex, England: Valentine Mitchell, 2007); Regula Ludi, "Michael Bazyler's Holocaust Justice," UCLA Center for European and Eurasian Studies, Paper 1 (2003), available at http://repositories.cdlib .org/cgi/viewcontent.cgi?article=1002&context=international/cees, last accessed June 30, 2008.

18. Gideon Taylor, "Where Morality Meets Money," in Bazyler and Alford, *Holocaust Restitution*, 165. Taylor is executive vice president of the Claims Conference.

19. Israel Singer, "Why Now?" *Cardozo Law Review* 20 (1998): 426; John Authers, "Making Good Again: German Compensation for Forced and Slave Laborers," in Pablo De Greiff, ed., *The Handbook of Reparations* (Oxford: Oxford University Press, 2006), 145.

20. Deborah Sturman, "Germany's Reexamination of Its Past through the Lens of the Holocaust Litigation," in Bazyler and Alford, *Holocaust Restitution*, 221.

21. Peter Hayes, "The Ambiguities of Evil and Justice: Degussa, Robert Pross, and the Jewish Slave Laborers at Gleiwitz," in Jonathan Petropoulos and John K. Roth, eds., *Gray Zones: Ambiguity and Compromise in the Holocaust and Its Aftermath* (New York: Berghahn, 2005), 8.

22. Tom Segev, *The Seventh Million: The Israelis and the Holocaust* (New York: Hill and Wang, 1993), 251. Marilyn Henry observes that "the idea of individual compensation was anathema to many in the 1950s: it was seen as blood money. Israel's claim against Germany was a deliberately cold mathematical calculation based on the costs of settling refugees. It was the only way to stomach a deal with Germany—an important one that built the port, phone and power systems. The idea was that if the destitute state of 1953 could build its infrastructure, everyone would benefit." "Metro Views: Did the State Rob Holocaust Survivors?" *Jerusalem Post*, June 29, 2008.

23. Ronald W. Zweig, *The Gold Train: The Destruction of the Jews and the Second World War's Most Terrible Robbery* (London: Allen Lane, 2002), 5.

24. See the comments of John Borneman, "Money and Memory: Transvaluing the Redress of Loss," in Dan Diner and Gotthart Wunberg, eds., *Restitution and Memory: Material Restoration in Europe* (New York: Berghahn, 2007), 27–50.

25. Adrian Vermeule, "Reparations as Rough Justice," John M. Olin Law & Economics Working Paper No. 260, University of Chicago Law School, September 2005, 3, available at http://papers.ssrn.com/s013/papers.cfm?abstract_id=813086, last accessed July 1, 2008.

26. Michael Ignatieff, "Blood Money," *New York Times*, September 10, 2000. See his quotation on page 8, above.

27. Vermeule, "Reparations as Rough Justice," 15.

28. Gideon Taylor, "Where Morality Meets Money," in Bazyler and Alford, *Holocaust Restitution*, 168.

29. Stuart Eizenstat, *Imperfect Justice: Looted Assets, Slave Labor, and the Unfinished Business of World War II* (New York: Public Affairs, 2003), 345.

30. Jane Fritsch, "$52 Million for Lawyers' Fees in Nazi-Era Slave Labor Suits," *New York Times*, June 15, 2001; Nathaniel Popper, "Lawyers' Fees Questioned in Gold Train Settlement," *Forward*, July 1, 2005. Michael Bazyler's reported observations on this settlement are instructive: "Like a number of legal authorities who commented on the case, Bazyler said the settlement was remarkable given the case's lack of legal merit, particularly because of the lack of evidence linking the contents of the train to any individual survivor. 'The lawyers were legal magicians.'" Ibid. Cf. Roman Kent, "It's Not about the Money," in Bazyler and Alford, *Holocaust Restitution*, 206.

31. David Rohde, "Holocaust Survivors Urge Quick Payments in Swiss Settlement and Assail Legal Fees," *New York Times*, November 30, 1999; Fritsch, "$52 Million for Lawyers' Fees."

32. Stuart E. Eizenstat, "Remarks at the 12th and Concluding Plenary on the German Foundation, July 17, 2000, available at http://germany.usembassy.gov/germany/img/assets/8497/eizenstat071700.pdf, last accessed July 2, 2008.

33. Bazyler, *Holocaust Justice*, 46.

34. Idem, "Suing Hitler's Willing Business Partners: American Justice and Holocaust Morality," *Jewish Political Studies Review* 16 (2004), available at http://www.jcpa.org/phas/phas-bazyler-f04.htm, last accessed July 2, 2008.

35. Burt Neuborne, letter to *The Nation*, October 23, 2000; Bazyler, *Holocaust Justice*, 45.

36. Nathaniel Popper, "Top Lawyer on Holocaust Restitution Cases Taking Flak over Fee Request," *Forward*, January 13, 2006; Peter Lattman, "Holocaust Survivors Angry over NYU Professor Burt Neuborne's Fees," Wall Street Journal Law Blog, February 27, 2006, available at http://blogs.wsj.com/law/2006/02/27/holocaust-survivors-angry-at-nyu-law-professor-burt-neubornes-fees/, last accessed July 2, 2008. See the exchange between Menachem Z. Rosesaft, "Profiting from the Holocaust," *Los Angeles Times*, November 19, 2006, and the reply by Burt Neuborne, "What Profit? I Gave Up $10 Million," *Los Angeles Times*, November 19, 2006. See also, most recently, Joseph Goldstein, "Holocaust Victim's Lawyer Asks for Interest on His Fee," *New York Sun*, January 28, 2008.

37. Theodore Eisenberg and Geoffrey P. Miller, "Attorney's Fees in Class Action Settlements: An Empirical Study," *Journal of Empirical Legal Studies* 1 (2004): 27–78.

38. "Editorial: A Disputed Fee," *New York Times*, March 26, 2007. The *Times* referred to "slipshod hourly records," survivors' claims about high hourly rates, and confusion about whether Mr. Neuborne was forgoing all fees or only some.

39. Eizenstat, *Imperfect Justice*, 345.

40. See Joel Siegel, "Getting His Due," *New York Magazine*, October 2, 2006.

41. Noeleen G. Walder, "Lawyer Disbarred for Failing to Pay Sanctions, Fees in Holocaust Case," Law.com, December 12, 2008, available at http://www.law.com/jsp/article.jsp?id=1202426698941, last accessed March 10, 2009. The *New York Times* reports Fagan's first reaction on hearing about Nazi gold and the Swiss banks: "I thought, 'Oh my goodness, I'm a lawyer, here are defendants. I don't know who the plaintiffs are, I

don't know who the plaintiffs are going to be, but someone is going to pay.'" Barry Meier, "An Avenger's Path: A Special Report. Lawyer in Holocaust Case Faces Litany of Complaints," *New York Times*, September 8, 2000; Jacob Gershman, "Attorney Accused of Misappropriating Funds," *New York Sun*, January 5, 2005; Daniel Wise, "Lawyer Sanctioned in Holocaust Suit," Law.com, August 23, 2005, available at http://www.law.com, last accessed July 2, 2008; Robert Wiener, "Shoa Reparations Attorney Faces Disbarment," *New Jersey Jewish News*, February 7, 2008.

42. Joshua Pantesco, "Melvyn Weiss Indicted on Milberg Weiss Conspiracy Charges," *Jurist: Legal News & Research*, September 20, 2007, available at http://jurist .law.pitt.edu/paperchase/2007/09/melvyn-weiss-indicted-on-milberg-weiss.php, last accessed July 3, 2008. For a brief description of how the scheme worked, see "Jailing the Bogeyman," *The Economist*, June 5, 2008.

43. John Authers and Richard Wolffe, *The Victim's Fortune: Inside the Epic Battle over the Debts of the Holocaust* (New York: Perennial, 2002), 81. See also Eizenstat, *Imperfect Justice*, 118; and the profile by Robert Lenzner and Emily Lambert, "Mr. Class Action," *Forbes*, February 16, 2004.

44. Tiffany Hsu and Thomas S. Mulligan, "Melvyn Weiss Sentenced in Class Action Kickback Scheme," *Los Angeles Times*, June 3, 2008; Amanda Bronsad, "Melvyn Weiss Draws 30-Month Prison Term for Kickback Scheme," *National Law Journal*, June 9, 2008.

45. As an editorial in the *Wall Street Journal* put it, "Milberg was a corrupt enterprise that perpetrated a vast fraud on our system of justice." "The Firm," *Wall Street Journal*, June 18, 2008. See also Jonathan D. Glater, "High-Profile Trial Lawyer Agrees to Guilty Plea," *New York Times*, March 21, 2008; Peter Elkind, "Mortal Blow to a Once-Mighty Firm," *Fortune*, March 25, 2008; "A Fall and a Lesson," *Washington Post*, April 9, 2008; Joe Nocera, "Serving Time, but Lacking Remorse," *New York Times*, June 7, 2008; Jonathan D. Glater, "To the Trenches: The Tort War Is Raging On," *New York Times*, June 22, 2008.

46. "Resign, Mr. Quackenbush," *Los Angeles Times*, May 7, 2000; "The Downfall of California's Insurance Commissioner," *Insurance Journal*, July 10, 2000.

47. Nacha Cattan, "Restitution Leader Disbarred by Court after Investigation of Job Misconduct," *Forward*, September 5, 2003; Tom Schoenberg, "The Unraveling of Neal Sher," Law.com, September 12, 2003, available at http://www.law.com/jsp/law/ LawArticleFriendly.jsp?id=900005536542, last accessed September 15, 2008.

48. Michael Cooper, "Hevesi Resigns, Pleading Guilty to Fraud Count," *New York Times*, December 22, 2006; Danny Hakim and Mary Williams Walsh, "Hevesi's Sons and Aides Face Pension Fund Investigation," *New York Times*, July 15, 2007; Danny Hakim, "Disgraced Comptroller Assails Cuomo and DiNapoli," *New York Times*, July 20, 2007.

49. Founded in 1988, the March of the Living is a Holocaust-education and Israel awareness program for Jewish youth in which groups of young people from various countries travel to Holocaust sites in Poland, followed by a visit to Israel.

50. "Hirchson May Turn State Witness," *Jerusalem Post*, March 21, 2007; Maria Colvin, "Minister Quizzed over Holocaust Cash," Timesonline, March 25, 2007, available at http://www.timesonline.co.uk/tol/news/world/middle_east/article1563803.ece, last accessed September 15, 2008; "Hirchson Should Bow Out," *Jerusalem Post*, March 24, 2007; Authers and Wolffe, *Victim's Fortune*, 375.

51. "Shoah March Offices Used for Political Activity?" Ynetnews.com, available at

http://www.ynetnews.com/Ext/Comp/ArticleLayout/CdaArticlePrintPreview/
1,2506,L-3265850,00.html, last accessed July 3, 2008. See also Tomer Zarchin, "Hirchson Faces Embezzlement Charges, Won't Request Immunity," *Haaretz*, May 5, 2008; Amit Benaroia and Ofra Edelman, "Hirchson Indictment: NIS 72,000 in Drugs, NIS 62,000 in Restaurant Meals," *Haaretz*, May 6, 2008.

52. Adam Nagourney, "The 1998 Campaign: The Senate; Jewish Vote Becomes Battleground in Tight Race for Senate," *New York Times*, October 19, 1998; Kevin Flynn, "The 1998 Elections: New York State—the Voters; Schumer Showed Strength across the State, Even in Some of D'Amato's Strongholds," *New York Times*, November 5, 1998.

53. Russ Baker, "Judgment Day for Senator Pothole," *Newsday*, May 7, 2002.

54. Amiram Barkat, "Where Was Edgar Bronfman?" *Haaretz*, February 22, 2007; Amiram Barkat, "World Jewish Congress Fires Chairman Israel Singer in Surprise Move," *Haaretz*, March 15, 2007; Stephanie Storm, "World Jewish Congress Dismisses Leader," *New York Times*, March 16, 2007; Nathaniel Popper, "Ugly Allegations Fly as Fabled WJC Duo Splits," *Forward*, March 23, 2007; Stephanie Storm, "New Accusations Are Raised after Firing in Jewish Group," *New York Times*, April 6, 2007; Etgar Lefkovits, "Bronfman: I Fired Singer to Avoid IRS Penalty," *Jerusalem Post*, April 8, 2007; Stephanie Strom, "President of Jewish Congress Resigns after 3 Years' Turmoil," *New York Times*, May 8, 2007.

55. Marie Colvin, "Minister Quizzed over Holocaust Cash," *Sunday Times*, March 25, 2007; "Shoah March Offices Used for Political Activity?" for questions raised about connections between ICHIEC money sent to Israel, ostensibly to support the "March of the Living," and extending to a "bewildering network of non-profit organizations and money transfers." See also Marilyn Henry, "Metro Views: Did the State Rob Holocaust Survivors?" *Jerusalem Post*, June 29, 2008; and Raul Teitelbaum, *Die biologische Lösung: Wie die Shoah "wiedergutgemacht" wurde*, trans. Bettina Malka-Igelbusch (Springe, Germany: Dietrich zu Klampen, 2008).

56. Marilyn Henry, "Metro Views: An Endeavor Cloaked in Sanctity," *Jerusalem Post*, February 4, 2008.

57. Michael J. Bazyler, "The Holocaust Restitution Movement in Comparative Perspective," *Berkeley Journal of International Law* 20 (2002): 11.

58. *Kelberine v. Société Internationale*, Etc., 363 F.2d 989, 995 (D.C. Cir. 1966), quoted in Shari C. Reig, "The Swiss Banks Holocaust Settlement," presented at the Conference on Reparations for Victims of Genocide, Crimes against Humanity and War Crimes: Systems in Place and Systems in the Making, the Peace Palace, The Hague, the Netherlands, March 1–2, 2007, 11, available at http://www.redress.org/PeacePalace/Holcaust SettlementSR.pdf, last accessed July 7, 2008.

59. Eva Hoffman, *After Such Knowledge: Memory, History, and the Legacy of the Holocaust* (New York: Public Affairs, 2004), 267, emphasis in original.

60. Si Frumkin, "Why Won't Those SOBs Give Me My Money? A Survivor's Perspective," in Bazyler and Alford, *Holocaust Restitution*, 100.

61. Christopher Kutz, "Justice in Reparations: The Cost of Memory and the Value of Talk," *Philosophy & Public Affairs* 32 (2004): 283.

62. Tzvetan Todorov, *Les Abus de la mémoire* ([Paris]: Arléa, 1995), 14; idem, "The Touvier Trial," in Richard J. Goslan, ed., *Memory, the Holocaust, and French Justice: The Bouisquet and Touvier Affairs* (Hanover, N.H.: University Press of New England, 1996), 177.

63. Charles Maier, "A Surfeit of Memory? Reflections on History, Melancholy and Denial," *History & Memory* 5 (1993): 144.

64. Henry Rousso, *The Haunting Past: History, Memory, and Justice in Contemporary France,* trans. Ralph Schoolcraft (Philadelphia: University of Pennsylvania Press, 1988), 4, emphasis in original.

65. Ibid., 9.

66. Ibid., 7, 16.

67. Richard Evans, "History, Memory, and the Law: The Historian as Expert Witness," *History and Theory* 41 (2002): 345.

68. An exception to this generalization may well be the increasing sophistication of provenance research by both museums and plaintiffs' lawyers concerned with the restitution of art stolen by the Nazis. On the development of this field and some recent examples see Jonathan Petropoulos, "Provenance Research as History: Reconstructed Collections and National Socialist Art Looting," *Contemporary Austrian Studies* 14 (2006): 373–81.

69. Jeremy Waldron, "Superseding Historic Injustice," *Ethics* 103 (1992): 5.

70. Suzette M. Malveau, "Statutes of Limitations: A Policy Analysis in the Context of Reparations Litigation," *George Washington Law Review* 74 (2005): 116.

71. Peer Zumbansen, "Globalization and the Law: Deciphering the Message of Transnational Human Rights Litigation," *German Law Journal* 5 (2004): 1515.

72. Authers and Wolffe, *Victim's Fortune,* 387. For an elaboration of this theme, focusing on the settlement with German industry, see Bazyler, *Holocaust Justice,* 101–6.

73. Elazar Barkan, *The Guilt of Nations: Restitution and Negotiating Historical Injustices* (New York: Norton, 2000), ix, 15, 308–9.

74. Burt Neuborne, "Holocaust Reparations Litigation: Lessons for the Slavery Reparations Movement," *New York University Annual Survey of American Law* 58 (2003): 618.

75. Bazyler, *Holocaust Justice,* 307–28.

76. Ibid., 327.

77. Ibid., 328–30.

78. Michael J. Bazyler, "The Holocaust Restitution in Comparative Perspective," *Berkeley Journal of International Law* 20 (2002): 44. For a related view, see Beth Stephens, "The Amorality of Profit: Transnational Corporations and Human Rights," *Berkeley Journal of International Law* 20 (2002): 45–90.

79. Eizenstat, *Imperfect Justice,* 365–72.

80. Burt Neuborne, "A Tale of Two Cities: Administering the Holocaust Settlements in Brooklyn and Berlin," in Bazyler and Alford, *Holocaust Restitution,* 74–77.

81. David Rohde, "The World; The Lawsuits Pile Up, Matching the List of Atrocities," *New York Times,* September 13, 1998.

82. Morris Ratner and Caryn Becker, "The Legacy of Holocaust Class Action Suits: Have They Broken Ground for Other Cases of Historical Wrongs?" in Bazyler and Alford, *Holocaust Restitution,* 348–49.

83. Idem, "Unfinished Business of the Unfinished Business of World War II," in Bazyler and Alford, *Holocaust Restitution,* 297.

84. Idem, "Preliminary Reflections on Aspects of Holocaust-Era Litigation in American Courts," *Washington University Law Quarterly* 80 (2002): 831–32; Justin H. Roy, "Strengthening Human Rights Protection: Why the Holocaust Slave Labor Claims

Should Be Litigated," *The Scholar* 1 (1999): 153–205; Thane Rosenbaum, "The Holocaust's Defrauded Survivors," *International Herald Tribune,* June 17, 2007.

85. Relevant here is increasing evidence of a declining influence of American Supreme Court decisions internationally. See Adam Liptak, "Supreme Court's Global Influence Is Waning," *New York Times,* September 18, 2008. On the general point, see Detlev F. Vagts, "Restitution for Historic Wrongs: The American Courts and International Law," *American Journal of International Law* 92 (1998): 232–35; Michele Taruffo, "Some Remarks on Group Litigation in Comparative Perspective," *Duke Journal of Comparative & International Law* 11 (2001): 404–21; Antoine Garapon, *Peut-on réparer l'Histoire? Colonisation, esclavage, Shoah* (Paris: Odile Jacob, 2008); and Regula Ludi, "Michael Bazyler's Holocaust Justice," UCLA Center for European and Eurasian Studies, Paper 1 (2003), available at http://repositories.cdlib.org/cgi/viewcontent.cgi?article=1002&context= international/cees, last accessed July 9, 2008.

86. Jonathan D. Glater, "To the Trenches: The Tort War Is Raging On," *New York Times,* June 22, 2008.

87. Paul R. Dubinsky, "Justice for the Collective: The Limits of the Human Rights Class Action," *Michigan Law Review* 102 (2004): 1176.

88. Dinah Shelton, "The World of Atonement: Reparations for Historical Injustice," *Netherlands International Law Review* 50 (2003): 291.

89. Ibid., 302. This even seems to be the case in the world of art. "With litigation costs rising far above the price most could pay to repossess family artwork, and with the legal questions brought up in such litigation turning on such esoteric aspects of a situation as choice of law and intricate domestic legal idiosyncrasies, returning looted artwork has become more of a diplomatic gesture than enforcement of actual law." Molly Ann Torsen, "National Reactions to Cultural Property Looting in Nazi Germany: A Window on Individual Effort and International Disarray," *Electronic Journal of Comparative Law* 9 (December 2005), available at http://www.ejcl.org/94/art94-1.html, last accessed July 11, 2008.

90. In what I interpret to be a concurring view, Martha Minow writes: "Symbolic reparations and negotiated settlements, rather than restitution of preexisting entitlements, offer a path through the political, moral, and legal morass." *Between Vengeance and Forgiveness: Facing History after Genocide and Mass Violence* (Boston: Beacon Press, 1998), 112. For a recent call in the art world for attending to the public interest, rather than restitution claims by distant relatives, see Norman Rosenthal, "The Time Has Come for a Statute of Limitations," *The Art Newspaper,* November 12, 2008.

91. Frank Bruni, "A Voice for Jews Shows Range and Resonance," *New York Times,* February 16, 1997.

Index

GEORGE L. MOSSE SERIES
IN MODERN EUROPEAN CULTURAL AND
INTELLECTUAL HISTORY

Series Editors

Stanley G. Payne, David J. Sorkin, and John S. Tortorice

Advisory Board

Steven E. Aschheim
Hebrew University of Jerusalem

Annette Becker
Université Paris X–Nanterre

Christopher Browning
*University of North Carolina at
Chapel Hill*

Natalie Zemon Davis
University of Toronto

Saul Friedländer
University of California, Los Angeles

Emilio Gentile
Università di Roma "La Sapienza"

Gert Hekma
University of Amsterdam

Stanley G. Payne
University of Wisconsin–Madison

Anson Rabinbach
Princeton University

David J. Sorkin
University of Wisconsin–Madison

John S. Tortorice
University of Wisconsin–Madison

Joan Wallach Scott
Institute for Advanced Study

Jay Winter
Yale University

Collected Memories: Holocaust History and Postwar Testimony
Christopher Browning

Cataclysms: A History of the Twentieth Century from Europe's Edge
Dan Diner; translated by William Templer with Joel Golb

La Grande Italia: The Myth of the Nation in the Twentieth Century
Emilio Gentile; translated by Suzanne Dingee and Jennifer Pudney

*Carl Schmitt and the Jews: The "Jewish Question," the Holocaust, and
    German Legal Theory*
Raphael Gross; translated by Joel Golb

Some Measure of Justice: The Holocaust Era Restitution Campaign of the 1990s
Michael R. Marrus

Confronting History: A Memoir
George L. Mosse

Nazi Culture: Intellectual, Cultural, and Social Life in the Third Reich
George L. Mosse

What History Tells: George L. Mosse and the Culture of Modern Europe
Stanley G. Payne, David J. Sorkin, and John S. Tortorice

The Jews in Mussolini's Italy: From Equality to Persecution
Michele Sarfatti; translated by John and Anne C. Tedeschi

*Jews and Other Germans: Civil Society, Religious Diversity, and Urban Politics in Breslau,
    1860–1925*
Till van Rahden; translated by Marcus Brainard

An Uncompromising Generation: The Nazi Leadership of the Reich Security Main Office
Michael Wildt; translated by Tom Lampert

D 818 .M37 2009
Marrus, Michael Robert.
Some measure of justice